THE RETURN OF THE

Annette Michelson, Rosalind Krauss, Yve-Alain Bois, Benjamin Buchloh, Hal Foster, Denis Hollier, and Silvia Kolbowski, editors

Broodthaers, edited by Benjamin H. D. Buchloh

AIDS: Cultural Analysis/Cultural Activism, edited by Douglas Crimp

Aberrations, by Jurgis Baltrušaitis

Against Architecture: The Writings of Georges Bataille, by Denis Hollier

Painting as Model, by Yve-Alain Bois

The Destruction of Tilted Arc: *Documents,* edited by Clara Weyergraf-Serra and Martha Buskirk

The Woman in Question, edited by Parveen Adams and Elizabeth Cowie

Techniques of the Observer: On Vision and Modernity in the Nineteenth Century, by Jonathan Crary

The Subjectivity Effect in Western Literary Tradition: Essays toward the Release of Shakespeare's Will, by Joel Fineman

Looking Awry: An Introduction to Jacques Lacan through Popular Culture, by Slavoj Žižek

Cinema, Censorship, and the State: The Writings of Nagisa Oshima, by Nagisa Oshima

The Optical Unconscious, by Rosalind E. Krauss

Gesture and Speech, by André Leroi-Gourhan

Compulsive Beauty, by Hal Foster

Continuous Project Altered Daily: The Writings of Robert Morris, by Robert Morris

Read My Desire: Lacan against the Historicists, by Joan Copjec

Fast Cars, Clean Bodies: Decolonization and the Reordering of French Culture, by Kristin Ross

Kant after Duchamp, by Thierry de Duve

The Duchamp Effect, edited by Martha Buskirk and Mignon Nixon

The Return of the Real: The Avant-Garde at the End of the Century, by Hal Foster

The Return of the Real

The Avant-Garde at the End of the Century

Hal Foster

An OCTOBER Book

The MIT Press
Cambridge, Massachusetts
London, England

This book was set in Bembo by Graphic Composition, Inc.

Printed and bound in the United States of America.

Library of Congress Cataloging-in-Publication Data

Foster, Hal.
    The return of the real : the avant-garde at the end of the century / Hal Foster.
        p.   cm.
    "An October book."
    Includes bibliographical references and index.
    ISBN 0-262-06187-2 (hc : alk. paper). — ISBN 0-262-56107-7 (pb : alk. paper)
        1. Art criticism—History—20th century.   2. Avant-garde (Aesthetics)—History—20th
    century.   3. Art, Modern—20th century.   I. Title
    N7475.F67   1996
    701'.18'09045—dc20   96-18323
                                                                              CIP

The following illustrations are reproduced by permission:

Marcel Duchamp: *Box in a Valise*, 1941, *Etant donnés*, 1946–66, *With My Tongue in My Cheek*,
1959, © 1997 Artists Rights Society (ARS), New York/ADAGP, Paris.

Richard Estes: *Double Self-Portrait*, 1976, © 1997 Richard Estes/Licensed by VAGA, New York/
Marlborough Gallery, New York.

Jasper Johns: *Target with Plaster Casts*, 1955, *Painted Bronze*, 1960, © 1997 Jasper Johns/Licensed
by VAGA, New York.

Donald Judd: *Untitled*, 1962, *Untitled*, 1966, © 1997 Estate of Donald Judd/Licensed by VAGA,
New York.

Robert Rauschenberg: *Factum I* and *II*, 1957, © 1997 Robert Rauschenberg/Licensed by VAGA,
New York.

Richard Serra: *One Ton Prop*, 1969, © 1997 Richard Serra/Artists Rights Society (ARS), New
York.

Andy Warhol: *Ambulance Disaster*, 1963, *National Velvet*, 1963, *Tunafish Disaster*, 1963, *White Burning Car III*, 1963, © 1997 1997 Andy Warhol Foundation for the Visual Arts/Artist Rights Society (ARS), New York

10   9   8

For Thatcher Bailey
Charles Wright
Ron Clark

Contents

Robert Morris, *Untitled,* 1977.

INTRODUCTION

Not long ago I stood with a friend next to an art work made of four wood beams laid in a long rectangle, with a mirror set behind each corner so as to reflect the others. My friend, a conceptual artist, and I talked about the minimalist basis of such work: its reception by critics then, its elaboration by artists later, its significance for practitioners today, all of which are concerns of this book as well. Taken by our talk, we hardly noticed his little girl as she played on the beams. But then, signaled by her mother, we looked up to see her pass through the looking glass. Into the hall of mirrors, the *mise-en-abîme* of beams, she moved farther and farther from us, and as she passed into the distance, she passed into the past as well.

Yet suddenly there she was right behind us: all she had done was skip along the beams around the room. And there we were, a critic and an artist informed in contemporary art, taken to school by a six-year-old, our theory no match for her practice. For her playing of the piece conveyed not only specific concerns of minimalist work—the tensions among the spaces we feel, the images we see, and the forms we know—but also general shifts in art over the last three decades—new interventions into space, different constructions of viewing, and expanded definitions of art. Her performance became allegorical as well, for she described a paradoxical figure *in space,* a recession that is also a return, that evoked for me the paradoxical figure *in time* described by the avant-garde. For even as the avant-garde recedes into the past, it also returns from the future, repositioned by innovative art in the present. This strange temporality, lost in stories of twentieth-century art, is a principal subject of this book.

Partial in interests (I am silent about many events) and parochial in examples (I remain a critic based in New York), this book is not a history: it focuses on several models of art and theory over the last three decades alone. Yet neither does it celebrate the false pluralism of the posthistorical museum, market, and academy in which anything goes (as long as accepted forms predominate). On the contrary, it insists that specific genealogies of innovative art and theory exist over this time, and it traces these genealogies through signal transformations. Crucial here is the relation between *turns* in critical models and *returns* of historical practices (broached in chapter 1): how does a *re*connection with a past practice support a *dis*connection from a present practice and/or a development of a new one? No question is more important for the neo-avant-garde addressed in this book—that is, art since 1960 that refashions avant-garde devices (e.g., the constructivist analysis of the object, the photomontage refunctioning of the image, the readymade critique of the exhibition) to contemporary ends.

The question of historical returns is old in art history; indeed, in the form of the renaissance of classical antiquity, it is foundational. Concerned to comprehend diverse cultures in a single narrative, the Hegelian founders of the academic discipline represented these returns as dialectical moves that advanced the story of Western art, and they offered appropriate figures for this historical narrative (thus Alois Riegl proposed that art advances as a screw turns, while Heinrich Wölfflin offered the related image of a spiral).[1] Despite appearances, this notion of a dialectic was not rejected in modernism; at least in the Anglo-American formalist account, it was continued, in part, by other means. "Modernism has never meant anything like a break with the past," Clement Greenberg proclaimed in 1961, at the opening of the period that concerns me here; and in 1965 Michael Fried was explicit: "a dialectic of modernism has been at work in the visual arts for more than a century now."[2]

To be sure, these critics stressed the categorical being of visual art à la Kant, but they did so to preserve its historical life à la Hegel: art was urged to stick to its space, "its area of competence," so that it might survive, even thrive, in time, and so "maintain past standards of excellence."[3] Thus was formal modernism plotted along a temporal, diachronic, or vertical axis; in this respect it opposed an avant-gardist modernism that did intend "a break with the past"— that, concerned to extend the area of artistic competence, favored a spatial, synchronic, or horizontal axis. A chief merit of the neo-avant-garde addressed in this book is that it sought to keep these two axes in critical coordination. Like the late-modernist painting and sculpture advocated by formalist critics, it worked through its ambitious antecedents, and so sustained the vertical axis or historical dimension of art. At the same time it turned to past paradigms to open up present possibilities, and so developed the horizontal axis or social dimension of art as well.

Today the address of many ambitious practices is different. Sometimes the vertical axis is neglected in favor of the horizontal axis, and often the coordination of the two seems broken. In a way this problem may stem from the neo-avant-garde as well, in its implicit shift from a disciplinary criterion of *quality,* judged in relation to artistic standards of the past, to an avant-gardist value of *interest,* provoked through a testing of cultural limits in the present; for with this implicit shift (discussed in chapter 2) came a partial move from intrinsic forms of art to discursive problems around art. Yet the early neo-avant-garde alone did not effect this putative change from "a historical succession of techniques and styles" to "a simultaneity of the radically disparate."[4] Only with the ethnographic turn in contemporary art and theory, I argue in chapter 6, is the turn from medium-specific elaborations to debate-specific projects so pronounced.[5]

For the most part this horizontal expansion is welcome, for it has involved art and theory in sites and audiences long removed from them, and it has opened up other vertical axes, other historical dimensions, for creative work. Yet this move also prompts questions. First, there is the question of *value* invested in the canons of twentieth-century art. This value is not set: there is always formal invention to be redeployed, social meaning to be resignified, cultural capital to be reinvested. Simply to surrender this value is a great mistake, aesthetically and strategically. Second, there is the question of *expertise,* which also should not be dismissed as elitist. In this regard the horizontal expansion of art has placed an enormous burden on artists and viewers alike: as one moves from project to project, one must learn the discursive breadth as well as the historical depth of many different representations—like an anthropologist who enters a new culture with each new exhibition. This is very difficult (even for critics who do little else), and this difficulty may hinder consensus about the necessity of art, let alone conversation about the criteria of significant art. As different interpretive communities shout past each other or fall into silence, reactionary know-nothings can seize the public forum on contemporary art— which they have done to condemn it.

A primary concern of this book, then, is the coordination of diachronic (or historical) and synchronic (or social) axes in art and theory. Out of this concern come the two notions that govern the stories that I tell (in chapters 1 and 7 in particular). The first is the notion of *parallax,* which involves the apparent displacement of an object caused by the actual movement of its observer. This figure underscores both that our framings of the past depend on our positions in the present and that these positions are defined through such framings. It also shifts the terms of these definitions away from a logic of avant-gardist transgression toward a model of deconstructive (dis)placement, which is far more appropriate to contemporary practices (where the turn from interstitial "text" to institutional "frame" is pronounced). The reflexivity of the viewer inscribed in the notion of parallax is also advanced in the other notion fundamental to this book: *deferred action.* In Freud an event is registered as traumatic only through a later event that recodes it retroactively, in deferred action. Here I propose that the significance of avant-garde events is produced in an analogous way, through a complex relay of anticipation and reconstruction.

Taken together, then, the notions of parallax and deferred action refashion the cliché not only of the neo-avant-garde as merely redundant of the historical avant-garde, but also of the postmodern as only belated in relation to the mod-

historical + social contexts

ern. In so doing I hope that they nuance our accounts of aesthetic shifts and historical breaks as well. Finally, if this model of *retroaction* can contribute any symbolic resistance to the work of *retroversion* so pervasive in culture and politics today—that is, the reactionary undoing of the progressive transformations of the century—so much the better.[6]

This book traces a few genealogies of art and theory since 1960, but it does so to approach *actuality:* what produces a present as different, and how does a present focus a past in turn? This question also involves the relation of critical to historical work, and here no one escapes the present, not even art historians. Historical insight does not depend on contemporary advocacy, but an engagement in the present, whether artistic, theoretical, and/or political, seems requisite. Certainly innovative historians of modern art have long tended to be incisive critics of contemporary practices as well, and this parallactic view has often led to other criteria for both objects of study.[7]

I advance this point not to insinuate my name but to remark my difference. Prominent art historians like Michael Fried, Rosalind Krauss, and T. J. Clark differ in method and motive, but they share a deep conviction in modernist art, and this conviction is somehow generational. Critics formed in my milieu are more ambivalent about this art, not only because we received it as an official culture, but because we were initiated by practices that wished to break with its dominant models. So, too, the anxiety of influence that flowed from Pablo Picasso through the milieu of Jackson Pollock to ambitious artists in the 1960s had eased for us; one sign of our difference (for our predecessors, no doubt, of our decadence) is that the angel with whom we wrestled was Marcel Duchamp by way of Andy Warhol, more than Picasso by way of Pollock. Moreover, both these Oedipal narratives had passed through the crucible of feminism, which changed them profoundly.[8] Thus a critic like me invested in the minimalist geneaology of art must differ from one invoked by abstract expressionism: not indifferent to modernist art, he or she will not be entirely convinced by it either. Indeed, I argue in chapter 2, this point of initiation may position the critic on a crux of modernist art, and so lead him or her to attend to its contradictions more than to its triumphs.[9]

Like others in my milieu, then, I have some distance on modernist art, but I have little on critical theory. In particular I have little distance on the semiotic turn that refashioned much art and criticism on the model of the text in the middle to late 1970s (discussed in chapter 3), for I developed as a critic during this time, when theoretical production became as important as artistic production. (To many of us it was more provocative, innovative, urgent—but then there was no real contest between, say, the texts of Roland Barthes or Jacques Derrida and new-image painting or pop-historicist architecture.) Nevertheless, when it comes to critical theory, I have the interest of a second-generation initiate, not the zeal of a first-generation convert. With this slight distance I attempt to treat critical theory not only as a conceptual tool but as a symbolic, even symptomatic form.

Two retrospective intuitions might be ventured here. Since the middle 1970s critical theory has served as a secret continuation of modernism by other means: after the decline of late-modernist painting and sculpture, it occupied the position of high art, at least to the extent that it retained such values as difficulty and distinction after they had receded from artistic form. So, too, critical theory has served as a secret continuation of the avant-garde by other means: after the climax of the 1968 revolts, it also occupied the position of cultural politics, at least to the extent that radical rhetoric compensated a little for lost activism (in this respect critical theory is a neo-avant-garde in its own right). This double secret service—as a high-art surrogate and an avant-garde substitute—has attracted many different followers.

One way in which I treat critical theory as a historical object is to attend to its synchronic connections with advanced art. Since the 1960s the two have shared at least three areas of investigation: the structure of the sign, the constitution of the subject, and the siting of the institution (e.g., not only the roles of the museum and the academy but also the locations of art and theory). This book is concerned with these general areas, but it focuses on specific relations, such as the rapport between the minimalist geneaology of art and the phenomenological concern with the body on the one hand and the structuralist analysis of the sign on the other (discussed in chapter 2), or the affinity between the pop genealogy of art and the psychoanalytic account of visuality developed by Jacques Lacan around the same time (discussed in chapter 5). It also concentrates on particular moments when art and theory are repositioned by other forces: for example, when site-specific installations or photo-text collages replicate the very effects that they otherwise resist, the fragmentation of the commodity-sign (chapter 3); or when a critical method like deconstruction is turned into a cynical gambit of art-world positioning (chapter 4).

Whether one regards such moments as total failures or as partial exposés, they do raise the question of the *criticality* of contemporary art and theory (the historical development of this value is discussed in chapters 1 and 7). I have already pointed to a few aspects of the current crisis, such as a relative inattention to the historicity of art and a near eclipse of contestatory spaces. But these laments about a loss of historical purchase and critical distance are old refrains, and sometimes they express little more than the anxiety of the critic about a loss of function and power. Yet this does not make them misbegotten or narcissistic. What *is* the place of criticism in a visual culture that is evermore *administered*—from an art world dominated by promotional players with scant need for criticism, to a media world of communication-and-entertainment corporations with no interest whatsoever? And what *is* the place of criticism in a political culture that is evermore *affirmative*—especially in the midst of culture wars that prompt the right to threaten *love it or leave it* and the left to wonder *where am I in this picture?* Of course this very situation makes the old services of criticism evermore urgent as well—to question a political-economic status quo committed to its own reproduction and profit above all else, and to mediate between cultural groups that, deprived of a public sphere for open debate, can only appear sectarian. But to note the needs is not to improve the conditions.

Several factors hinder art criticism in particular. Neither advocated by the museum nor tolerated by the market, some critics have withdrawn to the academy, while others have joined the administration of the culture industry—the media, fashion, and so on. This is not a moral judgment: even within the time

spanned by this book the few spaces once allowed for art criticism have nar-
rowed dramatically, and critics have followed artists forced to exchange critical
practice for economic survival. A double switch in these positions has not
helped: as some artists abandoned critical practices, others adopted theoretical
positions as if they were readymade critiques, and some theorists embraced artistic postures just as naively.[10] If the artists hoped to be elevated by theory, the
theorists looked to be grounded in art; but often these two projections advanced
two misconceptions: that art is not theoretical, not productive of critical concepts, in its own right; and that theory is only supplemental, to be applied or
not as one sees fit. As a result there may be little *formal* difference between the
illustration of commodity aesthetics in art of the late 1980s, say, and the illustration of gender politics in art of the early 1990s. Often in the cynicism of the
first and in the voluntarism of the second, work on form is neglected—in the
first as futile, in the second as secondary. And sometimes these misconceptions—that art is not theoretical and/or political in its own terms, that theory
is ornamental and politics external—*disable* theoretical and political art, and do
so in the name of each.

   This is not to save theory from artists or art from politics; nor is it to aid
the theory-bashing of the media or the witch-hunting of the right. (Sometimes
theory *is* burdened linguistically and irresponsible politically, but that hardly
means, as the *New York Times* has it, that art criticism is so much jabberwocky
and that deconstruction is an apology for the Holocaust.) On the contrary, it is
to insist that critical theory is immanent to innovative art, and that the relative
autonomy of the aesthetic can be a critical resource. For these reasons I argue
against a premature dismissal of the avant-garde. As I note in chapter 1, the
avant-garde is obviously problematic (it can be hermetic, elitist, and so on); yet,
recoded in terms of resistant and/or alternative articulations of the artistic and
the political, it remains a construct that the left surrenders at its own loss. The
avant-garde has no patent on criticality, of course, but a commitment to such
practices does not exclude a commitment to others as well.

   To demand this multiple focus does add to the burden on progressive art
and criticism, and the situation in art and academy is hardly supportive. In both

worlds a political backlash has manipulated an economic downturn to produce a reactive climate in which the dominant call is a conservative cutback to authoritative (often authoritarian) traditions.[11] The great threat to art and academy, we are told, comes from miscreant artists and tenured radicals; but subsidized reactionaries tell us so, and these ideologues of conservative foundations have done the real damage, as public faith in art and academy is eroded through such fantasms of the artist and the academic. This is hardly a state secret: thus far the right has dictated the culture wars and dominated the public imaging of art and academy, as the layman is led to associate the first with pornography, the second with indoctrination, and both with a waste of taxpayer money. Such are the deserts of the rightist campaign: while the left talked about the political importance of culture, the right *practiced* it.[12] Its philosophers have succeeded where readers of Marx have not—they have transformed the world, and it will take a great struggle to transform it otherwise.

It may be petty to worry about art and academic worlds when cooperative state and social contract alike are trashed. Yet important battles are waged here too: the attacks on affirmative action and multicultural initiatives, on public funding and political correctness (a classic instance of a leftist critique turned into a rightist weapon). The revolution of the rich also shows its true colors in these worlds, for our current rulers have revealed a new disregard not only for social compensation but for cultural support (at least the old rich had the good grace to be arriviste). Finally, however, there is this fundamental stake in art and academy: the preservation, in an administered, affirmative culture, of spaces for critical debate and alternative vision.

Again, to (re)claim such spaces is not easy. On the one hand, it is a labor of *dis*articulation: to redefine cultural terms and recapture political positions. (Here one must dispel the reactionary fantasms of art and academy as well as disentangle leftist critiques of such institutions from rightist attacks.)[13] On the other hand, it is a labor of articulation: to mediate content and form, specific signifiers and institutional frames. This is a difficult task but not an impossible one; I address some practices that succeeded, however provisionally, in such (dis)articulations. One beginning is to recover critical practices interrupted by the neoconservative coup of the 1980s—which is precisely what some young artists, critics, and historians do today. This book is my contribution to this work.[14]

Chapter 1 prepares my discussion of critical models in art and theory since 1960 through a new articulation of historical and neo-avant-gardes. Chapter 2 presents minimalist art as a crux in this relation in the 1960s. Chapter 3 discusses the subsequent reformulation of the work of art as text in the 1970s. And chapter 4 recounts the eventual meltdown of this textual model in a pervasive conventionalism of the image in the 1980s. In chapters 5 and 6 two contemporary reactions to this double inflation of text and image are examined: a turn to the real as evoked through the violated body and/or the traumatic subject, and a turn to the referent as grounded in a given identity and/or a sited community. Finally, chapter 7 (which is more epilogue than conclusion) extends my discussion to three discourses crucial to art and theory over this time: the critique of the subject, the negotiation of the cultural other, and the role of technology. The chapters tell connected stories (to me it is very important to regain the efficacy of such narratives), but they need not be read consecutively.

I dedicate this book to three people who have kept critical spaces open for me: Thatcher Bailey, founder of Bay Press; Charles Wright, director of the Dia Art Center from 1986 to 1994; and Ron Clark, head of the Whitney Museum Independent Study Program. I grew up with Thatcher and Charlie in Seattle, and they supported me as a critic in New York—Thatcher as a publisher, Charlie as a sponsor, and both as friends for years. In the same spirit I want to thank other old friends (Andrew Price, John Teal, Rolfe Watson, and Bob Strong) and family (Jody, Andy, and Becca). Over a decade ago Ron Clark invited me to the Whitney Program, where I was director of critical and curatorial studies when this book was conceived. Our seminars with Mary Kelly remain important to me, and I extend my thanks to all participants in the program over the years. For intellectual community I am indebted to my friends at *October:* Yve-Alain Bois, Benjamin Buchloh, Denis Hollier, Silvia Kolbowski, Rosalind Krauss, Annette Michelson, and Mignon Nixon; as well as at Cornell: David

Bathrick, Susan Buck-Morss, Mark Seltzer, and Geoff Waite. (I am grateful to other friends as well, especially Michel Feher, Eric Santner, and Howard Singerman—too many to list.) Parts of this book were written at the Cornell Society for the Humanities, and I thank its directors, Jonathan Culler and Dominick LaCapra. Finally, I am indebted to Carolyn Anderson, Peter Brunt, Miwon Kwon, Helen Molesworth, Charles Reeve, Lawrence Shapiro, Blake Stimson, and Frazer Ward; they have taught me as much I have taught them. The same is true in other ways of Sandy, Tait, and Thatcher.

New York, Winter 1995

The Return of the Real

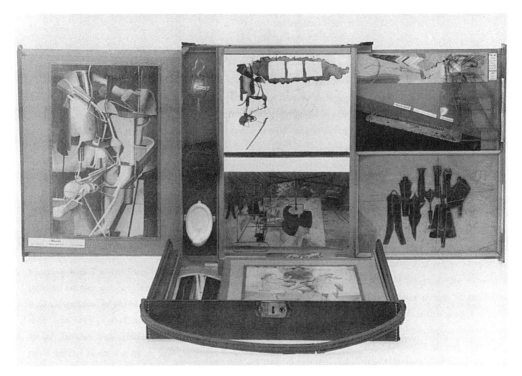

Marcel Duchamp, *Box-in-a-Valise,* deluxe edition, 1941, with miniatures (clockwise) of *The Bride* (1912), *Paris Air* (1919), *The Large Glass* (1915–23), *Tu m'* (1918), *Comb* (1916), *Nine Malic Molds* (1914–15), *Glider Containing a Water Mill* (1913–15), *Three Standard Stoppages* (1913–14), *Fountain* (1917), *Traveller's Folding Item* (1916).

WHO'S AFRAID OF THE NEO-AVANT-GARDE?

Postwar culture in North America and Western Europe is swamped by *neos* and *posts*. There are many repetitions and ruptures in this period: how do we distinguish them in kind? How do we tell the difference between a return to an archaic form of art that bolsters conservative tendencies in the present and a return to a lost model of art made to displace customary ways of working? Or, in the register of history, how do we tell the difference between an account written in support of the cultural status quo and an account that seeks to challenge it? In reality these returns are more complicated, even more compulsive, than I make them out to be—especially now, at the turn of the century, as revolutions at its beginning appear to be undone and as formations thought to be long dead stir again with uncanny life.

In postwar art to pose the question of repetition is to pose the question of the *neo-avant-garde,* a loose grouping of North American and Western European artists of the 1950s and 1960s who reprised such avant-garde devices of the 1910s and 1920s as collage and assemblage, the readymade and the grid, monochrome painting and constructed sculpture.[1] No rule governs the return of these devices: no one instance is strictly revisionist, radical, or compulsive. Here, however, I will focus on returns that aspire to a critical consciousness of both artistic conventions and historical conditions.

In "What is an Author?", a text written in early 1969 in the heyday of such returns, Michel Foucault writes in passing of Marx and Freud as "initiators of discursive practices," and he asks why a return is made at particular moments to the originary texts of Marxism and psychoanalysis, a return in the form of a rigorous reading.[2] The implication is that, if radical (in the sense of *radix:* to the root), the reading will not be another accretion of the discourse. On the contrary, it will cut through layers of paraphrase and pastiche that obscure its theoretical core and blunt its political edge. Foucault names no names, but clearly he has in mind the readings of Marx and Freud made by Louis Althusser and Jacques Lacan, respectively. (Again, he writes in early 1969, or four years after Althusser published *For Marx* and *Reading Capital* and three years after the *Ecrits* of Lacan appeared—and just months after May 1968, a revolutionary moment in constellation with other such moments in the past.) In both returns the stake is the *structure* of the discourse stripped of additions: not so much what Marxism or psychoanalysis means as *how* it means—and how it has transformed our conceptions of meaning. Thus in the early 1960s, after years of existentialist readings based on the early Marx, Althusser performs a structuralist reading based on the mature Marx of *Capital*. For Althusser this is the scientific Marx of an epistemological rupture that changed politics and philosophy forever, not the ideological Marx hung up on humanist problems such as alienation. For his part, in the early 1950s, after years of therapeutic adaptations of psychoanalysis, Lacan performs a linguistic reading of Freud. For Lacan this is the radical Freud who reveals our decentered relation to the language of our unconscious, not the humanist Freud of the ego psychologies dominant at the time.

The moves within these two returns are different: Althusser defines a *lost break* within Marx, whereas Lacan articulates a *latent connection* between Freud and Ferdinand de Saussure, the contemporaneous founder of structural linguistics, a connection implicit in Freud (for example, in his analysis of the dream as a process of condensation and displacement, a rebus of metaphor and metonymy) but impossible for him to think as such (given the epistemological limits of his own historical position).[3] But the method of these returns is similar: to focus on "the constructive omission" crucial to each discourse.[4] The motives are similar too: not only to restore the radical integrity of the discourse but to challenge its status in the present, the received ideas that deform its structure and restrict its efficacy. This is not to claim the final truth of such readings. On the contrary, it is to clarify their contingent strategy, which is to *re*connect with a lost practice in order to *dis*connect from a present way of working felt to be outmoded, misguided, or otherwise oppressive. The first move (*re*) is temporal, made in order, in a second, spatial move (*dis*), to open a new site for work.[5]

Now, amid all the repetitions in postwar art, are there any returns in this radical sense? None appear as historically focused and theoretically rigorous as the returns in Althusser and Lacan. Some recoveries are fast and furious, and they tend to reduce the past practice to a style or a theme that can be assimilated; such is often the fate of the found object in the 1950s and the readymade in the 1960s. Other recoveries are slow and partial, as in the case of Russian constructivism in the early 1960s, after decades of repression and misinformation in East and West alike.[6] Some old models of art appear to return independently, as with the various reinventions of monochrome painting in the 1950s and 1960s (Robert Rauschenberg, Ellsworth Kelly, Lucio Fontana, Yves Klein, Piero Manzoni, Ad Reinhardt, Robert Ryman, and so on). Other old models are combined in apparent contradiction, as when in the early 1960s artists like Dan Flavin and Carl Andre draw on such diverse precedents as Marcel Duchamp and Constantin Brancusi, Alexander Rodchenko and Kurt Schwitters, or when Donald Judd contrives an almost Borgesian array of precursors in his 1965 manifesto "Specific Objects." Paradoxically, at this crux of the postwar period, ambitious art is marked by an expansion of historical allusion as well as by a reduction of actual content. Indeed, such art often invokes different, even incommensurate models, but less to act them out in a hysterical pastiche (as in much art in the 1980s) than to work them through to a reflexive practice—to turn the very limitations of these models into a critical consciousness of history, artistic and otherwise. Thus there is method to the Judd list of precursors, especially where it appears most mad, as in its juxtaposition of the opposed positions of Duchamp and New York School painting. For Judd seeks not only to extract a new practice from these positions but to trump them as he goes—in this case to move beyond "objectivity" (whether in the nominalist version of Duchamp or in the formalist version of the New York School) to "specific objects."[7]

These moves involve the two returns in the late 1950s and early 1960s that might qualify as radical in the sense sketched above: the readymades of Duchampian dada and the contingent structures of Russian constructivism—that is, structures, like the counterreliefs of Tatlin or the hanging constructions of Rodchenko, that reflect both inwardly on material, form, and structure and outwardly on space, light, and context. Immediately two questions arise. Why do these returns occur then? And what relationship between moments of appearance and reappearance do they pose? Are the postwar moments passive repetitions of the prewar moments, or does the neo-avant-garde *act* on the historical avant-garde in ways that we can only now appreciate?

Let me respond to the historical question briefly; then I will focus on the theoretical question, which concerns avant-garde temporality and narrativity. My account of the return of the dadaist readymade and the constructivist structure will not come as a surprise. However different aesthetically and politically, both practices contest the bourgeois principles of autonomous art and expressive artist, the first through an embrace of everyday objects and a pose of aesthetic indifference, the second through the use of industrial materials and the transformation of the function of the artist (especially in the productivist phase of agitprop campaigns and factory projects).[8] Thus, for North American and Western European artists in the late 1950s and early 1960s, dada and constructivism offered two historical alternatives to the modernist model dominant at the time, the medium-specific formalism developed by Roger Fry and Clive Bell for postimpressionism and its aftermath, and refined by Clement Greenberg and Michael Fried for the New York School and its aftermath. Since this model was staked on the intrinsic autonomy of modernist painting in particular, pledged to the ideals of "significant form" (Bell) and "pure opticality" (Greenberg), discontented artists were drawn to the two movements that sought to exceed this apparent autonomy: to define the institution of art in an epistemological inquiry into its aesthetic categories and/or to destroy it in an anarchistic attack on its formal conventions, as did dada, or to transform it according to the materialist practices of a revolutionary society, as did Russian constructiv-ism—in any case to reposition art in relation not only to mundane space-time but to social practice. (Of course the neglect of these practices within the domi-nant account of modernism only added to the attraction, according to the old avant-gardist association of the critical with the marginal, of the subversive with the repressed.)

For the most part these recoveries were self-aware. Often trained in novel academic programs (the master of fine arts degree was developed at this time), many artists in the late 1950s and early 1960s studied prewar avant-gardes with a new theoretical rigor; and some began to practice as critics in ways distinct from belletristic or modernist-oracular precedents (think of the early texts of Robert Morris, Robert Smithson, Mel Bochner, and Dan Graham alone). In the United States this historical awareness was complicated by the reception of the avant-garde through the very institution that it often attacked—not only the museum of art but the museum of *modern* art. If artists in the 1950s had mostly recycled avant-garde devices, artists in the 1960s had to elaborate them critically; the pressure of historical awareness permitted nothing less. This com-plicated relation between prewar and postwar avant-gardes—the theoretical question of avant-garde causality, temporality, and narrativity—is crucial to comprehend today. Far from a quaint question, more and more depends on it: our very accounts of innovative Western art of the twentieth century as we come to its end.

Before I go further I should clarify two major presuppositions of my ar-gument: the value of the construct of the avant-garde and the need for new narratives of its history. By now the problems of the avant-garde are familiar: the ideology of progress, the presumption of originality, the elitist hermeticism, the historical exclusivity, the appropriation by the culture industry, and so on. Yet it remains a crucial coarticulation of artistic and political forms. *And it is this coarticulation of the artistic and the political that a posthistorical account of the neo-avant-garde, as well as an eclectic notion of the postmodern, serve to undo. Thus the need for new genealogies of the avant-garde that complicate its past and support its future.* My

Alexander Rodchenko, with constructions, c. 1922.

Carl Andre, with sawed sculptures, c. 1959–60.

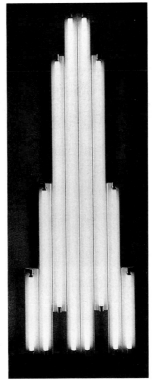

Vladimir Tatlin, *Monument for the Third International,* 1920, model.

Dan Flavin, *"Monument" for V. Tatlin,* 1969.

model of the avant-garde is too partial and canonical, but I offer it as a theoretical case study only, to be tested on other practices.[9] I also offer it in the belief that a revaluation of a canon is as significant as its expansion or its disruption.

THEORY OF THE AVANT-GARDE I

The central text on these questions remains *Theory of the Avant-Garde* by the German critic Peter Bürger. Over twenty years old, it still frames intelligent discussions of historical and neo-avant-gardes (Bürger first made these terms current), so even today it is important to work through his thesis. Some of his blind spots are now well marked.[10] His description is often inexact, and his definition overly selective (Bürger focuses on the early readymades of Duchamp, the early chance experiments of André Breton and Louis Aragon, the early photomontages of John Heartfield). Moreover, his very premise—that *one* theory can comprehend *the* avant-garde, that all its activities can be subsumed under the project to destroy the false autonomy of bourgeois art—is problematic. Yet these problems pale next to his dismissal of the postwar avant-garde as merely *neo,* as so much repetition in bad faith that cancels the prewar critique of the institution of art.

Here Bürger projects the historical avant-garde as an *absolute origin* whose aesthetic transformations are fully significant and historically effective in the first instance. This is tenuous from several points of view. For a poststructuralist critic such a claim of self-presence is suspect; for a theorist of reception it is impossible. Did Duchamp *appear* as "Duchamp"? Of course not, yet he is often presented as born full-blown from his own forehead. Did *Les Demoiselles d'Avignon* of Picasso *emerge* as the crux of modernist painting that it is now taken to be? Obviously not, yet it is often treated as immaculate in conception and reception alike. The status of Duchamp as well as *Les Demoiselles* is a retroactive effect of countless artistic responses and critical readings, and so it goes across the dialogical space-time of avant-garde practice and institutional reception. This blind spot in Bürger concerning the deferred temporality of artistic signification is ironic, for he is often praised for his attention to the historicity of aesthetic categories, and to a certain degree this praise is earned.[11] So where does he go astray? Do conventional notions of historicity not allow for such delays?

Bürger begins with the premise, which permits one to historicize in a Marxist way, of "a *connection* between the development of [an] object and the possibility of [its] cognition" (li).[12] According to this premise, our understanding of an art can be only as advanced as the art, and this leads Bürger to his principal argument: the avant-garde critique of bourgeois art depended on the development of this art, in particular on three stages within its history. The first stage occurs by the end of the eighteenth century when the autonomy of art is proclaimed as an ideal, in Enlightenment aesthetics. The second stage occurs by the end of the nineteenth century when this autonomy is made over into the very subject of art, that is, in art that aspires not only to abstract form but to an aestheticist withdrawal from the world. And the third stage occurs at the beginning of this century when this aestheticist withdrawal comes under attack by the historical avant-garde, for example, in the explicit productivist demand that art regain a use value, or the implicit dadaist demand that it acknowledge its uselessness value—that its withdrawal from the cultural order may be an affirmation of this order as well.[13] Although Bürger insists that this development is uneven and contradictory (he alludes to the notion of the "nonsynchronous" developed by Ernst Bloch), he still narrates it as an *evolution*. Perhaps Bürger could not conceive it otherwise, given his strict reading of the Marxist connection between object and understanding. But this residual evolutionism has troublesome effects.

Marx advances this premise of connection in a text that Bürger cites but does not discuss, the introduction to *Grundrisse* (1858), the draft notes preparatory to *Capital* (volume 1, 1867). At one point in these sketches Marx muses that his fundamental insights—not only the labor theory of value but the historical dynamic of class conflict—could not be articulated until his own time, the era of an advanced bourgeoisie.

> Bourgeois society is the most developed and the most complex historic organization of production. The categories which express its

relations, the comprehension of its structure, thereby also allows
insights into the structure and the relations of production of all the
vanished social formations out of whose ruins and elements it built
itself up, whose mere nuances have developed explicit significance
within it, etc. Human anatomy contains a key to the anatomy of the
ape. The intimations of higher development among the subordinate
animal species, however, can be understood only after the higher
development is known. The bourgeois economy thus supplies the
key to the ancient, etc.[14]

This analogy between socioeconomic evolution and anatomical evolution is
telling. Evoked as an illustration of development as recapitulation, it is neither
accidental nor arbitrary. It is part of the ideology of his time, and it arises almost
naturally in his text. And that is the problem, for to model historical development after biological development *is* to naturalize it, despite the fact that Marx
was the first to define this move as ideological par excellence. This is not to
dispute that our understanding can be only as developed as its object, but it is
to question how we think this connection, how we think causality, temporality,
and narrativity, how immediate we deem them to be. Clearly they cannot be
thought in terms of historicism, defined most simply as the conflation of *before*
and *after* with *cause* and *effect,* as the presumption that the prior event produces
the later one. Despite many critiques in different disciplines, historicism still
pervades art history, especially modernist studies, as it has from its great Hegelian founders to influential curators and critics like Alfred Barr and Clement
Greenberg and beyond.[15] Above all else it is this persistent historicism that condemns contemporary art as belated, redundant, repetitious.

Along with a tendency to take the avant-garde rhetoric of rupture at its
own word, this residual evolutionism leads Bürger to present history as both
punctual and final. Thus for him a work of art, a shift in aesthetics, happens all at
once, entirely significant in its first moment of appearance, and it happens once
and for all, so that any elaboration can only be a rehearsal. This conception of
history as punctual and final underlies his narrative of the historical avant-garde

as pure origin and the neo-avant-garde as riven repetition. This is bad enough, but things get worse, for to repeat the historical avant-garde, according to Bürger, is to cancel its critique of the institution of autonomous art; more, it is to invert this critique into an affirmation of autonomous art. Thus, if ready-mades and collages challenged the bourgeois principles of expressive artist and organic art work, neo-readymades and neo-collages reinstate these principles, reintegrate them through repetition. So, too, if dada attacks audience and market alike, neo-dada gestures are adapted to them, as viewers are not only prepared for such shock but hungry for its titillation. And so on down the line: for Bürger the repetition of the historical avant-garde by the neo-avant-garde can only turn the anti-aesthetic into the artistic, the transgressive into the institutional.

Of course there is truth here. For example, the proto-pop and *nouveau-réaliste* reception of the readymade did tend to render it aesthetic, to recoup it as an art-commodity. When Johns bronzed and painted his two Ballantine ales (upon a remark of Willem de Kooning, legend has it, that Leo Castelli could sell anything as art, even beer cans), he did reduce the Duchampian ambiguity of the urinal or the bottle rack as a (non)work of art; his materials alone signified the artistic. So, too, when Arman collected and composed his assisted ready-mades, he did invert the Duchampian principle of aesthetic indifference; his assemblages flaunted either transgression or taste. More egregiously, with figures like Yves Klein dadaist provocation was turned into bourgeois spectacle, "an avant-garde of dissipated scandals," as Smithson remarked in 1966.[16] But this is not the entire story of the neo-avant-garde, nor does it end there; indeed, one project in the 1960s, I will argue, is to *critique* the old charlatanry of the bohemian artist as well as the new institutionality of the avant-garde.[17] Yet the story does end there for Bürger, mostly because he fails to recognize the ambitious art of his time, a fatal flaw of many philosophers of art. As a result he can only see the neo-avant-garde in toto as futile and degenerate in romantic relation to the historical avant-garde, onto which he thus projects not only a magical effectivity but a pristine authenticity. Here, despite his grounding in Benjamin, Bürger affirms the very values of authenticity, originality, and singu-

Jasper Johns, *Painted Bronze*, 1960.

larity that Benjamin held in suspicion. Critical of the avant-garde in other respects, Bürger remains within its value system here.

However simple, his structure of heroic past versus failed present is not stable. Sometimes the *successes* credited to the historical avant-garde are difficult to distinguish from the *failures* ascribed to the neo-avant-garde. For example, Bürger argues that the historical avant-garde reveals artistic "styles" to be historical conventions and treats historical conventions as practical "means" (18–19), a double move fundamental to its critique of art as somehow beyond history and without purpose. But this move from styles to means, this passage from a "historical succession of techniques" to a posthistorical "simultaneity of the radically disparate" (63), would seem to push art into the arbitrary. If this is so, how is the supposed arbitrariness of the historical avant-garde different from the alleged absurdity of the neo-avant-garde, "a manifestation that is void of sense and that permits the positing of any meaning whatever" (61)?[18] There is a difference, to be sure, but one of degree not of kind, which points to a flow between the two avant-gardes that Bürger does not otherwise allow.

My purpose is not to pick apart this text twenty years after the fact; in any case its important thesis is too influential to dismiss out of hand. Rather I want to improve on it if I can, to complicate it through its own ambiguities—in particular to intimate *a temporal exchange between historical and neo avant-gardes, a complex relation of anticipation and reconstruction.* The Bürger narrative of direct cause and effect, of lapsarian before and after, of heroic origin and farcical repetition, will no longer do. Many of us recite this narrative without much thought—but with great condescension toward the very possibility of contemporary art.

At times Bürger approaches such complication, but ultimately he resists it. This is most manifest in his account of the failure of the avant-garde. For Bürger the historical avant-garde *also* failed—the dadaists to destroy traditional art categories, the surrealists to reconcile subjective transgression and social revolution, the constructivists to make the cultural means of production collective—but it failed heroically, tragically. Merely to fail *again,* as the neo-avant-garde does according to Bürger, is at best pathetic and farcical, at worst cynical and opportunistic. Here Bürger echoes the famous remark of Marx in *The Eighteenth Brumaire of Louis Bonaparte* (1852), mischievously attributed to Hegel, that all great events of world history occur twice, the first time as tragedy, the second time as farce. (Marx was concerned with the return of Napoleon, master of the first French Empire, in the guise of his nephew Louis Bonaparte, servant of the second French Empire.) This trope of tragedy followed by farce is seductive—its cynicism is a protective response to many historical ironies—but it hardly suffices as a theoretical model, let alone as a historical analysis. Yet it pervades attitudes toward contemporary art and culture, where it first *constructs* the contemporary as *post*historical, a simulacral world of failed repetitions and pathetic pastiches, and then *condemns* it as such from a mythical point of critical escape beyond it all. Ultimately *this* point is posthistorical, and its perspective is most mythical where it purports to be most critical.[19]

For Bürger the failure of both historical and neo-avant-gardes spills us all into pluralistic irrelevance, "the positing of any meaning whatever." And he concludes that "no movement in the arts today can legitimately claim to be historically more advanced *as art* than any other" (63). This despair is also seductive—it has the pathos of all Frankfurt School melancholia—but its fixation on the past is the other face of the cynicism about the present that Bürger both scorns and supports.[20] And the conclusion is *mistaken* historically, politically, and ethically. First, it neglects the very lesson of the avant-garde that Bürger teaches elsewhere: the historicity of *all* art, including the contemporary. It also neglects that an understanding of this historicity may be *one* criterion by which art can claim to be advanced as art today. (In other words, recognition of conventions need not issue in the "simultaneity of the radically disparate"; on the contrary, it can prompt a sense of the radically necessary.) Second, it ignores that, rather than invert the prewar critique of the institution of art, the neo-avant-garde has worked to extend it. It also ignores that in doing so the neo-avant-garde has produced new aesthetic experiences, cognitive connections, and political interventions, and that these openings may make up *another* criterion by which art can claim to be advanced today. Bürger does not see these openings, again in part because he is blind to the ambitious art of his time. Here, then, I want to explore such possibilities, and to do so initially in the form of an hypothesis: *rather than cancel the project of the historical avant-garde, might the neo-avant-garde comprehend it for the first time?* I say "comprehend," not "complete": the project of the avant-garde is no more concluded in its neo moment than it is enacted in its historical moment. In art as in psychoanalysis, creative critique is *interminable,* and that is a good thing (at least in art).[21]

THEORY OF THE AVANT-GARDE II

Immodestly enough, I want to do to Bürger what Marx did to Hegel: to right his concept of the dialectic. Again, the aim of the avant-garde for Bürger is to destroy the institution of autonomous art in order to reconnect art and life. Like the structure of heroic past and failed present, however, this formulation only seems simple. For what is art and what is life here? Already the opposition tends to cede to art the autonomy that is in question, and to position life at a point beyond reach. In this very formulation, then, the avant-garde project is predisposed to failure, with the sole exception of movements set in the midst of revolutions (this is another reason why Russian constructivism is so often privileged by artists and critics on the left). To make matters more difficult, life is conceived here paradoxically—not only as remote but also as immediate, as if it were simply *there* to rush in like so much air once the hermetic seal of convention is broken. This dadaist ideology of immediate experience, to which Benjamin is also inclined, leads Bürger to read the avant-garde as transgression pure and simple.[22] More specifically, it prompts him to see its primary device, the ready-made, as a sheer thing-of-the-world, an account that occludes its use not only as an epistemological provocation in the historical avant-garde but also as an institutional probe in the neo–avant-garde.

In short, Bürger takes the romantic rhetoric of the avant-garde, of rupture and revolution, at its own word. In so doing he misses crucial dimensions of its practice. For example, he misses its *mimetic* dimension, whereby the avant-garde mimes the degraded world of capitalist modernity in order not to embrace it

15

but to mock it (as in Cologne dada). He also misses its *utopian* dimension, whereby the avant-garde proposes not what can be so much as what *cannot* be—again as a critique of what is (as in de Stijl). To speak of the avant-garde in these terms of rhetoric is not to dismiss it as merely rhetorical. Rather it is to situate its attacks as both contextual and performative. *Contexual* in that the cabaret nihilism of the Zurich branch of dada critically elaborated the nihilism of World War I, or that the aesthetic anarchism of the Berlin branch of dada critically elaborated the anarchism of a country defeated militarily and torn up politically. And *performative* in the sense that both these attacks on art were waged, necessarily, in relation to its languages, institutions, and structures of meaning, expectation, and reception. It is in this *rhetorical* relation that avant-garde rupture and revolution are located.

This formulation blunts the sharp critique of the avant-garde project associated with Jürgen Habermas, which goes beyond Bürger. Not only did the avant-garde fail, Habermas argues, it was always already false, "a nonsense experiment." "Nothing remains from a desublimated meaning or a destructured form; an emancipatory effect does not follow."[23] Some respondents to Bürger push this critique further. In its attempt to negate art, they argue, the avant-garde *preserves* the category of art-as-such. Thus, rather than a break with the ideology of aesthetic autonomy, it is but "a reversal phenomenon on the identical ideological level."[24] This critique is pointed, to be sure, but it is pointed at the wrong target—that is, if we understand the avant-garde attack as rhetorical in the immanent sense sketched above. For the most acute avant-garde artists such as Duchamp, the aim is neither an abstract negation of art nor a romantic reconciliation with life but a perpetual testing of the conventions of both. Thus, rather than false, circular, and otherwise affirmative, avant-garde practice at its best is contradictory, mobile, and otherwise diabolical. The same is true of neo-avant-garde practice at its best, even the early versions of Rauschenberg or Allan Kaprow. "Painting relates to both art and life" runs a famous Rauschenberg motto. "Neither is made. (I try to act in that gap between the two.)"[25] Note that he says "gap": the work is to sustain a tension between art and life, not somehow to reconnect the two. And even Kaprow, the neo-avant-gardist most loyal to the line of reconnection, seeks not to undo the "traditional identities" of art forms—this is a given for him—but to test the "frames or formats" of aesthetic experience as defined at a particular time and place. This testing of frames or formats drives the neo-avant-garde in its contemporary phases, and it does so in directions that cannot be foreseen.[26]

At this point I need to take my thesis about the avant-garde a step further, one that may lead to another way—with Bürger, beyond Bürger—to narrate its project. What was effected by the signal acts of the historical avant-garde, as when Alexander Rodchenko presented painting as three panels of primary colors in 1921? "I reduced painting to its logical conclusion," the great constructivist remarked in 1939, "and exhibited three canvases: red, blue, and yellow. I affirmed: this is the end of painting. These are the primary colors. Every plane is a discrete plane and there will be no more representation."[27] Here Rodchenko declares the *end* of painting, but what he demonstrates is the *conventionality* of painting: that it could be delimited to primary colors on discrete canvases in his artistic-political context with its specific permissions and pressures—this is the crucial qualification. *And nothing explicit is demonstrated about the institution of art.* Obviously convention and institution cannot be separated, but neither are they identical. On the one hand, the institution of art does not totally govern aesthetic conventions (this is too determinist); on the other hand, these conventions do not totally comprise the institution of art (this is too formalist). In other words, the institution of art may *enframe* aesthetic conventions, but it does not *constitute* them. This heuristic difference may help us to distinguish the emphases of historical and neo-avant-gardes: if the historical avant-garde focuses on the conventional, the neo-avant-garde concentrates on the institutional.

A related argument can be advanced about Duchamp, as when he signed a rotated urinal with a pseudonym in 1917. Rather than define the fundamental properties of a given medium from within as do the Rodchenko monochromes, the Duchamp readymade articulates the enunciative conditions of the art work from without, with an alien object. But the effect is still to reveal the conventional limits of art in a particular time and place—this again is the crucial qualification (obviously the contexts of New York dada in 1917 and Soviet

Alexander Rodchenko, *Pure Colors: Red, Yellow, Blue,* 1921.

Daniel Buren, photo/souvenir of one of 200 green-and-white papers posted in Paris and environs, 1968.

constructivism in 1921 are radically different). Here, too, apart from the local outrage provoked by the vulgar object, the institution of art is not much defined. Indeed, the famous rejection of *Fountain* by the Society of Independent Artists exposed the discursive parameters of this institution more than the work per se.[28] In any case, like the Rodchenko, the Duchamp is a declaration, a performative: Rodchenko "affirms"; Duchamp "chooses." Neither work purports to be an analysis, let alone a deconstruction. The modern status of painting as made-for-exhibition is preserved by the monochrome (it may even be perfected there), and the museum-gallery nexus is left intact by the readymade.

Such are the limitations underscored fifty years later by artists like Marcel Broodthaers, Daniel Buren, Michael Asher, and Hans Haacke, who were concerned to elaborate these same paradigms in order to investigate this exhibition status and that institutional nexus systematically.[29] To my mind this is the essential relation between these particular historical and neo-avant-garde practices. First, artists like Flavin, Andre, Judd, and Morris in the early 1960s, and then artists like Broodthaers, Buren, Asher, and Haacke in the late 1960s, develop the critique of the conventions of the traditional mediums, as performed by dada, constructivism, and other historical avant-gardes, into an investigation of the institution of art, its perceptual and cognitive, structural and discursive parameters. *This is to advance three claims: (1) the institution of art is grasped as such not with the historical avant-garde but with the neo-avant-garde; (2) the neo-avant-garde at its best addresses this institution with a creative analysis at once specific and deconstructive (not a nihilistic attack at once abstract and anarchistic, as often with the historical avant-garde); and (3) rather than cancel the historical avant-garde, the neo-avant-garde enacts its project for the first time—a first time that, again, is theoretically endless.* This is one way to right the Bürger dialectic of the avant-garde.

RESISTANCE AND RECOLLECTION

Yet my thesis has its own problems. First, there is the historical irony that the institution of art, the museum above all else, has changed beyond recognition, a development that demands the continual transformation of its avant-garde critique as well. A reconnection of art and life *has* occurred, but under the terms of the culture industry, not the avant-garde, some devices of which were long ago assimilated into the operations of spectacular culture (in part through the very repetitions of the neo-avant-garde). This much is due the devil, but only this much.[30] Rather than render the avant-garde null and void, these developments have produced new spaces of critical play and prompted new modes of institutional analysis. And this reworking of the avant-garde in terms of aesthetic forms, cultural-political strategies, and social positionings has proved the most vital project in art and criticism over the last three decades at least.

However, this is but one historical problem; there are theoretical difficulties with my thesis as well. Again, terms like historical and neo-avant-garde may be at once too general and too exclusive to use effectively today. I noted some drawbacks of the first term; if the second is to be retained at all, at least two moments in the initial neo-avant-garde alone must be distinguished: the first represented here by Rauschenberg and Kaprow in the 1950s, the second by Broodthaers and Buren in the 1960s.[31] As the *first* neo-avant-garde recovers the historical avant-garde, dada in particular, it does so often literally, through a reprise of its basic devices, the effect of which is *less to transform the institution of art than to transform the avant-garde into an institution.* This is one ruse of history to grant Bürger, but rather than dismiss it as farce we might attempt to understand it—here in analogy with the Freudian model of repression and repetition.[32] On this model, if the historical avant-garde was *repressed* institutionally, it was *repeated* in the first neo-avant-garde rather than, in the Freudian distinction, *recollected,* its contradictions worked through. If this analogy between repression and reception holds, then in its first repetition the avant-garde was made to appear historical before it was allowed to become effective, that is, before its aesthetic-political ramifications could be sorted out, let alone elaborated. On the Freudian analogy this is repetition, indeed reception, as *resistance.* And it need not be reactionary; one purpose of the Freudian analogy is to suggest that resistance is unknowing, indeed that it is a process of unknowing. Thus, for example, as early as Rauschenberg and Johns there is a Duchamp genre in the making, a reification not only at odds with his practice but paradoxically in

Marcel Broodthaers, *Musée d'Art Moderne, Département des Aigles, Section des Figures,* 1972, detail.

Michael Asher, *Untitled,* 1979, installation, the Art Institute of Chicago.

advance of its recognition. This reification may also occur in resistance to his practice—to its final work (*Etants donnés,* 1946–66), to some of its principles, to many of its ramifications.

In any case the becoming-institutional of the avant-garde does not doom all art thereafter to so much affectation and/or entertainment. It prompts in a *second* neo-avant-garde a critique of this process of acculturation and/or accommodation. Such is the principal subject of an artist like Broodthaers, whose extraordinary tableaux evoke cultural reification only to transform it into a critical poetic. Broodthaers often used shelled things like eggs and mussels to render this hardening at once literal and allegorical, in a word, reflexive—as if the best defense against reification were a preemptive embrace that was also a dire exposé. In this strategy, whose precedent dates to Baudelaire at least, a personal reification is *assumed*—sometimes homeopathically, sometimes apotropaically—against a social reification that is *enforced.*[33]

More generally, this becoming-institutional prompts in the second neo-avant-garde a creative analysis of the limitations of both historical and first neo-avant-gardes. Thus, to pursue one aspect of the reception of Duchamp, in several texts since the late 1960s Buren has questioned the dadaist ideology of immediate experience, or the "petit-bourgeois anarchist radicality" of Duchampian acts. And in many works over the same period he has combined the monochrome and the readymade into a device of standard stripes in order to explore further what these old paradigms sought to expose, only in part to occlude: "the parameters of artistic production and reception."[34] This elaboration is a collective labor that cuts across entire generations of neo-avant-garde artists: to develop paradigms like the readymade from an object that purports to be transgressive in its very facticity (as in its first neo repetition), to a proposition that explores the enunciative dimension of the work of art (as in conceptual art), to a device that addresses the seriality of objects and images in advanced capitalism (as in minimalist and pop art), to a marker of physical presence (as in site-specific art of the 1970s), to a form of critical mimicry of various discourses (as in allegorical art of the 1980s involved with mythical images from both high

art and mass media), and, finally, to a probe of sexual, ethnic, and social differences today (as in the work of such diverse artists as Sherrie Levine, David
Hammons, and Robert Gober). In this way the so-called *failure* of both historical and first neo-avant-gardes to destroy the institution of art has *enabled* the
deconstructive testing of this institution by the second neo-avant-garde—a testing that, again, is now extended to other institutions and discourses in the ambitious art of the present.[35]

But lest I render this second neo-avant-garde heroic, it is important to
note that its critique can also be turned on it. If the historical and the first neo-
avant-gardes often suffered from anarchistic tendencies, the second neo-avant-
garde sometimes succumbs to apocalyptic impulses. "Perhaps the only thing
one can do after having seen a canvas like ours," Buren remarks in one such
moment in February 1968, "is total revolution."[36] This is indeed the language
of 1968, and artists like Buren often use it: his work proceeds from "the extinction" of the studio, he writes in "The Function of the Studio" (1971); it is
pledged not merely to "contradict" the game of art but to "abolish" its rules
altogether.[37] This rhetoric, which is more situationist than situated, echoes the
oracular, often macho pronouncements of the high modernists. Our present is
bereft of this sense of imminent revolution; it is also chastened by feminist critiques of revolutionary language and cautioned by postcolonial concerns about
the exclusivity not only of art institutions but of critical discourses as well. As a
result contemporary artists concerned to develop the institutional analysis of
the second neo-avant-garde have moved away from grand *oppositions* to subtle
displacements (I think of artists from Louise Lawler and Silvia Kolbowski to
Christopher Williams and Andrea Fraser) and/or strategic *collaborations* with
different groups (Fred Wilson and Mark Dion are representative here). This is
one way in which the critique of the avant-garde continues, indeed one way
in which the avant-garde continues. And this is not a recipe for hermeticism or
formalism, as is sometimes alleged; it is a formula of practice. It is also a precondition of any contemporary understanding of the different phases of the avant-
garde.

Hans Haacke, *MetroMobilitan*, 1985.

Fred Wilson, *Mining the Museum,* 1992, detail of slave manacles repositioned in metalwork display, Maryland Historical Society.

DEFERRED ACTION

Perhaps now we can return to the initial question: how to narrate this revised relation between historical and neo-avant-gardes? The premise that an understanding of an art can only be as developed as the art must be retained, but again not along historicist lines, whether in analogy to anatomical development (as momentarily in Marx) or in analogy to rhetorical development, of origin followed by repetition, of tragedy followed by farce (as persistently in Bürger). Different models of causality, temporality, and narrativity are required; far too much is at stake in practice, pedagogy, and politics not to challenge the blindered ones that are in place.

In order to advance a model of my own I need to foreground an assumption already at work in this text: that history, in particular modernist history, is often conceived, secretly or otherwise, on the model of the individual subject, indeed *as a subject*. This is plain enough when a given history is narrated in terms of evolution or progression, as often in the late nineteenth century, or conversely in terms of devolution or regression, as often in the early twentieth century (the last trope is pervasive in modernist studies from Georg Lukács to the present). But this modeling of history continues in contemporary criticism even when it assumes the death of the subject, for often the subject only returns at the level of ideology (for example, the Nazi subject), the nation (now imagined as a psychic entity more than as a body politic), and so on. As is clear from my treatment of the art institution as a subject capable of repression and resistance, I am as guilty of this vice as the next critic, but rather than give it up I want to make it a virtue. For if this analogy to the individual subject is all but structural to historical studies, why not apply the most sophisticated model of the subject, the psychoanalytic one, and do so in a manifest way?[38]

In his best moments Freud captures the psychic temporality of the subject, which is so different from the biological temporality of the body, the epistemological analogy that informs Bürger via Marx. (I say in his best moments for, just as Marx often escapes the modeling of the historical on the biological, Freud often succumbs to it in his reliance on developmental stages and

Lamarckian associations.) For Freud, especially as read through Lacan, subjectivity is not set once and for all; it is structured as a relay of anticipations and reconstructions of traumatic events. "It always takes two traumas to make a trauma," comments Jean Laplanche, who has done much to clarify the different temporal models in Freudian thought.[39] One event is only registered through another that recodes it; we come to be who we are only in deferred action (*Nachträglichkeit*). It is this analogy that I want to enlist for modernist studies at the end of the century: *historical and neo-avant-gardes are constituted in a similar way, as a continual process of protension and retension, a complex relay of anticipated futures and reconstructed pasts—in short, in a deferred action that throws over any simple scheme of before and after, cause and effect, origin and repetition.*[40]

On this analogy the avant-garde work is never historically effective or fully significant in its initial moments. It cannot be because it is traumatic—a hole in the symbolic order of its time that is not prepared for it, that cannot receive it, at least not immediately, at least not without structural change. (This is the other scene of art that critics and historians need to register: not only symbolic disconnections but *failures to signify.*)[41] This trauma points to another function in the repetition of avant-garde events like the readymade and the monochrome—not only to deepen such holes but to bind them as well. And this function points to another problem mentioned at the outset: how are we to distinguish the two operations, the first disruptive, the second restorative? Can they be separated?[42] There are related repetitions in the Freudian model that I have also smuggled into my text: some in which the trauma is acted out hysterically, as the first neo-avant-garde acts out the anarchistic attacks of the historical avant-garde; others in which the trauma is worked through laboriously, as later neo-avant-gardes develop these attacks, at once abstract and literal, into performances that are immanent and allegorical. In all these ways the neo-avant-garde acts on the historical avant-garde as it is acted on by it; it is less *neo* than *nachträglich;* and the avant-garde project in general develops in deferred action. Once repressed in part, the avant-garde did return, and it continues to return, but *it returns from the future:* such is its paradoxical temporality.[43] So what's neo about the neo-avant-garde? And who's afraid of it anyway?

Marcel Duchamp, *Given: 1. the Waterfall, 2. the Illuminating Gas,* 1946–66, detail.

Silvia Kolbowski, *Already,* 1992, detail.

I want to return briefly to the strategy of the return with which I began. Whether the artistic recoveries of the 1960s are as radical as the theoretical readings of Marx, Freud, or Nietzsche during the same period cannot be decided. What is certain is that these returns are as fundamental to postmodernist art as they are to poststructuralist theory: both make their breaks through such recoveries. But then these breaks are not total, and we have to revise our notion of epistemological rupture. Here, too, the notion of deferred action is useful, for *rather than break with the fundamental practices and discourses of modernity, the signal practices and discourses of postmodernity have advanced in a* nachträglich *relation to them.*[44]

Beyond this general *nachträglich* relation, both postmodernist art and poststructuralist theory have developed the specific questions that deferred action poses: questions of repetition, difference, and deferral; of causality, temporality, and narrativity. Apart from repetition and return stressed here, temporality and textuality are the twin obsessions of the neo-avant-gardes—not only the introduction of time and text into spatial and visual art (the famous debate between minimalist artists and formalist critics, discussed in chapter 2, is but one battle in this long war), but also the theoretical elaboration of museological temporality and cultural intertextuality (announced by artists like Smithson and developed by artists like Lothar Baumgarten in the present). Here I want only to register that similar questions, posed in different ways, have also impelled crucial philosophies of the period: the elaboration of *Nachträglichkeit* in Lacan, the critique of causality in Althusser, the genealogies of discourses in Foucault, the reading of repetition in Gilles Deleuze, the complication of feminist temporality in Julia Kristeva, the articulation of *différance* in Jacques Derrida.[45] "It is the very idea of a *first time* which becomes enigmatic," Derrida writes in "Freud and the Scene of Writing" (1966), a fundamental text of this entire antifoundational era. "It is thus the delay which is in the beginning."[46] So it is for the avant-garde as well.

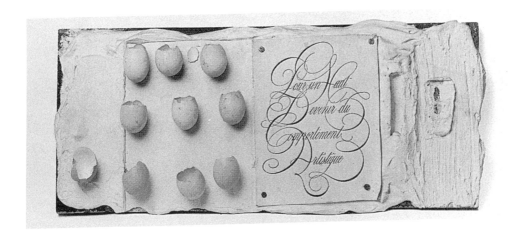

Marcel Broodthaers, *Pour un Haut Devenir du Comportement Artistique*, 1964.

David Hammons, *Bliz-aard Ball Sale*, 1983.

Larry Bell, *Untitled*, 1965.

The Crux of Minimalism

ABC art, primary structures, literalist art, minimalism: most of the terms for the relevant work of Carl Andre, Larry Bell, Dan Flavin, Donald Judd, Sol LeWitt, Robert Morris, Richard Serra, and others suggest that this art is not only inexpressive but almost infantile. Often dismissed in the 1960s as reductive, minimalism was often regarded in the 1980s as irrelevant, and both trashings are too vehement to be only a matter of art-world polemics. Beyond the vested interests of artists and critics pledged to humanist ideals and/or iconographic images in art, these trashings of minimalism were conditioned by two related events: in the 1960s by a specific sense that minimalism consummated one formalist model of modernism, completed and broke with it at once; and in the 1980s by a general reaction that used a trashing of the 1960s to justify a return to tradition in art and elsewhere. For just as rightists in the 1950s sought to bury the radicalism of the 1930s, so rightists in the 1980s sought to cancel the cultural claims and to reverse the political gains of the 1960s, so traumatic were they to these neoconservatives. Nothing much changed for the Gingrich radicals of the early 1990s, and political passion against the 1960s runs as high as ever today.[1]

So what is at stake in this trashing is history, in which minimalism is hardly a dead issue, least of all to those who would make it so. It is, however, a perjured one, for in the 1980s minimalism was represented as reductive and *retardataire* in order to make neo-expressionism appear expansive and vanguard, and in this way the different cultural politics of the minimalist 1960s and the neo-expressionist 1980s were misconstrued. For all its apparent freedoms, neo-expressionism participated in the cultural regressions of the Reagan-Bush era, while for all its apparent restrictions, minimalism opened up a new field of art, one that advanced work of the present continues to explore—or so it will be the burden of this chapter to prove. To do so, the reception of minimalism must first be set in place, then a counter-memory posed via a reading of its funda-mental texts. Next this counter-memory will be used to define the dialectical involvements of minimalism with both late-modernist and neo-avant-garde art, which in turn will suggest a genealogy of art from the 1960s to the present. In this genealogy minimalism will figure not as a distant dead end but as a contem-porary crux, a paradigm shift toward postmodernist practices that continue to be elaborated today. Finally this genealogy will lead back to the 1960s, that is, to the place of minimalism in this critical conjuncture of postwar culture, poli-tics, and economics.[2]

RECEPTION: "I OBJECT TO THE WHOLE REDUCTION IDEA"

On first glance it all looks so simple, yet in each body of work a perceptual ambiguity complicates things. At odds with the specific objects of Judd is his nonspecific composition ("one thing after another").[3] And just as the given gestalts of Morris are more contingent than ideal, so the blunt slabs of Serra are redefined by our perception of them in time. Meanwhile, the latticed logic of LeWitt can be obsessive, almost mad;[4] and even as the perfect cubes of Bell appear hermetically closed, they mirror the outside world. So what you see is what you see, as Frank Stella famously said,[5] but things are never as simple as they seem: the positivism of minimalism notwithstanding, perception is made reflexive in these works and so rendered complex.

Although the experiential surprise of minimalism is difficult to recapture, its conceptual provocation remains, for minimalism breaks with the transcen-dental space of most modernist art (if not with the immanent space of the dada-

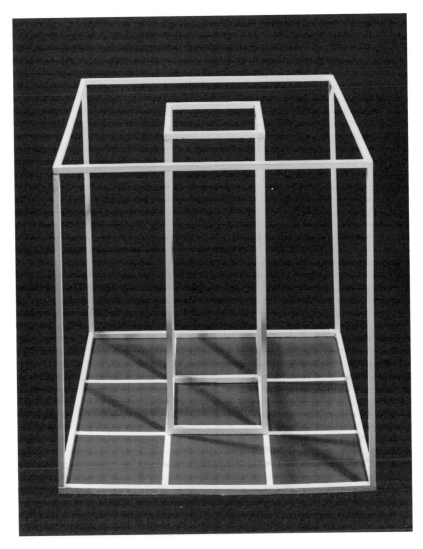

Sol LeWitt, *A 9* (from "Serial Project #1"), 1966.

ist readymade or the constructivist relief). Not only does minimalism reject the anthropomorphic basis of most traditional sculpture (still residual in the gestures of abstract-expressionist work), but it also refuses the siteless realm of most abstract sculpture. In short, with minimalism sculpture no longer stands apart, on a pedestal or as pure art, but is repositioned among objects and redefined in terms of place. In this transformation the viewer, refused the safe, sovereign space of formal art, is cast back on the here and now; and rather than scan the surface of a work for a topographical mapping of the properties of its medium, he or she is prompted to explore the perceptual consequences of a particular intervention in a given site. This is the fundamental reorientation that minimalism inaugurates.

Made explicit by later artists, this reorientation was sensed by early critics, most of whom lamented it as a loss for art. Yet in the moralistic charge that minimalism was reductive lay the critical perception that it pushed art toward the quotidian, the utilitarian, the nonartistic. For Clement Greenberg the minimalists confused the innovative with the outlandish and so pursued extraneous effects rather than essential qualities of art. This was why they worked in three dimensions (note that he does not call this work "sculpture"), a zone in which what is specific for Judd is arbitrary for Greenberg: "Minimalist works are readable as art, as almost anything is today—including a door, a table, or a blank sheet of paper."[6] Greenberg intended this remark as a scourge, but to the likes of John Cage it was an avant-gardist challenge: "We must bring about a music which is like furniture."[7] And this challenge was indeed taken up, via Robert Rauschenberg, Jasper Johns, Cage, and Merce Cunningham, in minimalist art (e.g., Judd and Morris), music (e.g., Philip Glass), dance (e.g., Yvonne Rainer), and theater (e.g., Robert Wilson), if rarely in the interests of a restored use value for culture.[8] In this reorientation Greenberg smelled a rat: the arbitrary, the avant-gardist, in a word, Marcel Duchamp. As we saw in chapter 1, this intuition of the return of the readymade paradigm in particular and the avant-gardist attack on the institution of art in general was common among both advocates and detractors of minimalism, and it is one I want to develop here.

For Richard Wollheim, too, the art content of minimalism was minimal; indeed, it was he who introduced the term, by which he meant that the work

Richard Serra, *One Ton Prop (House of Cards),* 1969.

of art was to be considered in terms less of execution or construction than "of decision or dismantling."[9] This aesthetic possibility is still taken as a threat in the guild of high art; here Greenberg defends against it: "Minimal art remains too much a feat of ideation." If the first great misreading is that minimalism is reductive, the second is that it is idealist. This was no less a misreading, made by some conceptual artists too, when it was meant positively: that minimalism captures pure forms, maps logical structures, or depicts abstract thought. For it is precisely such metaphysical dualisms of subject and object that minimalism seeks to overcome in phenomenological experience. Thus, far from idealist, minimalist work complicates the purity of conception with the contingency of perception, of the body in a particular space and time. (Consider how Serra pressures the Platonic idea of the cube in *House of Cards* [1969], a massively fragile propping of lead slabs.) And far from conceptual, minimalism is not "based on systems built beforehand, a priori systems," or so Judd argued in 1966.[10] However, more important to minimalism than this perceptual positivism is its avant-gardist comprehension of art in terms of its conventionality.[11] In short, minimalism is as self-critical as any late-modernist art, but its analysis tends toward the epistemological more than the ontological, for it focuses on the perceptual conditions and conventional limits of art more than on its formal essence and categorical being. It is this orientation that is so often mistaken as "conceptual."

In this way the stake of minimalism is the nature of meaning and the status of the subject, both of which are held to be public, not private, produced in a physical interface with the actual world, not in a mental space of idealist conception.[12] Minimalism thus contradicts the two dominant models of the abstract expressionist, the artist as existential creator (advanced by Harold Rosenberg) and the artist as formal critic (advanced by Greenberg). In so doing it also challenges the two central positions in modern aesthetics that these two models of the artist represent, the first expressionist, the second formalist. More importantly, with its stress on the temporality of perception, minimalism threatens the disciplinary order of modern aesthetics in which visual art is held to be strictly spatial. It is for this category mistake that Michael Fried condemned

Eva Hesse, *Hang-Up,* 1965–66.

minimalism—and rightly so from his position, for minimalism did prompt a concern with time, as well as an interest in reception in process art, body art, performance, site-specific work, and so on. Indeed, it is difficult to see the work that follows minimalism as entirely present, to be grasped in a single glance, a transcendental moment of grace, as Fried demands of modernist art at the end of his famous attack on minimalism, "Art and Objecthood" (1967).[13]

As minimalism challenges this order of modern aesthetics, it also contradicts its idealist model of consciousness. For Rosalind Krauss this is the central import of the minimalist attack on anthropomorphism and illusionism, for in her account these categories constitute not only an outmoded paradigm of art but an ideological model of meaning. In "Specific Objects" (1965) Judd had already associated relational composition with a "discredited" rationalism. In "Sense and Sensibility: Reflection on Post '60s Sculpture" (1973) Krauss poses a further analogy between illusionism and intentionality. For an intention to become an idea, she argues, an illusionist space of consciousness must be posited, and this space is idealist. Thus, to avoid the relational and the illusionist, as minimalism sought to do through its insistence on nonhierarchical orderings and literal readings, is in principle to avoid the aesthetic correlates of this ideological idealism as well.

This reading of minimalism warrants a digression. In her phenomenological account of minimalism, of minimalism *as* a phenomenology, Krauss insists on the inseparability of the temporal and the spatial in our reading of this art. Indeed, in *Passages in Modern Sculpture* (1977) she rethinks the modernist history of the medium through this inseparability (which her very title advances). In effect Krauss gives us a minimalist history of modernist sculpture in which minimalism emerges as the penultimate move in its long passage "from a static, idealized medium to a temporal and material one."[14] Here, rather than posit minimalism as a break with modernist practice (the conclusion to which her subsequent criticism tends),[15] she projects a minimalist recognition back onto modernism so that she can then read minimalism as a modernist epitome. Yet this is only one half of the story: minimalism is an apogee of modernism, but it is no less a break with it.

Of special interest here is the anachronism of this minimalist reading of modernist sculpture, which Krauss justifies in this way: "The history of modern sculpture coincides with the development of two bodies of thought, phenomenology and structural linguistics, in which meaning is understood to depend on the way that any form of being contains the latent experience of its opposite: simultaneity always containing an implicit experience of sequence."[16] It is true that, as represented by Edmund Husserl and Ferdinand de Saussure, phenomenology and structural linguistics did emerge with high modernism. Yet neither discourse was current among artists until the 1960s, that is, until the time of minimalism, and when they did reemerge they were in tension.[17] For example, structuralism was more critical of idealist consciousness and humanist history than was phenomenology; phenomenology was questioned because such notions were held to be residual in it. Now if this is so, and if minimalism is phenomenological at base, one might question how radical *its* critique of these notions is. For instance, just as phenomenology undercuts the idealism of the Cartesian "I think," so minimalism undercuts the existentialism of the abstract-expressionist "I express," but both substitute an "I perceive" that leaves meaning lodged in the subject. One way to ease this bind is to stress the structuralist dimension of the minimalist conjuncture, and to argue that minimalism is also involved in a structural analysis of pictorial and sculptural signifiers. Thus, while some artists (like Robert Irwin) develop the phenomenological dimension of minimalism, others (like Michael Asher) develop its structural analysis of these signifiers.

Minimalism does announce a new interest in the body—again, not in the form of an anthropomorphic image or in the suggestion of an illusionist space of consciousness, but rather in the *presence* of its objects, unitary and symmetrical as they often are (as Fried saw), just like people. And this implication of presence does lead to a new concern with perception, that is, to a new concern with the subject. Yet a problem emerges here too, for minimalism considers perception in phenomenological terms, as somehow before or outside history, language, sexuality, and power. In other words, it does not regard the subject as a sexed body positioned in a symbolic order any more than it regards the gallery or the museum as an ideological apparatus. To ask minimalism for a full critique of the subject may be anachronistic as well; it may be to read it too

43

much in terms of subsequent art and theory. Yet this question also points to the historical and ideological limits of minimalism—limits tested by its critical followers. For if minimalism does initiate a critique of the subject, it does so in abstract terms, and as subsequent art and theory develop this critique, they also come to question minimalism (this is especially true of some feminist art). Such is the difficulty of a genealogical tracing of its legacy, which here must await an analysis of the discourse of minimalism in its own time.

DISCOURSE: "THERE IS NO WAY YOU CAN FRAME IT"

In its own time the discourse of minimalism was dominated by three texts: "Specific Objects" by Donald Judd (1965), "Notes on Sculpture, Parts 1 and 2" by Robert Morris (1966), and "Art and Objecthood" by Michael Fried (1967).[18] Although well known, they manifest both the claims and the contradictions of minimalism in ways that are not well understood.

The year of "Specific Objects," 1965, was also the year that Greenberg revised his position paper, "Modernist Painting," which followed by four years his landmark collection of essays *Art and Culture*. In this context the first two claims made by Judd—that minimalism is neither "painting nor sculpture" and that "linear history has unraveled somewhat"—defy both categorical imperatives and historicist tendencies in Greenbergian modernism. Yet this extreme defiance developed as excessive devotion. For example, the reservation voiced by Greenberg about *some* painting after cubism—that its content is too governed by its edge—is elaborated by Judd into a brief against *all* modernist painting—that its flat, rectangular format "determines and limits the arrangement of whatever is on and inside it."[19] Here, as Judd extends Greenberg, he breaks with him, for what Greenberg regards as a definitional essence of painting Judd takes as a conventional limit, literally a frame to exceed. This break is attempted through a turn to specific objects, which he positions in relation to late-modernist *painting* (again, as represented by David Smith and di Suvero, late-modernist sculpture remains too mired in anthropomorphic composition and/or gesture). In short, *Judd reads the putatively Greenbergian call for an objective painting so literally as to exceed painting altogether in the creation of objects.* For what can be

---

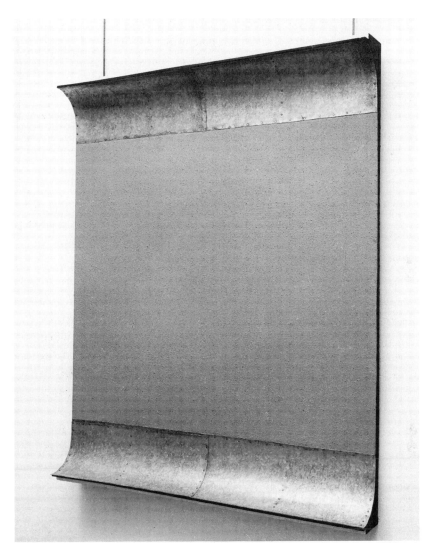

Donald Judd, *Untitled,* 1962.

more objective, more specific, than an object in actual space? Moved to fulfill the late-modernist project, Judd breaks with it, as is clear from his list of proto-types: Duchamp readymades, Johns cast objects, Rauschenberg combines, John Chamberlain scrap-metal sculptures, Stella shaped canvases, and so on—all rejects from the Greenberg canon.

This list suggests another consequence of the minimalist supersession of late-modernist art. According to Judd, some of these precursors assumed that "painting and sculpture have become set forms," that is, forms whose conventionality could not be elaborated further. "The use of three dimensions," he claims (note that Judd too does not term minimalism "sculpture"), "isn't the use of a given form" in this reified sense. In this other realm of objects, he suggests, *any* form, material, or process can be used. This expansion opens up criticism too, as Judd is led by his own logic to this infamous avant-gardist position: "A work of art needs only to be interesting." Here, consciously or not, *interest* is posed against the great Greenbergian shibboleth *quality*. Whereas quality is judged by reference to the standards not only of the old masters but of the great moderns, interest is provoked through the testing of aesthetic categories and the transgressing of set forms. In short, quality is a criterion of normative criticism, an encomium bestowed upon aesthetic refinement; interest is an avant-gardist term, often measured in terms of epistemological disruption. It too can become normative, but it can also license critical inquiry and aesthetic play.[20]

In "Specific Objects," then, the mandate that late-modernist art pursue objectivity is completed only to be exceeded, as Judd and company come out the other side of the objecthood of painting into the realm of objects. In "Notes on Sculpture, Parts 1 and 2" Robert Morris presents a different scenario in which minimalism is again set in a complicated relation to late-modernist discourse.

As Morris retains the category of sculpture, he implicitly disagrees with Judd on the genesis of minimalism. Sculpture was never "involved with illusionism," pictorial as this category is, and neither is minimalism. Far from a break with sculpture, minimalism realizes "the autonomous and literal nature of sculpture . . . that it have its own, equally literal space." At first glance this statement seems contradictory, for its two adjectives conflate the positions held by Greenberg and Judd respectively: the demand for autonomy and the demand for literalism. Yet this is precisely how Morris sees minimalism, as a provisional resolution of this contradiction, for he defines its unitary forms as *both* autonomous and literal. With minimalist gestalts, Morris writes, "one sees and immediately 'believes' that the pattern of one's mind corresponds to the existential fact of the object." His is the most nuanced discussion of the quintessentially minimalist tension between "the known constant and the experienced variable." Although Morris sometimes privileges the unitary form as prior to the specific object (in a way that the anti-idealism of minimalism otherwise does not), he usually presents the two as bound qua gestalt "cohesively and indivisibly together." This unity is necessary for Morris to retain the category of sculpture and to posit shape as its essential characteristic.

Yet this argument also appears circular. Morris first defines modernist sculpture in terms of minimalism (that it be literal) and then defines minimalism in terms of modernist sculpture (that it be autonomous). He then arrives at the very property, shape, that a year later Fried will pose as the essential value of *painting*. Part 1 of "Notes on Sculpture" ends in this way: "The magnification of this single most important sculptural value . . . establishes both a new limit and a new freedom for sculpture." The paradoxical nature of this statement suggests the tensions in minimalist discourse as well as the instabilities of aesthetic categories at this time. *For minimalism is both a contraction of sculpture to the modernist pure object and an expansion of sculpture beyond recognition.*

In Part 2 of "Notes on Sculpture" Morris addresses this paradoxical situation. First he defines the "new limit" for sculpture by reference to a remark by Tony Smith that situates minimalist work somewhere between the object and the monument, around the scale of the human body.[21] Then in an incisive move Morris redefines this scale in terms of address (from private object to public monument), that is, in terms of *reception*—a shift in orientation from the object to the viewer that turns the "new limit" for sculpture into its "new freedom." However, one intermediate step is needed, and so Morris returns to the mini-

Tony Smith, *Die,* 1962.

Robert Morris, *Untitled*, 1965.

malist gestalts. These unitary forms are used not only to "set the work beyond retardataire Cubist esthetics," he argues now, but, more importantly, to "take relationships out of the work and make them a function of space, light, and the viewer's field of vision."

In this way, as Judd exceeds Greenberg, so Morris exceeds both, for here, in 1966, a new space of "object/subject terms" is acknowledged. The minimalist suppression of anthropomorphic images and gestures is more than a reaction against the abstract-expressionist model of art; it is a "death of the author" (as Roland Barthes would call it in 1968) that is at the same time a birth of the viewer: "The object is but one of the terms of the newer esthetic. . . . One is more aware than before that he himself is establishing relationships as he apprehends the object from the various positions and under varying conditions of light and spatial context." Here we are at the edge of "sculpture in the expanded field" (as Krauss would call it in 1978). Yet even as Morris announces this new freedom, he seems ambivalent about it: in a flurry of contradictory statements he both pulls back ("that the space of the room becomes of such importance does not mean that an environmental situation is being established") and pushes forward ("Why not put the work outside and further change the terms?").

Finally, "Notes on Sculpture, Parts 1 and 2" is caught in the contradictions of its moment. On the one hand Morris insists that sculpture remain autonomous; on the other hand he suggests that "some of the new work has expanded the terms of sculpture" to the point where the object is "but one of" them. It is this expanded field, foreseen by Morris, that Michael Fried in "Art and Objecthood" is pledged to forestall.

More fully than Judd and Morris, Fried comprehends minimalism in its threat to formalist modernism, which is why he prosecutes it with such passion. First Fried details the minimalist crime: an attempt to displace late-modernist art by means of a literal reading that confuses the transcendental "presentness" of art with the mundane "presence" of things. According to Fried, the essential difference is that minimalist art seeks "to discover and project objecthood as such," whereas late-modernist art aspires "to defeat or suspend" this objecthood. Here, he contends, "the critical factor is *shape*," which, far from an essential sculptural value (as Morris would have it), is an essential pictorial value. Indeed, only if it "compels conviction as shape" can the late-modernist painting of Kenneth Noland, Jules Olitski, and Stella suspend objecthood, transcend the literalism of minimalism, and so achieve presentness.[22]

Given this difference, Fried must next show why minimalist literalism is "antithetical to art." To this end he argues that the presence of the minimalist object is that of a personage in disguise, a presence that produces a *situation* that, however provocative, is extrinsic to visual art. Here Fried also cites Smith on the scale of minimalism, but in order to recast it as an art of abstract statues, hardly as radically anti-anthropomorphic as its advocates claim. And yet his primary point is not to show up minimalism as secretly anthropomorphic but to present it as "incurably theatrical," for, according to the crucial hypothesis of "Art and Objecthood," "theatre is now the negation of art."

In order to support this hypothesis, Fried makes a strange detour: a gloss on an anecdote, again told by Tony Smith, about a nighttime ride on the unfinished New Jersey Turnpike in the early 1950s. For this proto-minimalist artist and architect the experience was somehow aesthetic but not quite art:

> The experience of the road was something mapped out but not socially recognized. I thought to myself, it ought to be clear that's the end of art. Most painting looks pretty pictorial after that. There is no way you can frame it, you just have to experience it.[23]

What was revealed to Smith, Fried argues, was the "conventional nature of art." "And this Smith seems to have understood not as laying bare the essence of art, but as announcing its end."

Here is marked the crux not only of the Friedian case against minimalism but of the minimalist break with late modernism. For in this epiphany about the conventionality of art is foretold the heretical stake of minimalism and its neo-avant-garde successors: not to discover the essence of art à la Greenberg but to transgress its institutional limits ("there is no way you can frame it"), to negate its formal autonomy ("you just have to experience it"), precisely to

---

announce its end.[24] For Fried as for Greenberg such avant-gardism is infantile: hardly a dialectical sublation of art into life, minimalist transgression obtains only the literalism of a frameless event or object "as it *happens,* as it merely *is*." Fried terms this minimalist literalism "theatrical" because it involves mundane time, a property that he deems improper to visual art. Thus, even if the institutional autonomy of art is not threatened by minimalism, the old Enlightenment order of the arts (the temporal versus the spatial arts) is endangered. This is why "theatre is now the negation of art," and why minimalism must be condemned.

At this point the prosecution of minimalism becomes a testament to formalist modernism, replete with the celebrated principles that "the concept of art" is "meaningful only *within* the individual arts" and "what lies *between* the arts is theatre."[25] Here, then, even as the order of Enlightenment aesthetics is disrupted on all sides in practice, it is reaffirmed in theory. And, finally, against this practice, against the hellish "endlessness" of minimalist theatre, Fried opposes the sublime "instantaneousness" of the modernist work, "which at every moment . . . is wholly manifest." More than a historical paradigm, even more than an aesthetic essence, this becomes, at the end of "Art and Objecthood," a spiritual imperative: "Presentness is grace."[26]

With its condemnation of theatrical art and its insistence on individual grace, this brief against minimalism is distinctly puritanical (its epigraph concerning the presentness of God refers to the Puritan theologian Jonathan Edwards). And its aesthetic does depend on an act of faith. Against avant-gardist atheism we are asked to believe in consensual quality, "specifically, the conviction that a particular painting or sculpture or poem or piece of music can or cannot support comparison with past work within that art whose quality is not in doubt." As Judd implicitly countered quality with interest, so Fried explicitly counters interest with *conviction,* which, like Greenberg, he attempts to save from subjectivism by an appeal to quasi-objective standards of taste, that is, to a particular judgment of an exclusive history of art. In short, beyond respect for the old decorum of the arts, Fried requests devotion to art, and in the words "compel conviction" are exposed the disciplinary underpinnings of this aesthetic. Apparently, the real threat of the minimalist paradigm is not only that it may disrupt the autonomy of art but that it may corrupt belief in art, that it may sap its conviction value. Here the doctrine of aesthetic autonomy returns in a late guise, and it suggests that rather than separate from religion (as Enlightenment aesthetics sometimes proposed to be), autonomous art is, in part, a secret substitute for religion—that is, a secret substitute for the moral disciplining of the subject that religion once provided.[27]

In the end the complication of minimalism for Fried comes clear in a long footnote in which he glosses a remark by Greenberg that "a stretched or tacked-up canvas already exists as a picture—though not necessarily as a *successful* one."[28] Fried must qualify this avant-gardist intimation that modernist art voids the conventional, for otherwise it might allow recognition of minimalism as advanced art. So first he distinguishes between the "irreducible essence of art" and the "minimal conditions" for its recognition as such. Then he argues that this essence is *conditional,* but not to the point where it becomes *conventional,* that is, to the point where aesthetic autonomy is threatened: "This is not to say that painting *has no essence;* it *is* to claim that that essence—i.e., that which compels conviction—is largely determined by, and therefore changes continually in response to, the vital work of the recent past." This formula is an affirmation of categorical limits ("painting") and institutional norms ("the vital work") in the face of the minimalist threat to both. As such it attempts to resolve the contradictions of late-modernist discourse inherited from Greenberg—but in a way that remains *within* this discourse and stands *against* its supersession in minimalism.

GENEALOGIES: "ROOT, HOG OR DIE"

Fried is an excellent critic of minimalism not because he is right to condemn it but because in order to do so persuasively he has to understand it, and this is to understand its threat to late modernism. Again, Fried sees minimalism as a corruption of late modernism "by a sensibility *already* theatrical, already (to say the worst) corrupted or perverted by theatre." In this reading minimalism develops out of late modernism, only to break it apart (the Latin *corrumpere,* the root of *corrupt,* means "to break"), contaminated as minimalism already is by theatre. But theatre here represents more than a concern with time alien to visual art; it is also, as "the negation of art," a code word for avant-gardism. We arrive, then, at this equation: *minimalism breaks with late modernism through a partial reprise of the historical avant-garde, specifically its disruption of the formal categories of institutional art.* To understand minimalism—that is, to understand its significance for advanced art since its time—both parts of this equation must be grasped at once.

First the minimalist break: rhetorically at least, minimalism is inaugurated when Judd reads late modernism so literally that he answers its call for self-critical objectivity perversely with specific *objects.* Morris seeks to reconcile this new minimalist literalism with the old modernist autonomy by means of the gestalt, only thereby to shift the focus from the object to its perception, to its *situation.* Fried then rises to condemn this theatrical move as a threat to artistic decorum and a corruption of artistic conviction; in so doing he exposes the disciplinary basis of his formalist aesthetics. In this general scenario, then, minimalism emerges as a dialectical moment of a "new limit and a new freedom" for art, in which sculpture is reduced one moment to the status of a thing "between an object and a monument" and expanded the next moment to an experience of sites "mapped out" but "not socially recognized" (in his anecdote Smith mentions "turnpikes, air strips, drill grounds," the very expanded field condemned by Fried but explored by Smithson and many others). In short, *minimalism appears as a historical crux in which the formalist autonomy of art is at once achieved and broken up,* in which the ideal of pure art becomes the reality of one more specific object among others.

This last point leads to the other side of the minimalist rupture, for if minimalism breaks with late-modernist art, by the same token it prepares the postmodernist art to come.[29] Yet before this genealogy is sketched, the avant-gardist part of the minimalist equation must be grasped. In chapter 1 I discussed the return of the transgressive avant-garde (especially Duchampian dada and Russian constructivism) in art of the 1960s, which poses the problem of its delay in the previous decades. To a great extent this avant-garde was suppressed

Robert Smithson, *Spiral Jetty,* 1969–70, details.

by Nazism and Stalinism, but it was also detained in North America by a combination of old anti-modernist forces and new Cold War politics, which tended to reduce the avant-garde to bolshevism *tout court*.[30] This North American delay allowed the dominance of Greenbergian formalism, which not only overbore the transgressive avant-garde institutionally but almost defined it out of existence. Thus, for Greenberg in "Avant-Garde and Kitsch" (1939/1961), the aim of the avant-garde is not at all to sublate art *into* life but rather to purify art *of* life—to save it from debasement by mass-cultural kitsch and abandonment by bourgeois patronage. In effect, this formalist avant-garde sought to *preserve* what the transgressive avant-garde sought to *transform:* the institutional autonomy of art. Faced with this account, the minimalists looked to the transgressive avant-garde for alternative models of practice. Thus Andre turned to Alexander Rodchenko and Constantin Brancusi, Flavin to Vladimir Tatlin, many others to Duchamp, and so on. In this way minimalism became one site of a general return of this avant-garde—a return that, with the force of the repressed, opened up the disciplinary order of late modernism.

This avant-gardist connection may explain why, in the very first sentence of "Art and Objecthood," Fried brands minimalism as "largely ideological" when most critics saw it as largely *non*ideological, altogether minimal in content, a zero degree of art. One implication here is that minimalism is an aesthetic fraud that corrupts conviction in art, but there is another: that minimalism presents a self-conscious position *on* art, which might allow it not only to comprehend modernist art as an institutional discourse, an array of other "largely ideological" positions, but also to intervene in this discourse *as* such a position. Again, this is an avant-gardist recognition (Fried smelled the same rat as Greenberg: Duchamp and disciples), but minimalism does more than repeat it, for, as I argued in chapter 1, only with minimalism does this understanding become self-conscious. That is, only in the early 1960s is the institutionality not only of art but also of the avant-garde first appreciated and then exploited.[31]

For many critics the failure of the historical avant-garde to integrate art into life renders this avant-gardist project futile. "Since now the protest of the historical avant-garde against art as an institution is accepted as *art*," Peter Bürger writes in *Theory of the Avant-Garde* (1974), "the gesture of the neo-avant-garde becomes inauthentic."[32] But this failure of the transgressive avant-garde in the 1910s and 1920s as well as of the first neo-avant-garde in the 1950s is not total; at a bare minimum it prompts a practical critique of the institution of art, the tradition of the avant-garde, and other discourses in a *second* neo-avant-garde that emerges in the 1960s. In this second neo-avant-garde, in which minimalism as well as pop art figure prominently, the aim is twofold at least: on the one hand, to reflect on the contextual conditions of art, as in minimalism, in order to expand its parameters; and on the other hand, to exploit the conventionality of the avant-garde, as in pop, in order to comment on modernist and mass-cultural formations alike. Both steps are important to the institutional critique that follows in art of the late 1960s and early 1970s.

Finally, however, my claim that the mission of the avant-garde is comprehended, if not completed, only with the neo-avant-garde furthered by minimalism and pop rests on this belief: the break that Bürger considers the ultimate significance of the avant-garde is only achieved by this neo-avant-garde in its contestation of formalist modernism.

> The meaning of the break in the history of art that the historical avant-garde movements provoked [Bürger writes] does not consist in the destruction of art as an institution, but in the destruction of the possibility of positing aesthetic norms as valid ones. This has consequences for scholarly dealings with works of art; the normative examination is replaced by a functional analysis, the object of whose investigation would be social effect (function) of a work and a sociologically definable public within an already existing institutional frame.[33]

Only with minimalism is such "normative examination"—in my account the categorical approach of Greenbergian formalism—revealed to be prejudicial. And with this revelation come the two shifts that I have stressed: the *normative* criterion of *quality* is displaced by the *experimental* value of *interest,* and art is seen to develop less by the *refinement* of the given forms of art (in which the pure is pursued, the extraneous expunged) than by the *redefinition* of such aesthetic categories. In this way the object of critical investigation becomes less the essence of a medium than "the social effect (function) of a work" and, more importantly, the intent of artistic intervention becomes less to secure a transcendental conviction in art than to undertake an immanent testing of its discursive rules and institutional regulations. Indeed, this last point may provide a provisional distinction between formalist, modernist art and avant-gardist, postmodernist art: to compel conviction versus to cast doubt; to seek the essential versus to reveal the conditional.

None of this develops as smoothly or as completely as I imply here. Nevertheless, if minimalism and pop do mark a historical crux, then, again, they will suggest not only a perspective on modernist art but also a genealogy of postmodernist art. This genealogy cannot be a stylistic history of influence or evolution (in which minimalism "reduces" the art object, say, so that conceptualism may then "dematerialize" it altogether), nor can it be a psychological account of generational conflicts or periodic reactions (as with the trashings of the 1960s with which I began). Again, only an analysis that allows for both parts of the minimalist equation—the break with late modernism and the return of the avant-garde—can begin to account for the advanced art of the last thirty-five years or so.

A few readings of recent art approach minimalism and pop as such a crux, either as a break with the aesthetic order of late modernism or as a reprise of the critical strategies of the readymade (but not both); they are significant for what they exclude as well as include. In two essays from 1979 Douglas Crimp and Craig Owens depart from the aesthetic order mapped out by Fried in "Art and Objecthood."[34] For Crimp it is theatrical presence, condemned by Fried and repressed in late-modernist art, that returns in the performance and video art of the early 1970s, to be recontained in the pictures of Cindy Sherman, Sherrie Levine, and others in the late 1970s. For Owens it is linguistic temporality that returns to disrupt the visual spatiality of late-modernist art: the textual decenterings of the art object in the site/nonsite works of Smithson, for example, or the allegorical collisions of aesthetic categories in the performances of Laurie Anderson. Yet, however much they comprehend, both scenarios overlook crucial developments: the first neglects the institutional critique that emerges from minimalism, and the second does not question the historical forces at work in the textual fragmentation of art after minimalism. Moreover, both critics· accept the terms offered by Fried, which are not deconstructed so much as reversed. In this way his negative terms, the theatrical and the temporal, are only revalued as positive, and his late-modernist schema remains in place, indeed in force.[35]

As an analysis of perception, minimalism prepared a further analysis of the conditions of perception. This led to a critique of the spaces of art (as in the work of Michael Asher), of its exhibition conventions (as in Daniel Buren), of its commodity status (as in Hans Haacke)—in short, to a critique of the institution of art. For critics like Benjamin Buchloh this history is mostly a genealogy of the presentational strategies of the readymade. Yet, as we have seen, this narrative also leaves out a crucial concern: the sexual-linguistic constitution of the subject. For the most part this concern is left out of the art as well, for, again, even as minimalism turned from the objective orientation of formalism to the subjective orientation of phenomenology, it tended to position artist and viewer alike not only as historically innocent but as sexually indifferent, and the same holds for much conceptual and institution-critical work that followed minimalism. This omission is addressed in feminist art from the middle 1970s through the middle 1980s, and in this investigation such disparate artists as Mary Kelly and Silvia Kolbowski, Barbara Kruger and Sherrie Levine, Louise Lawler and Martha Rosler turned to images and discourses adjacent to the art world, especially to representations of women in mass culture and to constructions of femininity in psychoanalytic theory. This is the most productive critique of minimalism to date, and it is elaborated in practice.

Recently the status of minimalism has changed once more. On the one hand, it recedes from us as an archival object as the 1960s become an historical period.[36] On the other hand, it rushes toward us as artists seek an alternative to practices of the 1970s and 1980s. This return is a mixed event: often rather than a working through of the problems left by minimalism, it appears strategic and/ or reactive. Thus there are strategic revisions of minimalism that refashion it in iconographic, expressive, and/or spectacular themes—as if to attack it with the very terms that it opposed. So, too, there are reactive versions of minimalism that pit it against subsequent work—that pose its phenomenological intimation of the body, say, against the psychoanalytic definition of the subject in feminist art of the 1970s and 1980s (which here becomes the object of resentment). In this way, even as minimalism became a set style long ago, its value is still not set, and this is further evidence of its crucial status in postwar art.[37]

A POP-MINI-SERIES: "A SCHIZOPHRENIC CLATTERING"

Finally, in order to understand the crux of minimalism we must reposition it in its own time. One way to do so is to juxtapose minimalism with pop art, as related responses to the same moment in the dialectic of modernism and mass culture. In this account both minimalism and pop confront, on the one hand, the rarefied high art of late modernism and, on the other hand, the spectacular culture of advanced capitalism, and both are soon overwhelmed by these forces. Thus pop may seek to use mass culture in order to test high art, but its dominant effect is to recoup the low for the high, the categories of which remain mostly intact. And minimalism may resist both high art and low culture in order to regain a transformative autonomy of aesthetic practice, but its dominant effect is to allow this autonomy to be dispersed across an expanded field of cultural activity.[38] In the case of pop, then, the fabled integration of high art and low culture is attained, but mostly in the interests of the culture industry, to which, with Warhol and others, the avant-garde becomes as much a subcontractor as an antagonist. In the case of minimalism the fabled autonomy of art is achieved, but mostly to be corrupted, broken up, dispersed.

What forces effect this integration and that corruption? The best clues are the pop embrace and the minimalist refusal of low culture, both of which point to a new order of serial production and consumption. In this light the minimalist stress on perceptual presence resists mass-mediated representations.

Donald Judd, *Untitled*, 1966.

Moreover, the minimalist insistence on specific objects counters simulacral images—even as minimalism, like pop, also employs serial forms and techniques. In short, the minimalist emphasis on the physical here-and-now is not only an enthusiasm for phenomenology, nor is the minimalist suspicion about artistic subjectivity only an embrace of structuralism. In part the first critiques, even as the second reflects, a reification of history and a fragmentation of the subject associated since Georg Lukács with the dynamic of capitalism. As I argue in chapter 3, these historical processes reach a new intensive level in the 1960s—to the point, Fredric Jameson has claimed, where they effect an "eclipse, finally, of all depth, especially *historicity* itself, with the subsequent appearance of pastiche and nostalgia art."[39] Such an eclipse is projected by minimalism and pop alike, with each so insistent on the externality, indeed the superficiality, of contemporary representations, meanings, experiences. Certainly pastiche and nostalgia, the twin reactions to this putative eclipse of historical depth, dominate the cultural wares of the 1970s and 1980s.

Minimalism may resist the spectacular image and the disembodied subject of advanced capitalism, while pop may embrace them. But in the end minimalism may resist these effects only to advance them too.[40] This notion will remain conjectural, however, at the homological level of reflections or the mechanistic level of responses, unless a local link between artistic forms and socio-economic forces in the 1960s is found. One such link is provided by the readymade: both minimalism and pop use the readymade not only thematically but formally, even structurally—as a way à la Judd to put one thing after the other, to avoid the idealist rationalism of traditional composition.[41] But to what order do these minimalist industrial objects and pop art simulacra point? To work in a series, to serial production and consumption, to the socio-economic order of one-thing-after-another.

Of course seriality precedes minimalism and pop. Indeed, this procedure penetrated art when its old transcendental orders (God, pristine nature, Platonic forms, artistic genius) began to fall apart. For once these orders were lost as referents or guarantees, "the oeuvre [became] the original" and "each painting [became] a discontinuous term of an indefinite series, and thus legible first not in its relation to the world but in its relation to other paintings by the same artist."[42] Such seriality is not evident much before industrial production, which more than any other force eroded the old orders of art, especially pristine nature. Ironically, even as artists from Claude Monet to Jackson Pollock wrested original impressions from this reified nature, they succumbed to seriality through this very struggle. This succumbing to seriality is fundamental to the becoming-abstract of art. Nevertheless, in abstract art seriality still pertains to the pictorial ordering of the motif more than to the technical production of the work.

In time, however, seriality could not be avoided, and this recognition led to demonstrations and counter-demonstrations of its logic. Consider, for example, how Rauschenberg tests this logic in *Factum I* and *II* (1957), each canvas filled with found images and aleatory gestures that are repeated, imperfectly, in the other. *Yet not until minimalism and pop is serial production made consistently integral to the technical production of the work of art.* More than any mundane content, this integration makes such art "signify in the same mode as objects in their everydayness, that is, in their latent *systematic*."[43] And more than any cool sensibility, this integration severs such art not only from artistic subjectivity (perhaps the last transcendental order of art) but also from representational models.[44] In this way minimalism rids art of the anthropomorphic and the representational not through anti-illusionist ideology so much as through serial production. For abstraction tends only to *sublate* representation, to preserve it in cancellation, whereas repetition, the (re)production of simulacra, tends to *subvert* representation, to undercut its referential logic. (In future histories of artistic paradigms, repetition, not abstraction, may be seen to supersede representation—or at least to disrupt it most effectively.)[45]

Since the Industrial Revolution a contradiction has existed between the craft basis of visual art and the industrial order of social life. Much sculpture since Rodin seeks to resolve this contradiction between "individual aesthetic creation" and "collective social production," especially in the turn to processes like welding and to paradigms like the readymade.[46] With minimalism and pop this contradiction is at once so attenuated (as in the minimalist concern with

Robert Rauschenberg, *Factum I* and *II*, 1957.

nuances of perception) and so collapsed (as in the Warholian motto "I want to be a machine") that it stands revealed as a principal dynamic of modernist art. In this regard, too, the seriality of minimalism and pop is indicative of advanced-capitalist production and consumption, for both register the penetration of industrial modes into spheres (art, leisure, sport) that were once removed from them. As the economist Ernest Mandel has written: "Far from representing a 'post-industrial society,' late capitalism thus constitutes *generalized universal industrialization* for the first time in history. Mechanization, standardization, over-specialization, and parcellization of labour, which in the past determined only the realm of commodity production in actual industry, now penetrate into all sectors of social life."[47] Both minimalism and pop resist some aspects of this logic, exploit others (like mechanization and standardization), and foretell still others. For in serial production a degree of difference between commodity-signs becomes necessary; this distinguishes it from mass production. Indeed, in our political economy of commodity-signs it is difference that we consume.[48]

This logic of difference and repetition is second nature to us today, but it was not so patent thirty-five years ago. Yet this logic structured minimalism and pop: in minimalism it is evident in the tension between different specific objects and repetitive serial ordering, and in pop in the production of different images through repetitive procedures (like silkscreening). Again, this serial structure integrates minimalism and pop, like no other art before them, into our systematic world of serial objects, images, people. Finally, more than any industrial technique in minimalism or mass-cultural content in pop, this logic, long since general to both high art and low culture, has redefined the lines between the two.

Although this logic qualifies the transgressive value of minimalism and pop, neither art merely reflects it. Both play with this logic too; that is, both release difference and repetition in sometimes subversive ways. As Gilles Deleuze, the great philosopher of these forces, wrote in 1969:

> The more our daily life appears standardised, stereotyped and subject to an accelerated reproduction of objects of consumption, the

Window display with paintings by Andy Warhol, Bonwit Teller, New York, 1961.

more art must be injected into it in order to extract from it that little difference which plays simultaneously between other levels of repetition, and even in order to make the two extremes resonate— namely, the habitual series of consumption and the instinctual series of destruction and death. Art thereby connects the tableau of cruelty with that of stupidity, and discovers underneath consumption a schizophrenic clattering of the jaws, and underneath the most ignoble destructions of war, still more processes of consumption. It aesthetically reproduces the illusions and mystifications which make up the essence of this civilisation, in order that Difference may at last be expressed.[49]

As Deleuze suggests, the artistic crux marked by minimalism and pop must be related to other ruptures of the 1960s—social and economic, theoretical and political. Somehow the new immanence of art with minimalism and pop is connected *not only* with the new immanence of critical theory (the poststructuralist shift from transcendental causes to immanent effects), *but also* with the new immanence of North American capital in the 1960s. Somehow, too, the transgressions of institutional art with minimalism and pop are associated *not only* with the transgressions of sexist and racist institutions by women, African-Americans, students, and others, *but also* with the transgressions of North American power in the 1960s.

The diagram of these connections is very difficult to produce; certainly it cannot be drawn with the conventional tools of art criticism, semiotic analysis, or social art history alone.[50] At risk in such mappings is the specific location of the art, but the relations between minimalism and pop and the greater forces of the time are also crucial to record. Could it be, for example, that the historical consciousness of this neo-avant-garde—the recognition of the conventionality of art and avant-garde alike—depends on the privileged perspective that advanced capitalism offers its culture for the first time in the 1960s?

Andy Warhol, *Tunafish Disaster,* 1963.

Gordon Matta–Clark, *Splitting,* 1974.

3

THE PASSION OF THE SIGN

Advanced art in the 1960s was caught between two opposed imperatives: on the one hand to achieve an autonomy of art as demanded by the dominant logic of late modernism; on the other hand to break up this autonomous art across an expanded field of culture that was largely textual in nature—textual in that language became important (as in much conceptual art) and that a decentering of subject and object alike became paramount (as in much site-specific art). This tension between the autonomy of the artistic sign and its dispersal across new forms and/or its combination with mass-cultural ones governed the relation not only between minimalism and pop, say, but also between the reflexive cinema of the North American independents (e.g., Michael Snow) and the allusive cinema of the French new wave (e.g., Jean-Luc Godard). By the 1970s, however, the textual term of this dialectic was ascendant in practice and theory alike. In this chapter I will consider this *textual turn*—initially through the debates on postmodernism that developed then as well.

In the late 1970s these debates began to divide into two basic positions, the first aligned with neoconservative politics, the second associated with post-structuralist theory. In all apparent ways these two versions of postmodernism were very much opposed. Thus, after the supposed amnesia of modernist abstraction, the neoconservative version of postmodernism proclaimed the *return* of cultural memory in the form of historical representations in art and architecture. So, too, after the supposed death of the author, it announced the return of the heroic figure of the artist and the architect. For its part the poststructuralist version of postmodernism advanced a *critique* of these same categories of representation and authorship. This opposition continued on other fronts as well. Thus the neoconservative version of postmodernism tended to counter the modernist fetish of form with a loose practice of *pastiche,* the supposed populism of which often covered an elitist coding of references. For its part the poststructuralist version of postmodernism worked to exceed both formal aesthetic categories (the disciplinary order of painting, sculpture, and so on) and traditional cultural distinctions (high versus mass culture, autonomous versus utilitarian art) with a new model of art as *text.* And so this battle was fought.

Yet, however opposed, these two positions on postmodernism were also connected, as a third position on postmodernism, which drew on the Marxist mandate to relate cultural forms of signification to socio-economic modes of production, was at pains to show.[1] According to this position, the pastiche of the neoconservative version of postmodernism did not recover historical representation or artistic authorship any more than the textuality of the poststructuralist version deconstructed these categories on its own terms. Rather, both practices, pastiche and textuality, were referred to a general crisis in representation and authorship, a crisis that far exceeded them. In particular, whether in the guise of a neo-expressionist painting by Julian Schabel or a multimedia performance by Laurie Anderson, a historicist building by Michael Graves or a deconstructivist project by Peter Eisenman, both practices were related to a qualitative shift in the capitalist dynamic of reification and fragmentation.[2]

Long ago in *History and Class Consciousness* (1923) Georg Lukács revealed this dynamic of reification and fragmentation to be fundamental to capitalist society. Then, in the midst of a monopoly capitalism based on mass production, Lukács was concerned with the reification and fragmentation of *the object,* especially in assembly-line production. Today, in the midst of an advanced capitalism based on serial consumption, we are witness to a further reification and fragmentation—of *the sign.* One way to narrate these vicissitudes of the sign, its passion under advanced capitalism, is to consider certain practices of art and theory in the 1970s and 1980s. For the reification and fragmentation of the sign, if not grasped as such in these practices, is nonetheless at work there, or so I want to suggest. So, too, I want to suggest that related poststructuralist concepts of the time often made internal this dynamic of reification and fragmentation, and nowhere more so than when they presumed to be most post-Marxist, most critical of the concept of totality. Such a symptomatic reading of art and theory runs the risk, also associated with the Lukács legacy, of cultural practices reduced to socio-economic forces. Here, however, my premise is not that art and theory reflect any socio-economic moment, but rather that they are marked by its contradictions, and that cultural categories, including concepts of the sign, thus possess a historicity that it is one task of criticism to apprehend.

But what is it to suggest that the sign has a specific history? Of course, any such history is a myth, one that presumes a totalistic view that is very much out of critical fashion today.[3] Nevertheless, it remains important to attempt such histories, for they enable one, however provisionally, to connect phenomena that both require and resist connection—perhaps now more than ever before. As we saw at the end of chapter 2, phenomena as diverse as postmodernist art, poststructuralist theory, and advanced-capitalist society are extremely difficult to mediate, and the attempt to do so may only reflect on a critic who is both presumptuous and anxious (in a word, paranoid). Yet relationships among such phenomena do exist, and some can be understood, at least in part, in terms of the reification and fragmentation of the sign. This penetration of the sign by capital is not metaphorical; in chapter 2 I noted some of its effects in the 1960s, as when serial production and consumption became integral to the work of art. But only in the 1970s and 1980s is this penetration elaborated, indirectly to be sure, in practice and theory alike. This is the story I want to tell here, again in broad, often heuristic terms.

AUTONOMOUS ART AND TEXTUAL CULTURE

Several genealogies of the sign under capitalism can be contrived, and I will trace a few here in order to reinscribe them later in relation to art and theory of the 1970s and 1980s. I derive the first two genealogies from signal poststructuralist texts by Roland Barthes and Jacques Derrida: *S/Z* (1970), in which Barthes decodes the 1830 story "Sarrazine" by Honoré de Balzac, and "Structure, Sign, and Play in the Discourse of Human Sciences" (1966), in which Derrida deconstructs the structural anthropology of Claude Lévi-Strauss. These two texts suggest a way not only to relate the sign to two epochal shifts, the first associated with market capitalism, the second with high modernism, but also to relate poststructuralist theory to a further shift in our own period.

In *S/Z* Barthes is on the lookout for cracks in the symbolic order of the Parisian world of the Balzac story. Linguistic and narrative, sexual and psychological, social and political, these cracks emanate from the center of the text, the castrato Zambinella, a figure whose relation to sexual identity and symbolic order alike is enigmatic, to say the least (he is thought to be a woman).[4] Early in the story, in a comment on the mysterious keepers of the opera singer, the narrator laments that the new order of capitalist exchange has corrupted the old reading of class membership: "No one asks to see your family tree because everyone knows how much it cost." Provoked by this statement, Barthes conceives the *historical* passage from an old feudal regime of hierarchical origins, of fixed wealth of land and gold, to a new bourgeois regime of equivalent signs, of promiscuous paper money, in terms of a *semiotic* shift from the order of the index, of a fixed marking of identity, to the order of the sign, of a relative mobility of position: "The difference between feudal society and bourgeois society, index and sign, is this: the index has an origin, the sign does not: to shift from index to sign is to abolish the last (or first) limit, the origin, the basis, the prop, to enter into the limitless process of equivalences, representations that nothing will ever stop, orient, fix, sanction . . . the signs (monetary, sexual) are wild because . . . the two elements *interchange,* signified and signifier revolving in an endless process: what is bought can be sold, the signified can become the signifier, and so on."[5]

Here Barthes relates the passage from index to sign to the spread of *market* capitalism, the socio-economic order out of which modern art developed. Yet he describes this passage in terms more appropriate to the socio-economic order of *advanced* capitalism: "a limitless process of equivalences." Might this condition of "wild signs" be emergent in the historical moment witnessed by Balzac, but not dominant until our own moment, so often described as a world of spectacular simulacra—not dominant, that is, until the conjuncture from which Barthes writes 140 years after Balzac? In other words, might Barthes here project certain aspects of a contemporary economy back onto its historical beginnings? If this is so, his retrospective reading suggests that the shift from the order of the index to that of the sign is completed (at least to the point where it can be understood as such) only in the present of his own text. And below I argue such a shift was indeed registered in recent art.

Derrida also appears to project a poststructuralist concept of the sign onto a past moment. Yet, unlike Barthes, he does so not in relation to the semiotic order of market capitalism and early modernism, but implicitly in relation to the semiotic order of high modernism, which is also the moment of *monopoly* capitalism. In "Structure, Sign, and Play in the Discourse of Human Sciences" Derrida writes of the epistemological rupture produced in structural linguistics. For Derrida this rupture compels us to think structure apart from a fixed center or a central presence. The celebrated passage reads: "This was the moment when language invaded the universal problematic, the moment when, in the absence of a center or origin, everything became discourse . . . that is to say, a system in which the central signified, the original or transcendental signified, is never absolutely present outside a system of differences. The absence of transcendental signified extends the domain and play of signification infinitely."[6]

Pressed to specify this decentering, Derrida alludes to the critique of truth in Nietzsche, the critique of self-presence in Freud, and the critique of metaphysics in Heidegger (he has already assumed the critique of the referential model of language in Saussure). Taken together, these allusions may allow us to relate the epistemological rupture remarked by Derrida in structural linguistics to the artistic rupture inaugurated in high modernism. And in retrospect—that is, in an instance of the deferred (*nachträglich*) relation of postmodern to modern discourses noted in chapter 1—this connection between structural linguistics and high modernism has become clear in our own time. (To cite but one example from recent criticism: "The extraordinary contribution of [cubist] collage is that it is the first instance within the pictorial arts of anything like a systematic exploration of the conditions of representability entailed by the sign.")[7] Significantly, however, Derrida refuses to locate this decentering historically. "It is no doubt part of the totality of an era, our own," he states enigmatically, "but still it has always already begun to proclaim itself."[8] Here Derrida seems to intimate the preconditions of his own recognition—that this traumatic decentering of structure is only grasped as such in his own poststructuralist present. Like "the limitless process of equivalences" in Barthes, then, the infinite "play of signification" in Derrida may be prepared in a past moment (in Barthes that of market capitalism, in Derrida that of high modernism), but it is only achieved in our own advanced-capitalist, postmodernist present. If this is so, the poststructuralisms of Barthes and Derrida are also symptomatic discourses. They may comprehend past ruptures in the sign, but they also intimate a present rupture that they *cannot* comprehend for the simple reason that they participate in it.[9]

Two different genealogies of the sign might clarify this symptomatic aspect of poststructuralism. For both Jean Baudrillard and Fredric Jameson the passage from structural linguistics to poststructuralist semiotics is a process of abstraction: in the first instance the referent is bracketed; in the second the signified is loosened, redefined as another signifier. A related passage occurs in advanced art of this century: first the referent is abstracted in high modernism, as in the characteristic nonobjectivity of its art and architecture, then the signified is released in postmodernism, as in our media world of simulacral images (Baudrillard) and schizophrenic signifiers (Jameson). This suggests a connection between structural linguistics and high modernism on the one hand, and poststructuralist semiotics and postmodernism on the other. But what *makes* these connections?

For both Baudrillard and Jameson the ultimate agent of this abstraction of the sign is capital. "For finally it was capital," Baudrillard writes, "which was the first to feed throughout its history on the destruction of every referent . . .

of original image

in order to establish its radical law of equivalence and exchange."[10] Jameson narrates this "destruction" in terms of reification:

> In a first moment [that of structural linguistics and high modernism], reification "liberated" the sign from its referent, but this is not a force to be released with impunity. Now, in a second moment [that of poststructuralist semiotics and postmodernism], it continues its work of dissolution, penetrating the interior of the sign itself and liberating the signifier from the signified, or from the meaning proper. This play, no longer of a realm of signs, but of pure or literal signifiers freed from the ballast of their signifieds, their former meanings, now generates a new kind of textuality in all the arts.[11]

Below I will test this model of a "new kind of textuality in all the arts," but first its aggressive historicism must be tempered. For the dissolution of the sign is not as final as Jameson suggests; there are always resistances to factor in, let alone other stories to consider. Nevertheless, the dominant logic of modernist art was indeed to bracket the referent. Again, this was done to approach an *autonomy* of the sign, and here the painting of Piet Mondrian, rigorous in its pursuit of transcendental purity, is paradigmatic. But the referent was also bracketed in order to explore the *arbitrariness* of the sign, an exploration that could be analytical, as it was in early cubism (especially in collages and constructions); anarchistic, as it was in early dada or early futurism (especially in poetry and performances); or transformative, as it was in early Russian constructivism (especially when laboratory experiments were pushed toward social practice).

In this way the modernist "liberation" of the sign was more varied in artistic form and political value than Jameson implies; it also did not pass directly into a postmodernist "play" of signifiers. For example, in the late modernism of abstract-expressionist and color-field painting, the autonomy of the sign was reestablished as the primary criterion of art. Moreover, this purity of painting was set up by its principal advocate, Clement Greenberg, in express opposition to the dadaist counter-principle of the arbitrariness of the sign. Yet just when semiotic autonomy seemed to be secured once and for all, semiotic arbitrariness was reasserted in turn, first with neo-dadaist figures like John Cage and then, within the very realm of painting, by figures like Robert Rauschenberg and Jasper Johns. Indeed, both artists pushed the arbitrariness of the sign to the point of the dissolution remarked by Jameson, to the point, that is, where signifiers (letters, numbers, and so on) became literal, "freed from the ballast of their signifieds." As we saw in chapter 2, this incipient textuality was both resisted and advanced by minimalism and pop, which participated in an expansion of artistic practice that, again, was largely textual. We return, then, to the initial question: under what pressures did this textual turn occur?

A test case might be helpful here. Frank Stella is an exemplary artist of late modernism, a principal proponent of the autonomy of painting. In his early work (c. 1958–60) he forces the picture (or depicted shape) into near coincidence with the picture support (or literal shape): in different ways the rectangle *of* the canvas is graphed *onto* the canvas again and again.[12] In his next phase (c. 1960–64) Stella first notches the rectangle, then supplements it with other support shapes that tend, however, to remain fundamental, such as the cross, the triangle, and the star: here, then, he is still concerned to ground the structure of painting in the stability of simple signs.[13] That he does so, however, under the pressure of the historical *in*stability of the sign is suggested by subsequent work in which the shapes become more complex, indeed eccentric. For example, in the "Protractor" paintings (1967–69) picture and support are at once so coterminous and so conflicted that the sign is held together under such pressure that its fundamental *dis*unity is exposed. By the middle 1970s Stella all but gives his work over to this instability. Indeed, he exacerbates it: first he quotes specific modernist styles (like cubism and constructivism), and then he simulates entire codes of historical painting, to the point in the early 1980s where fragments of the modernist grid, linear perspective, and the three grounds of landscape painting might collide in one construction. In this progression from simple forms to fragmentary signifiers Stella almost illustrates the dissolution of the sign associated with the abstractive dynamic of capital—a demonstration

Jasper Johns, *Target with Plaster Casts*, 1955.

that is less reflexive than symptomatic, less transformative than decorative.[14]

This disintegrative dynamic was at work in other art practices of the late 1960s and early 1970s as well; paradoxically, this alone may connect them. Some artists sought to *resist* the dissolution of the sign, to ground it in other ways—first in new materials and techniques (evident in minimalism, this fetishism became dominant in postminimalist experiments in process), then in actual bodies and sites (as in body art, site-specific art, performance). Meanwhile other artists worked to *exploit* the dissolution of the sign, to demonstrate either the reification of aesthetic language (as in the tautologies of much conceptual art) or its fragmentation (as in the ephemera of much installation art).[15] However, no one was able to grasp the dynamic of this dissolution in its own terms. There are partial exceptions, of course: especially in his textual site/nonsite works, Robert Smithson did reflect on a concept of structure apart from the concept of center à la Derrida, and Smithson did think this decentering as a disintegration. Yet he referred this disintegration to natural history and physical entropy more than to social history and capitalist reification and fragmentation. In this way the dissolution of the sign was performed in much North American art and criticism of the 1960s and the 1970s, but it was not understood as such—at least not until the end of the 1970s. And even then this understanding was only partial; indeed, the two texts that did the most to prepare this understanding are silent on the historical forces that produced the very passion of the sign that they otherwise recount.

INDEXICAL MARKS AND ALLEGORICAL IMPULSES

In "Notes on the Index: Seventies Art in America" (1977) Rosalind Krauss seeks a principle that might comprehend the pluralistic art of the decade, and she finds it not in the art-historical category of style but in the semiotic order of the index, that is, a mark like a footprint that makes its meaning through a direct relationship to its referent.[16] Immediately this model refocuses such characteristic art of the 1970s as body art and installation work as an indexical grounding of art in physical presence, on a body, in a site. Yet this shift to the

Frank Stella, *Darabjerd I*, 1967.

indexical, Krauss notes, had occurred long ago with Duchamp, who confronted in cubism the arbitrariness of the sign: "It was as if cubism forced for Duchamp the issue of whether pictorial language could continue to signify directly, could picture anything like an identifiable set of contents" (202). Duchamp responded to this crisis in two opposite ways. On the one hand he foregrounded the instability of the sign—in the slippages of the homonymous phrases scribbled on his roto-reliefs, for example, or in the confusions of the sexual identity of his alter ego Rrose Sélavy. On the other hand he grounded the sign in indexical marks, of which the painting *Tu M'* (1918) is a virtual catalogue, replete with shadow images of the readymades, a play of linguistic shifters in the title (*tu m'*/you me), and an index finger depicted by a sign painter. For Krauss these indexical operations govern the Duchampian oeuvre in its photographic manifestations (she reads *The Large Glass* "as a kind of photograph") as well as in its readymade manifestations, since the photograph as a "sub- or pre-symbolic" trace is inherently indexical and the readymade is "a sign which is inherently 'empty,' its signification a function of only this one instance, guaranteed by the existential presence of just this object" (206).

Krauss sees a related turn to indexical marking in art in the 1970s, examples of which might include the cuts into derelict buildings made by Gordon Matta-Clark and moldings of body parts and marginal spaces produced by Bruce Nauman.[17] The implication is that, like the young Duchamp, these artists also confronted a "trauma of signification": on the one hand, an abstraction of the referent, announced for Duchamp in cubism and for artists in the 1970s in minimalism; and, on the other hand, a predominance of the photographic, advanced for Duchamp by a new culture of mechanical reproduction and for artists in the 1970s by a new culture of serial consumption. Here again Krauss relates the indexical to the photographic, which she defines first as a "reduction of the conventional sign to a trace" and then, after Barthes, as a "message without a code" (211). To connect the indexical and the photographic in this way is to order the diverse forms of art in the 1970s under a single principle, "the registration of sheer physical presence." More importantly, it is to understand this registration as a substitute for a "language of aesthetic conventions" (209) that breaks down in the 1970s as it had in the time of the young Duchamp. In short, art in the 1970s also faced a "tremendous arbitrariness with regard to meaning," and its primary response was to resort to "the mute presence of an uncoded event" (212).[18]

"Notes on the Index" provides an incisive theory of much art in the 1970s, but its insight into structural logic makes for a blindness regarding historical and/or ideological process.[19] For example, the premise of this indexical model—that artistic signs can be empty, that cultural messages can exist without a code—was challenged by other artists of the time involved in a critique of art institutions and discourses, artists for whom no body or site, representation or event, could ever be purely present or completely codeless. As is now well known, some artists who elaborated on indexical art in the 1970s came to treat site-specificity in terms not of mute presence but of institutional power; one thinks of the interventions into art spaces by Michael Asher and others. So, too, other artists who elaborated on photography in the 1970s came to treat the documentary image not as a message without a code to explore but as an ideological function to critique; one thinks of the questioning of photographic authority by Martha Rosler and others. Just as artists like Asher concluded that, far from mute, institutional sites structure the speech of art, so artists like Rosler concluded that, far from codeless, photographic representations are codes that project an effect of the real through a process of connotation that Barthes once termed mythical.

To be fair, Krauss focuses on the structural logic of indexical art of the 1970s. This is a limitation, but it allows her to define this logic clearly enough that today, in retrospect, its historical preconditions also appear clear. The shift to indexical marks of presence in this art was prompted by a crisis in representation. On the one hand, this crisis was local: after the serial objects of minimalism and the simulacral images of pop (not to mention the immaterial demonstrations of conceptual work), the move to reground art was urgent, almost necessary. But this crisis was also general, prompted by a reification and fragmentation of the sign to which indexical art is but one indirect response. Such is the political unconscious of the semiotic breakdown registered in indexical

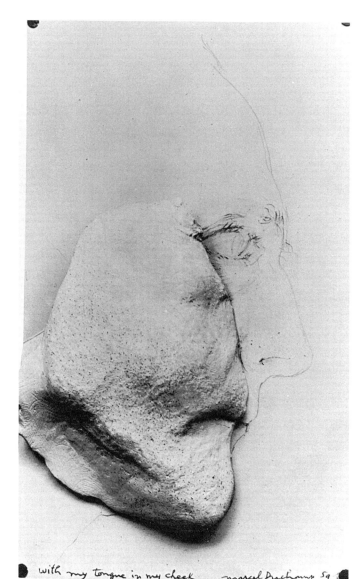

Marcel Duchamp, *With My Tongue in My Cheek*, 1959.

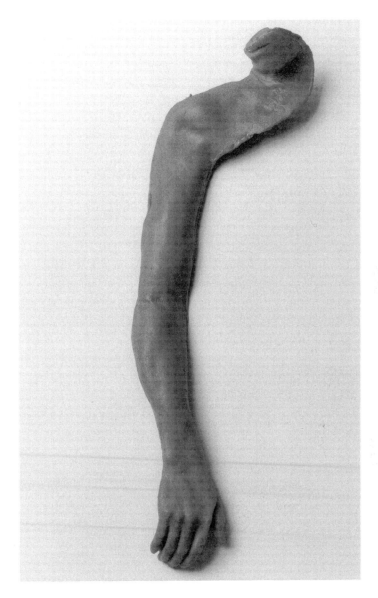

Bruce Nauman, *From Hand to Mouth,* 1967.

art, which, precisely because it was unconscious, could not be grasped in its own historical moment.

This reading must now be tested on the other major model of innovative art in the 1970s: that such art rejects the late-modernist purity of the work in favor of a postmodernist impurity of the text. Advanced by Craig Owens, this model might be taken to mark a further dissolution of the sign: from its *indexical* grounding in the *presence* of the body or the site to its *allegorical* dispersal as a *play* of signifiers. Yet this theory is also blind to the capitalist dynamic that influences its object. Like the indexical model, it focuses on internal transformations in the sign in a way that brackets the historical preconditions not only of its artistic object but of its own theoretical construction.

If "Notes on the Index" points to an erosion of specific artistic mediums (painting, sculpture, architecture), "Earthwords" (1979), a review of *The Writings of Robert Smithson,* points to a transgression of entire aesthetic categories (the visual versus the verbal, the spatial versus the temporal).[20] In this early text Owens links postmodernism in Smithson with poststructuralism in Derrida by means of the decentering at work in both practices. For Owens language erupts in art from the middle 1960s to the middle 1970s (in conceptual art, textual modes of documentation, artist writings), and this linguistic eruption dislocates the visual order of modernism and prepares the textual space of postmodernism.

In "The Allegorical Impulse" (1980) Owens again connects postmodernist fragmentation in art to poststructuralist decentering in language, here through the notion of allegory advanced by Walter Benjamin in *The Origin of German Tragic Drama* (1928; English translation, 1977). Postmodernist art is allegorical not only in its stress on ruinous spaces (as in emphemeral installations) and fragmentary images (as in appropriations from art history and mass media alike) but, more importantly, in its impulse to upset stylistic norms, to redefine conceptual categories, to challenge the modernist ideal of symbolic totality—in short, in its impulse to exploit the gap between signifier and signified. Owens cites these practices in particular: "appropriation, site-specificity, impermanence, accumulation, discursivity, hybridization."[21]

This model is useful, but it is also problematic. In terms of definition it is

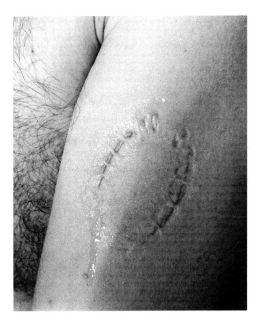

Vito Acconci, *Trademarks*, 1970.

problematic to oppose a symbolic impulse in modernism to an allegorical impulse in postmodernism, for the two imperatives—the first transcendental, totalistic, often utopian, the second immanent, contingent, somehow fallen—define one another, and they do so *within modernism*. The most celebrated definition of modern art presents the two impulses in this way: "By 'modernity' I mean the ephemeral, the fugitive, the contingent," Charles Baudelaire writes in *The Painter of Modern Life* (1863), "the half of art whose other half is the eternal and the immutable."[22] As Owens traces his genealogy of the allegorical impulse, he is led back via Benjamin to Baudelaire, that is, to the beginnings of modernism as it is traditionally defined.[23] In other words, rather than an absolute divide between modernism and postmodernism, we have another instance of the deferred action at work in our narratives of the two.

This model is also problematic in terms of method. Early in the essay Owens insists that the textuality of postmodernist art disrupts the autonomy of modernist art. At this point, then, the stake of postmodernism is still avant-gardist (that is, the allegorical mode is held to disrupt or to exceed the symbolic mode). Not yet in view are the historical preconditions, economic processes, and political ramifications of postmodernism. Thus even as Owens comments on history as decay in Benjamin, on reification of language in Smithson, on representations undone in postmodernism, he does not reflect on the forces that influence these deconstructions; they remain at the obscure level of artistic impulses.

In conclusion Owens depicts his own passion of the sign from modernism to postmodernism:

> Modernist theory presupposes that mimesis, the adequation of image to referent, can be bracketed or suspended, and that the art object itself can be substituted (metaphorically) for its referent. . . . For reasons that are beyond the scope of this essay, this fiction has become increasingly difficult to maintain. Postmodernism neither brackets nor suspends the referent but works to problematize the activity of reference (235).

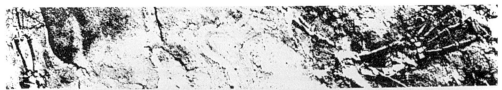

CRETACEOUS GLOBIGERINA OOZE AND THE BLUISH MUDS. *CRETA* THE LATIN WORD FOR CHALK (THE CHALK AGE). AN ARTICLE CALLED GROTTOES, GEOLOGY AND THE GOTHIC REVIVAL. PHILOSOPHIC ROMANCES. GREENSANDS ACCUMULATED OVER WIDE AREAS IN SHALLOW WATER. UPRAISED PLATEAUX IN AUSTRALIA. SEDIMENT SAMPLES. CONIFERS. REMAINS OF A FLIGHTLESS BIRD DISCOVERED IN A CHALK PIT. CAUSES OF EXTINCTION UNKNOWN. THE FABULOUS SEA-SERPENT. THE CLASSICAL ATTITUDE TOWARD MOUNTAINS IS GLOOMY. A DISPLAY OF PLASTER TRICERATOPS EGGS IN A GLASS CASE. THE ROCKS OF MONTANA. GLIBIGERINA CRETACEA ENLARGED 30 TIMES IN A BOOK. THE WEARING PROCESS CONTINUES. A CONSTANT GRINDING DOWN OF ROUGH TERRAINS. SOMETHING HAD FANGS 6 INCHES LONG. KILLED BY THE HEAT OF THE SUN. THE SACRED THEORY OF THE EARTH CAUSES BEWILDERMENT. SOME BOOKS CONCERNING THE DELUGE BRING CHAOS TO MANY. GRAY MISTS AND MUCH HEAT. PERPLEXED BY PEBBLE DEPOSITS. COLUMNS OF BASALT ILLUSTRATED IN DE RERUM FOSSILIUM. PAINTINGS OF CRETACEOUS PERIOD SHOWN AS *ARTIST'S CONCEPTIONS* ON LARGE PANELS. FROM 135 TO 70 MILLION YEARS AGO. TRAITE DE PETRIFICATIONS. WOODCUT SHOWING TWO STONES FALLING FROM THE HEAVENS DURING A STORM. A DEAD TORTOISE. IN THE ZONE OF AIR—THUNDERBOLTS, E.G. *CERANUNIUS*, BELEMNITE, ETC. CERTAIN BEDS OF THE KEOKUK IN THE CENTRAL MISSISSIPPI VALLEY. THE *FLAMING RAMPARTS OF THE WORLD* (LUCRETIUS), DE MINERALI-BUS BY ALBERTUS MAGNUS. FEATHER IMPRESSIONS EXHIBITED IN A PALEONTOLOGICAL MUSEUM. FOSSILIZED VENOM. THE TREE ONICA WHOSE TEARS HARDEN INTO THE MINERAL ONYX. (FROM THE HORTUS SANITATIS). SOME GRAINS OF SAND WERE SQUARE AND OTHERS PYRAMIDAL. CAMERAS LOST IN SHELLS AND SKELETONS.

JURASSIC A LABEL UNDER A STEGOSAURUS SKELETON. BONY PLATES. THREE OUNCES OF BRAIN. 45,000,000. NO WORDS COULD DESCRIBE IT. CRAGGY CLIFFS, INDEPENDENT OF LIFE. EXTENSIVE LAKES OR INLAND SEAS MARKED AS BLUE STRIPES ON AN OVAL MAP. PLASTIC SEAWEEDS IN THE MUSEUM. A GREAT COLLECTION OF FOSSILS IN THE ASHMOLEAN MUSEUM AT OXFORD. MUNDUS SUBTERRANEUS, KIRCHER AMSTERDAM 1678. STONE PLANTS. JOHN CLEVELAND'S NEWS FROM NEWCASTLE OR NEWCASTLE COAL PITS PUBLISHED IN 1659. AGE OF CYCADS. A FINE CHALKY DEPOSIT (PERHAPS DUST BLOWN FROM RAISED CORAL REEFS). MONO LAKE—THE DEAD SEA OF THE WEST. BELEMNITES SWARMED IN THE MUDDY SEAS. POETS CELEBRATING GROTTOES. THE RECENT MONKEY-PUZZLE HAS NOTHING TO DO WITH THE JURASSIC PERIOD. WELL-PRESERVED PTERODACTYLS. THE BURNET CONTROVERSY. MANY CRAWLED ON THE OCEAN FLOOR. DELTAIC SANDSTONES OUTCROPPING IN YORKSHIRE. A MODEL OF A BRYOZOA ONE MILLION TIMES LIFE SIZE. MEANDER-ING RIVERS. *GO MY SONS, BUY STOUT SHOES, CLIMB THE MOUNTAINS, SEARCH THE VALLEYS, DESERTS, THE SEA SHORES, AND THE DEEP RECESSES OF THE EARTH* (SEVERINUS). IN BRITAIN THE JURASSIC CONSISTS MAINLY OF OOLITES AND CLAYS. RHAETIC BEDS. SEVERAL LAND-MASSES NOT SHOWN ON A MAP. LUXURIANT VEGETATION. *PARADISE LOST.* INVASION OF THE OCEAN. ARCHAEOPTERYX. FLESH-EATERS WALKED ON THEIR HIND LEGS USING THEIR FORE LIMBS FOR GRABBING PREY. BONES WITH AIR CAVITIES SHOWN IN LINE DRAWING. LOW TIDE. DEAD JELLY-FISH IN A LAGOON. PAINTING OF FERN FOREST. POST CARDS OF ZION CANYON. A BOOK ON URANIUM. AN *ARTIST'S CONCEPTION* OF DINOSAURS IN A SWAMP. CHART TELLS OF THE EVOLUTION OF WASTE. OVER-EXPOSED PHOTOGRAPHS OF THE SUNDANCE SEA. A NOVEL ABOUT THE LIFE OF AN ICHTHYOSAUR. NO ICE SHEETS MARKED THE POLES. INFRA-RED PHOTOGRAPHS OF THE GULF OF GEOSYNCLINE.

TRIASSIC OBSCURE VALLEYS. DATA FROM DRILLED HOLES. *HE MAY EVEN NOW—IF I MAY USE THE PHRASE—BE WANDERING ON SOME PLESIOSAURUS-HAUNTED OLLITIC CORAL REEF, OR BESIDE THE LONELY SALINE LAKES OF THE TRIASSIC AGE* (H.G. WELLS). TRACKS OF DINOSAURS DISCOVERED AT TURNERS FALLS, ON THE CONNECTICUT RIVER IN MASSACHU-SETTS. THE COLUMNAR JOININGS OF THE PALISADES. INERT, ALL SLIDES INTO A LOST MOMENT. A CLIFF BELOW THE WEST END OF THE GEORGE WASHINGTON BRIDGE. VOLCANIC VAPORS. AT THE CHILLED ZONE. A RESTORED SECTION OF A TRIASSIC FAULT BLOCK SHOWING LAVA DIKES. A BOOK IS A PAPER STRATA. A COLORED PHOTOGRAPH OF THE PETRIFIED FOREST, ARIZONA. A LANDSLIDE OF MAPS. ECLIPSE OF THE MOON. GYPSUM. AN ILLUSTRATION FROM THE PALESTECTONIC ATLAS. DYING IN THE YUKON AMID THE PLUTONIC ROCKS. TECTONIC ISLANDS SURROUNDED BY GREEN FOAM. *...NOTHING CAN APPEAR MORE LIFELESS THAN THE CHAOS OF ROCKS...* (DARWIN). SOUTHERN ELLESMERE-LAND. ABUNDANT QUANTITIES OF GRANULAR MINERALS. THE EXHUMED PRE-LATE TRIASSIC PENEPLANE CAN BE SEEN NEAR THE GEORGE WASHINGTON BRIDGE. A GENERALIZED GEOLOGIC CROSS SECTION SHOWING MAGMA OFFSHOOTS. A DIAGRAM SHOWING A FAULT ZONE. WEDGES OF SEDIMENTARY STRATA. A PHOTOGRAPH OF *ROTTEN* DIABASE. RAPID HEAT LOSS. A RESTORATION OF A ICAROSAURUS. FALL ZONE. SWASH. 600,000 CUBIC YARDS OF SOMETHING. A BLOCK DIAGRAM SHOWING DRIFT. BARRIERS OF MUD, *THE EARLIEST OF THE THREE GEOLOGICAL PERIODS COMPRISED IN THE MESOZOIC ERA* (DICTIONARY OF GEOLOGICAL TERMS). BLACK HEATHS, WILD ROCKS, BLACK CRAGS, AND NAKED HILLS (CHARLES COTTON). IN THE WAKE OF LAVA FLOWS. CHOMATIC EMULSIONS OF NAMELESS ROCKS. A NARROW RANGE OF GREY TONALITIES. THE ANONYMOUS SURFACE UNIFORMITY OF MUSEUM PHOTOGRAPHS. DEGENERATE TECHNIQUES. DISPLAYS IN PLASTIC.

STRATA A GEOPHOTOGRAPHIC FICTION

Robert Smithson, *Strata: A Geophotographic Fiction,* 1972, detail.

This passage from a modernist *bracketing* of the referent to a postmodernist *breaking* of the sign recalls the accounts of Baudrillard and Jameson. Yet Owens does not foreground its capitalist dynamic as they do; he stops short of its historical determinations, which remain precisely beyond the scope of his poststructuralist model. (The word *capital* does not appear once in this long essay.) As a result Owens can only celebrate the problematization of reference in postmodernist art and poststructuralist theory in avant-gardist terms; he cannot problematize it in turn. This is not the path pursued by Benjamin, the intellectual guide of "The Allegorical Impulse." In his later writings on Baudelaire, Benjamin rethought the role of allegory within modern culture; that is, he rethought the dissolution of the sign in terms of the commodity-form. "The devaluation of the world of objects in allegory," he wrote in a celebrated aphorism, "is outdone within the world of objects itself by the commodity."[24] It is to this devaluation, as rehearsed both critically and cynically in contemporary art, that I now turn.

ALLEGORICAL PROCEDURES AND COMMODITY SIGNS

Like Krauss in "Notes on the Index," Owens in "The Allegorical Impulse" is not responsible for the conceptual limits of the time. There are particular reasons why, in North America in the late 1970s, postmodernist art was seen in terms of an allegorical textuality. The Benjaminian notion of allegory was received not only through *The Origin of German Tragic Drama* rather than the writings on Baudelaire (the *Passagen-Werk* was not published in German until 1982), but also through the deconstruction of Derrida and Paul de Man rather than the demystification of the Marxist tradition; as a result aporetic doubt tended to be privileged over ideology critique. Then, too, other models appropriate to related practices, such as the analysis of the artistic sign in institution-critical work and the questioning of its phallocentric subject in feminist art, were not well developed. The psychoanalytic feminist art that emerged in Britain in the middle 1970s was a particular blind spot; the conjuncture of political and theoretical movements (e.g., feminism, film theory, Lacan, Althusser) that prompted artists like Mary Kelly and Victor Burgin did not yet exist—or was not yet supported—in the same way here. However, a reading of institution-critical art had emerged by the early 1980s. Significantly, it too applied the Benjaminian concept of allegory, but in its Marxist reformulation as a mode of reflection, at once contemplative and critical, on the culture of the commodity.

Advanced by Benjamin Buchloh, this reading did relate "the allegorical procedures" in postmodernist art to the Marxist tradition of ideology critique. Like Owens, Buchloh privileged strategies of "appropriation and depletion of meaning, fragmentation and dialectical juxtaposition of fragments, and separation of signifier and signified."[25] But he positioned them differently, in a genealogy of art critical not only of the institution of art but also of the commodification of culture. In this way Buchloh returned allegorical art to its historical subject as defined by Benjamin: reification.

Yet a problem arose with this version of allegorical art too, for it tended toward a melancholic treatment both of society as so many opaque images and of history as so many distant ruins. Thus some art that Owens deemed allegorical (e.g., early work by Robert Longo, Jack Goldstein, Troy Brauntuch) could also be seen as melancholic in its mix of political resignation and fetishistic fascination (this is how Buchloh saw it). It could also be seen as spectacular, seduced to the point of replication by the advanced-capitalist transformation of objects, events, even people into images to consume (which is how I tended to see it). Indeed, by the early 1980s there emerged a general aesthetic of spectacle that reflected on such reification but did not challenge it.[26]

This aesthetic prepared the model that governed much art by the middle 1980s. After indexical markings and allegorical impulses, this model can be termed *conventionalist,* for, with the permission of a poststructuralism that was not well understood, it tended to treat all practices (artistic, social, and otherwise) as detached signifiers to be manipulated, ahistorical conventions to be consumed. Not restricted to any one style, conventionalism tended to reduce these practices to abstractions, indeed to simulacra. (Thus analytic abstraction might be reduced to diagrams in Day-Glo colors, or the Duchampian readymade to vacuum cleaners in Plexiglas displays.) In so doing conventionalism hardly contested our political economy of the commodity-sign as defined by

Baudrillard; on the contrary, it played into this new order in which practices are reduced not just to commodities but to simulacra for exchange. Now according to Baudrillard, just as the commodity is divided into use and exchange values, so is the sign divided into signified and signifier. Structurally, then, just as the commodity can assume the effects of signification, so can the sign assume the functions of exchange value. Indeed, on the basis of this structural chiasmus between commodity and sign he recasts structuralism as a secret ideological code of capitalism.[27] For Baudrillard this structural chiasmus has now become *actual:* we have entered a political economy of the commodity-sign, with epochal ramifications for political economy, art practice, and cultural criticism alike. In chapter 4 I argue that this conventionalism has become a pervasive aesthetic of our new order of capitalism. Suffice it to say here that in this art "the commodity has taken the place of the allegorical way of seeing" once again.[28]

Even in the early 1980s Buchloh sensed that allegorical art might only replicate, melancholically or cynically, the very reification that it addressed. Nevertheless, he insisted on its cognitive potential as well. Rather than merely rehearse the division of the commodity-sign, allegorical art might also turn this "splintering" into a critical procedure:

> The allegorical mind sides with the object and protests against its devaluation to the status of a commodity by devaluating it a second time in allegorical practice. In the splintering of signifier and signified, the allegorist subjects the sign to the same division of functions that the object has undergone in its transformation into a commodity. The repetition of the original act of depletion and the new attribution of meaning redeems the object (44).

Here Buchloh draws on Barthes in *Mythologies* (1957) in which the dominant culture is seen to operate through appropriation: it abstracts the specific signifieds of social groups into general signifiers that are then sold and consumed as cultural myths. (The operation is not as complicated as it sounds. Consider one trajectory of graffiti in the early 1980s from a specific, guerilla expression on the streets to a general, pop style in art, music, and fashion industries.) Against this appropriation Barthes proposed a counter-appropriation: "Truth to tell, the best weapon against myth is perhaps to mythify it in its turn, and to produce an *artificial myth:* and this reconstituted myth will in fact be a mythology. . . . All that is needed is to use it as a departure point for a third semiological chain, to take its signification as the first term of a second myth."[29]

To break apart the mythical sign, to reinscribe it in a critical montage, and then to circulate this artificial myth in turn: this is a strategy not only of much subcultural style but also of much appropriation art that flourished in the late 1970s and early 1980s. Thus, in her appropriations of modern masters, Sherrie Levine questioned the myths of original artist and unique artwork; so, too, in her photographs of contemporary art in its social settings, Louise Lawler questioned the myths of artistic autonomy and aesthetic disinterest; and in her contestations of sexual stereotypes Barbara Kruger questioned the myths of masculinity and femininity at work in art world and popular culture alike. (One could substitute other artists and other interests here: Victor Burgin, Barbara Bloom, Silvia Kolbowski, and so on.)

Yet a problem arose with this definition of allegorical art as well. It was too absolute to pronounce montage an "abused gadget . . . for sale," as Buchloh did in 1981, or to dismiss appropriation as a museum category, as Douglas Crimp did in 1983.[30] Nevertheless, when does montage recode, let alone redeem, the splintering of the commodity-sign, and when does it exacerbate it? When does appropriation double the mythical sign critically, and when does it replicate it, even reinforce it cynically? Is it ever purely the one or the other?

As early as 1970 Barthes had revised his project of myth robbery and ideology critique. On the one hand it might presume too much: a position of truth outside myth, a place of subjectivity beyond ideology. On the other hand it might lead to a form of sophistication in which contempt substitutes for critique. One must do more, Barthes argued, shake the sign, challenge the symbolic.[31] In some practices in the 1980s this mandate led to innovative work concerning the making of meaning and value, identity and privilege, in dominant artistic representations and cultural discourses. However, in other practices

Sherrie Levine, *President Profile 1*, 1979.

Barbara Kruger, *Untitled*, 1981–83.

it took on a different valence: not a recoding of the mythical commodity-sign so much as a fascination with its splintered signifiers. In this work the passion *of* the commodity-sign, its vicissitudes under advanced capitalism, was met by a passion *for* the commodity-sign, a fetishism of "the factitious, differential, encoded, systematized aspect of the object."[32] Sometimes this passion, this fetishism, made it difficult to distinguish, among postmodernist artists and post-structuralist critics alike, between *critics* of the reification and fragmentation of the sign and *connoisseurs* of this same process.

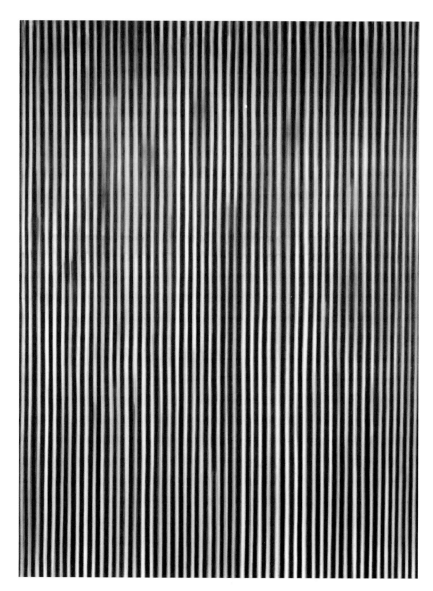

Ross Bleckner, *Fallen Sky,* 1981/1985.

4

In the textual turn of art in the 1970s, the field of aesthetic practice expanded, and the disciplinary limits of painting and sculpture broke down. In part this defetishized given forms of practice, yet new fetishisms soon replaced the old. As we saw in chapter 3, the two principal versions of postmodernist art tended to treat both art-historical and mass-cultural images as fetishes, that is, as so many detached signifiers to manipulate. By the middle 1980s entire genres and mediums (like abstraction and painting) were taken up in a conventionalist manner whereby complex historical practices were reduced to static signs that then stood as if out of time. In this chapter I will follow the trajectory of this *conventionalist aesthetic* through the 1980s.

SIMULATION PAINTING

By the middle 1980s there emerged in New York a geometric painting that, in keeping with the manic marketing of the time, was given two labels very quickly: neo-geo and simulationism. Associated with artists like Peter Halley and Ashley Bickerton, this work assumed an ironic distance from its own tradition of abstract painting. In effect it treated this tradition as a store of ready-mades to appropriate, and in strategy if not in appearance neo-geo was closer to appropriation art than to abstract painting.

The development of neo-geo out of appropriation art was direct in the case of Sherrie Levine. In two series of paintings on wood from the middle 1980s, Levine recalled two types of abstraction. First, her paintings of broad stripes and bright checkerboards evoked the analytic abstraction of Frank Stella, Robert Ryman, Brice Marden, and others. Yet, often rote in design and kitschy in color, they evoked this abstraction only to fall short of it, to fail it—which is to say, only to suggest that *it* had fallen short, that *it* had failed on its promise of pictorial purity, formal reflexivity, and so on. The same was true of her paintings of oval knots. Far from surrealist motifs of biomorphism or chance, these knots were plugs machined into place. Here the informal freedom of automatist abstraction was evoked, not the formal rigor of analytic abstraction, but again only to be mocked as false or forced. Both series thus cited modernist abstraction, but in a manner that drained it of aesthetic value, whether this was understood in terms of formal consciousness or aleatory unconsciousness. In this way abstraction was positioned as another set of styles among others, with as much or as little historical necessity as the next. More, it was positioned where its advocates feared it might fall all along: in the place of design, decoration, even kitsch. But did neo-geo artists like Levine receive abstraction as so reified, or did they participate in its emptying out?

This reduction of abstraction to design, decoration, even kitsch was extreme in the citation of op art by Ross Bleckner, Phillip Taaffe, and Peter Schuyff. As Bleckner noted in a characteristically sardonic way, op art was "quintessentially twentieth century: technologically oriented, disruptive, 'about perception,' naive, superficial, and, by most accounts, a failure."[1] A pop version of abstraction or an abstract form of pop, "it attempted to construct a conceptual relationship to abstract painting. It was a dead movement from its very inception."[2] In op art, then, abstraction was *already* reduced to design, and these neo-geo artists only reiterated this failure. But they reiterated it not in order to redeem it critically (this Benjaminian model was not considered possible, or not considered at all) but to compound it cynically. At times they appeared to mock this abstraction in order to distance it, to suggest that *it* was reified, failed, beyond redemption, not they. At other times they appeared to embrace this failure as if it were a form of protection: the paradoxical defense of the already defeated, the already dead. This move from an ironic posture to a failed, pathetic, even abject one became pronounced in art in the early 1990s, and in retrospect neo-geo appears as an early instance of this strategy—which is to say, perhaps, an early sign of a crisis in critical art.[3]

In either form, then, whether a parodic reduction of analytic abstraction or a campy recycling of op abstraction, neo-geo developed out of appropriation art. That is, it arose as the next move in the game: to appropriate modernist abstraction in order to mock its aspiration to originality and sublimity, or to play upon its failure.[4] Yet the nature of this move—back to painting, to the medium of the unique—contradicted the central critique in appropriation art of the original art work and the sublime aesthetic experience. Some, like the painter-critic Thomas Lawson, argued that this move was necessary, that the critique of painting could only be continued *within* painting, as if deconstructively, with painting used as camouflage for its own subversion.[5] Yet this argument was too sophisticated, which is to say, too sophistical, and, as we will see, the lines between deconstruction and complicity blurred.

The critique in appropriation art was often dubious in its own right, but at least it retained critique as a value. Moreover, it attempted to elaborate rather than to reverse the deconstructive techniques of related practices: conceptual art, institutional critique, feminist art, and so on. With artists like Bickerton, however, the "strategic inversion of many of the deconstructive techniques of the past decade or two" became programmatic.[6] Thus, even as his neo-geo work referred "to every station of its operational life, i.e., storage, shipping, gallery access, rack, reproduction, and on the wall,"[7] it did so in a way that turned the conceptual analysis of the art object, its discourses and institutions, into a closed device designed to implode (like a Rousselian machine) rather than to ramify (as in the reframings of art works in social settings by artists like Allan McCollum and Louise Lawler). It also treated this critique as a commodity—a critical point, but a cynical one if made in the explicit form *of* a commodity.

For Bickerton and others institutional critique had come to a dead end. Yet here, too, did they receive this critique as so reified—as an "absurd, pompous, saturated and elaborate system, of cul-de-sac meanings"—or did they

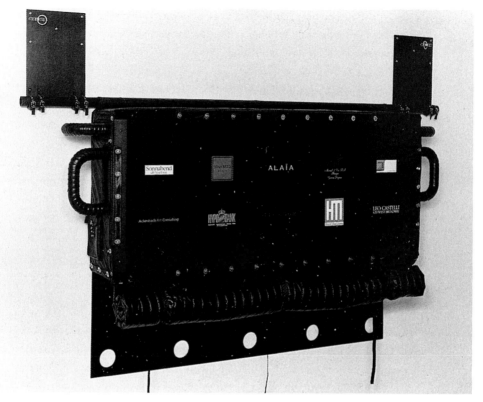

Ashley Bickerton, *Commercial Piece 1,* 1989.

render it so?[8] Certainly the negativity of neo-geo was defeatist more than dialectical, and sophisticated though it was, this defeatism was adolescent in the sense that, like the embrace of failure, it was both aggressive and defensive, a pose of recalcitrance that intimated a plea for acceptance. (This pose might speak to the great success of neo-geo with its patrons, who could condescend to it even as they were provoked by it. Bickerton even coined a term for this pose: "defiant complicity.")[9]

If neo-geo was not abstract painting except in appearance, appropriation art except in strategy, or institutional critique except in rhetoric, what was it? One way to define it is through its very ambiguity, particularly in relation to representation and abstraction. Neo-geo partook of both modes, but it did not treat them as opposed; or rather it did not attempt to reconcile them as if they were opposed. Instead it treated them as *already reconciled,* and this suggests a rethinking of the relationship between the two. As I argued in chapter 2, abstraction did not undo representation; rather, in the moment of high modernism, it repressed or (better) sublated representation, and in this sublation representation was preserved even as it was canceled.[10] Think of the residues of referentiality in the early compositions of Kandinsky or the early grids of Mondrian. Far from mistakes, these vestiges of riders and mountains in Kandinsky or traces of trees and piers in Mondrian were necessary to the abstraction. They not only defined it as such but also grounded it, rescued it from the arbitrary— and the arbitrary was a constant threat to abstraction, a threat courted by Kandinsky, resisted by Mondrian.

However, representation is not preserved in simulation, which is the mode that neo-geo approximated (hence its alternative name "simulationism"). In future art histories of the sign, representation may be superseded not by abstraction alone, as in our basic accounts of prewar art, but by simulation as well. For if abstraction tends only to *sublate* representation, simulation tends to *subvert* it, given that simulation can produce a representational effect without a referential connection to the world. The same is true of future social histories of the sign. Here, too, simulation may be seen to supersede representation, crucial as this mode is to the serial production of commodities and images in advanced-capitalist society.

———

But what exactly is simulation? Gilles Deleuze has distinguished the simulacrum from the copy in two ways: the copy is "endowed with resemblance," whereas the simulacrum need not be; and the copy produces the model as original, whereas the simulacrum "calls into question the very notion of the copy and the model."[11] This definition might lead us to revise our basic accounts of postwar art as well.[12] For example, pop art might appear less as a return to representation after abstract expressionism than as a turn to simulation—to the serial production of images whose connection to originals, let alone resemblance to referents, is often attenuated (especially in the work of Andy Warhol).[13] However, if simulation was thus released into art in the 1960s, it was not used reflexively there. This had to await the neo-pop appropriation art of Cindy Sherman, Richard Prince, Barbara Ess, and others in the late 1970s and early 1980s, which also marked less a return to representation (say, after the abstraction of postminimalism) than a troubling of representation through a turn to simulation.

What, then, is the status of simulation in neo-geo? It too can be taken as critical of representation, disruptive of its conceptual order. Consider how the generic abstractions of Levine seem to be neither originals nor copies, how they might disturb these representational categories. It can also be seen as critical of abstraction, disruptive of its historical logic. Consider here how the Levine paintings, if insinuated into the canon of recent abstraction (again, Stella, Ryman, Marden), might disturb this paternal lineage, this artistic patrimony. Yet this use of simulation remains tricky. For one thing it might evince a posthistorical perspective, according to which art appears stripped of its historical contexts and discursive connections—as if it were a synchronous array of so many styles, devices, or signifiers to collect, pastiche, or otherwise manipulate, again with no one deemed more necessary, pertinent, or advanced than the next. In this conventionalist ethos painting is then produced as little more than a sign of painting; or, as Bickerton remarked of an early series of work: "These are not paintings. They are paradigms of paintings."[14] *This is the rhetoric of an analytical metalanguage of painting, but the result is rather a posthistorical conventionalism of painting, a fetishism of its signifiers that occludes the historicity of its practices.* More than anything else this fetishism of the signifier delivers this art over to our political economy of the commodity-sign, of which it is an epitome rather than a critique.

Simulation is also not a force to be taken lightly outside of art. Along with old regimes of disciplinary surveillance and media spectacle, the simulation of events is an important form of social deterrence today, for how can one intervene in events when they are simulated or replaced by pseudo-events?[15] In this sense simulacral images may improve upon ideological representations; or as Jean Baudrillard writes: "Ideology only corresponds to a betrayal of reality by signs; simulation corresponds to a short-circuit of reality and its reduplication by signs."[16] But then many neo-geo artists sought to represent this reduplication by signs: the abstraction of advanced-capitalist models of space, as in the cell-and-conduit paintings of Halley; of technoscientific languages, as in the cybernetic paintings of Bickerton; of technological modes of vision, as in the spectacular paintings of Jack Goldstein; of scientific paradigms of (dis)order, as in the fractal paintings of James Welling; and of contemporary image processing in general, as in the hypermediated paintings of Meyer Vaisman and Oliver Wasow. The attempt to represent this extra-artistic order of abstraction might be taken as a cognitive project; it might even be associated with the "cognitive mapping" of advanced-capitalist systems advocated by Fredric Jameson.[17] Yet neo-geo did not situate us in this new order so much as it left us in aesthetic awe before its effects: it aspired to a contemporary version of the capitalist sublime.

What is it, then, to represent this extra-artistic abstraction? The old icons of modernity like the automobile, Jameson has argued, are now displaced by new emblems like the computer, which "are all sources of reproduction rather than 'production,' and are no longer sculptural solids in space."[18] As diffuse networks rather than discrete objects, they resist representation, as does advanced capitalism in general, an order all but global in its reach, everywhere and nowhere at once. This raises the stake of neo-geo painting, for in the attempt to represent such abstractive processes, artists like Halley might only simplify them. So, too, in the attempt to represent such abstractive effects, artists like Goldstein might only mystify them. Moreover, can these artists engage issues of a postindustrial society in a medium such as painting based in preindustrial craft? Although concerned with technoscientific systems, they produced works of art in

Peter Halley, *White Cell with Conduits,* 1985.

a traditional medium. And although not oblivious to this contradiction, they did not (perhaps could not) reflect on it in the paintings.

In the end the project to represent simulation might not only mystify it; it might also reduce simulation to the status of a theme. This suggests two things: that the use of theory in this art was illustrational, and that the use of simulation theory in particular was contrary to its own claims—for if simulation can be illustrated in painting, captured there as a theme, how disruptive is it to old orders of representation? Here simulation became mere "simulationism."

COMMODITY SCULPTURE

Along with simulation painting there emerged a kind of sculpture associated with artists like Jeff Koons and Haim Steinbach. This commodity sculpture developed out of appropriation art as well, and it too assumed an ironic distance from its own tradition, in this case the readymade. Just as simulation painting often treated abstraction as a readymade, commodity sculpture often treated the readymade as an abstraction, and just as simulation painting tended to reduce art to design and kitsch, commodity sculpture tended to substitute design and kitsch for art. In this sense the two activities were complementary, and both groups of artists delighted in these reductions and reversals as strategic moves in an apparent endgame of art. End*game,* not end: there is a difference between a posthistorical manipulation of conventions whose value is regarded as given or fixed and a historical transformation of practices whose value is elaborated or contested.[19] Unlike most modernist apocalypses of art (at least in ambition), this endgame rendered traditional categories more stable and artistic discourse more hermetic. There was no utopianism here; on the contrary, the impossibility of transcendence in art, of transgression into society, seemed part of the demonstration. In short, this endgame was business as usual for the art world, only more so; and it was mostly as a business that simulation painting and commodity sculpture were reported in the media.

There is another sense in which simulation painting and commodity sculpture must be seen together. Like pop and minimalism, they emerged as different responses to the same moment in the dialectic of high art and commodity culture—a late moment in which the criticality long generated out of this dialectic had waned. Whether one regards high art and commodity culture as diametrically opposed (as did the young Clement Greenberg in "Avant-Garde and Kitsch" [1939]) or as dialectically connected ("torn halves of an integral freedom, to which however they do not add up," as the young Theodor Adorno put it in 1936), the two near implosion by the moment of minimalism and pop.[20] Minimalism and pop often approximated a serial mode of *production* that related them like no previous art to our systematic world of commodities and images. With this serial mode of production came a different form of *consumption,* the object of which is not the use of this commodity or the meaning of that image so much as its difference as a sign from other signs; it is this difference that we fetishize, "the factitious, differential, encoded, systematized aspect of the object."[21] With minimalism and pop this form of consumption is in play in art as well; it informs our reading of the compositions of each. Once serial production and differential consumption penetrated art in this manner, the distinctions between high and low forms became blurred beyond a borrowing of images or a sharing of themes. Evident in minimalism and pop, this blurring appeared all but total in commodity sculpture. Just as simulation painting seemed to conflate representation and abstraction, commodity sculpture seemed to collapse high art and commodity culture programmatically. But has this high-low dialectic collapsed, or is it only transformed in a new political economy of the commodity-sign? I suggested above that simulation painting might *symptomatize* our fetishism of the signifier in this new economy; commodity sculpture seems to *thematize* this fetishism. Together the two comprise a virtual aesthetics of this economy.

Let me clarify this development with a historical sketch of the readymade in its various guises, for this device has served more than any other to articulate the tense relation between art and commodity. In 1914 Duchamp presented a product, a bottle rack, as a work of art. Immediately this object posed the question of *aesthetic* value, of what counts as art, and it intimated that, in a bourgeois context, this value depends on the autonomy of the object, that is, on its abstraction from the world. But retrospectively this object has prompted two contrary readings of value as well: on the one hand, that the work of art is also defined, as a commodity, in terms of *exchange* value (or, as Walter Benjamin put it, exhibition value); and, on the other hand, that the work of art might yet be defined, as a bottle rack (say), in terms of *use* value.[22] This conflict among different values is the crux of the critical ambiguity that the readymade device can put into play.

What happened to this critical ambiguity when in 1960, at the threshold of minimalism and pop, Jasper Johns bronzed two Ballantine ale cans on a base? Here aesthetic value is not in doubt, nor is its relation to exchange/exhibition value; the art status of the object is guaranteed by the bronze as well as by the presentation. The question of use value thus recedes; in fact it is canceled by aesthetic value as surely as the ale is canceled by the bronze. At the same time, however, the question of *consumption* comes to the fore in two ways that commodity sculpture seems to elaborate. First, the ale cans imply a relation between consumption and art *appreciation:* both involve products and/or signs to consume ("Ballantine," "Johns"). They also imply a further relation between consumption and art *collection.* This is a different kind of consumption, to be sure, consumption as expenditure; but it too cannot be separated from aesthetic value, for in part this expenditure confers aesthetic value upon the object, just as it confers sumptuary value (that is, prestige) upon its collector.

Next consider two familiar examples of commodity sculpture: *New Shelton Wet/Dry Double Decker* (1981), a display by Jeff Koons of two vacuum cleaners encased one above the other in Plexiglas and bathed in fluorescent light like mock relics, and *related and different* (1985), a display by Haim Steinbach of a pair of Air Jordans set on a formica shelf next to five plastic gold goblets like kitsch grails. *Almost explicitly here the connoisseur of the art work is positioned as a fetishist of the commodity-sign.* Art and commodity are made one; they are presented as signs for exchange; and they are appreciated—consumed—as such. So what relation do these readymades have to the articulations of Duchamp and Johns?

Again, however anarchistically, most Duchamp readymades proposed that objects of use value be substituted for objects of aesthetic and/or exchange/ exhibition value: a bottle rack in place of a sculpture or, reciprocally, "a

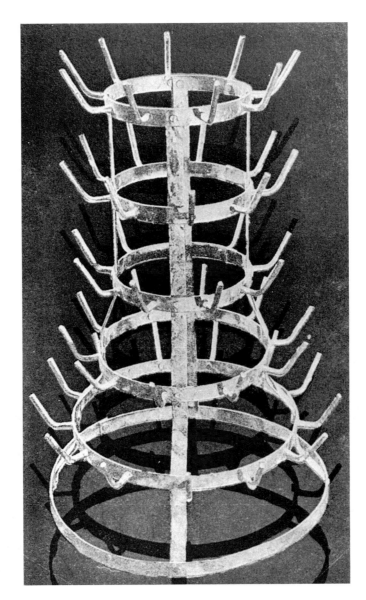

Marcel Duchamp, *Bottle Dryer,* 1914 (lost).

Jeff Koons, *New Shelton Wet/Dry Double Decker,* 1981.

Rembrandt used as an ironing board."[23] Most Koons and Steinbach readymades do the opposite: they present objects of exchange/exhibition in the place of art in a way that cancels use. One can use vacuum cleaners and basketball shoes, of course, but the display is the thing here: the cases in Koons, the shelves in Steinbach, the arrangement of the objects, the effect of the exhibition as a whole (this exhibition effect recouped whatever critical value installation art might have possessed). Like Johns, then, Koons and Steinbach *reverse* Duchamp on use value. But they also *trump* Johns on the significance of consumption along the lines of appreciation and collection traced above. In general they intimate that all these values—aesthetic, use, and exchange/exhibition—are now subsumed by *sign exchange value*. They suggest, in other words, that we covet and consume not the vacuum cleaners so much as the Sheltons, not the basketball shoes so much as the Air Jordans, and that this passion for the sign, this fetishism of the signifier, governs our reception of art as well: we covet and consume not the work per se so much as the Koons, the Steinbach. These brand names may be more exalted, but in part because they are more expensive. This brings us to the other dimension of sign exchange value, the sumptuary, for, again, it is extravagant expenditure that guarantees the exalted status of these objects.

Koons and Steinbach highlighted this sumptuary operation in art even as they were highlighted by it. As these artists rose in value on the market, so did the commodities they deployed. Koons commissioned crafted works at once elaborate and kitschy (e.g., whiskey decanters in the form of stainless steel train sets, entertainment celebrities in the form of porcelain statues), and Steinbach purchased conversation pieces at once extravagant and vulgar (e.g., trophies of exotic animals in the form of furniture). In this way they underscored an identity between coveted art work and luxury commodity as objects of desire and vehicles of distinction (pomp, prestige, power). Indeed, with evermore outlandish products and displays, Koons and Steinbach pushed the limits of this identity. In doing so they parodied the consumerist potlatch that preoccupied the Reaganomic elite in the middle 1980s even as they participated in this financial debauch.

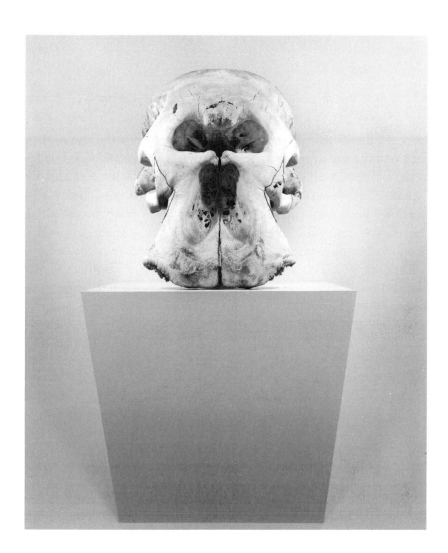

Haim Steinbach, *Untitled,* 1988, elephant skull and foot stools.

If Koons and Steinbach explored the social dimension of the commodity-sign in similar ways, they approached its structural dimension (again, "the facti-tious, differential, encoded, systematized aspect of the object") from different angles. Koons was drawn to the factitious or fetishistic aspect of the commod-ity-sign, Steinbach to its differential or encoded aspect. From the basketballs suspended in water tanks to the ad campaigns of personal promotion, Koons fixed on perfect objects and auratic images. Although he cloaked this fascination in the mystificatory terms of traditional aesthetics, the perfection in play here was that of the commodity fetish, the aura that of the glamorous celebrity. In effect Koons performed what Benjamin predicted long ago: the cultural need to compensate the lost aura of art with "the phony spell" of the commodity and the star.[24] Here, of course, the precedent is Warhol. "Some company re-cently was interested in buying my 'aura'," he wrote in *The Philosophy of Andy Warhol* (1975). "They didn't want my product. They kept saying, 'We want your aura.' I never figured out what they wanted."[25] Obviously Warhol is too modest here; he figured it out well enough. But it was left to Koons to make this shift from product to aura the very subject of an oeuvre, indeed the very operation of a career. In a sense this stockbroker-turned-artist presented *hype* as the advanced-capitalist substitute for aura.

If Koons illuminated the commodity fetish as perfect object, Steinbach illuminated it as differential sign. Set in clever juxtapositions of form and color, his objects are precisely "related and different," related as commodities, different as signs. Again, it is this relation-in-difference that we read, consume, fetishize, and Steinbach made us aware of it. In effect he gave us little pieces of a great puzzle: an economic system based on a principle of equivalence that no longer eradicates difference so much as recodes it, exploits it, puts it into play in a calculus of sign exchange. At the level of the art work this system appears as *design,* and in the Steinbach version its code seemed total. That is, it seemed to subsume any thing, however odd, and any arrangement, however surreal. It also seemed to overwhelm old oppositions of function and dysfunction, rationality and irrationality.[26]

If capitalist exchange is based on equivalence, there are two principal ways to challenge it symbolically. The first is to refer to an order of exchange based on a different principle: the ambivalence of gift exchange, say, rather than the equivalence of commodity exchange. This vision of a gift society bound by rituals of reciprocity has long intrigued anthropological critics of commodity society—from Marcel Mauss and Georges Bataille to the situationists and Baudrillard. But if this other order haunts our own, as they all suggest, it does so in a spectral way, and to invoke it in a gesture of resistance is romantic at best. The second strategy is to challenge our economy of equivalence from within, through a recoding of its commodity-signs. One aspect of this strategy, the appropriation of mass-cultural signs, is apparent in subcultural style, which has long played with given signs of class, race, and gender. This bricolage is also practiced in appropriation art, which repositions such signs in other ways, often in collision with high-art ones. Clearly the other aspect of this strategy, the appropriation of serial commodities, is operative in the work of Koons, Steinbach, and others—but to what end?

Sometimes the appropriations in commodity sculpture do estrange the object provocatively. Examples include the drowned basketballs of Koons, the found-object totem poles of Joel Otterson, the mechanical-electronic devices of Jon Kessler, and the old-master reconstructions of Justen Ladda (e.g., the *Praying Hands* of Dürer assembled out of *Tide* boxes). Such works alienate the commodity in ways that evoke the ambivalence of the surrealist object, if not the tribal gift. At other times, however, the appropriations in commodity sculpture do not estrange the object at all. On the contrary, they either trade on the equivalence of the commodity or exploit its fetishistic charms. In the first tendency, strong in Steinbach, the art object is presented directly as a commodity—as if in a suicidal strike against consumption that is also an ecstatic embrace of it. In the second tendency, strong in Koons, the lost aura of art is replaced with the false aura of the commodity—a paradoxical move, given that the commodity withered artistic aura in the first place; a problematic move as well, given that it turns the readymade from a device that demystifies art into one that remystifies it. In both tendencies, then, the readymade according to Duchamp is reversed, and explicitly the commodity takes the place of "the allegorical way of seeing."[27]

Notwithstanding the claims of criticality and sincerity made for Steinbach and Koons respectively, commodity sculpture comes down to this triumphal defeatism: this suicidal embrace and that cynical substitution are the only options for object making in a political economy of the commodity-sign. Yet several artists during these years belied this presumptive fatalism. Allan McCollum demonstrated the same positioning of art as object of desire and vehicle of prestige—only he withheld the goods, so to speak. Although his *Surrogates* and *Perfect Vehicles* are also signs for painting and sculpture respectively, they turn this conventionalism into an object of critical play; they frame the system of sign exchange value with witty irony, not cynical duplicity. To this end they focus less on the commodity than on the emotional politics of consumption; thus, rather than double the consumerist object suicidally, they mirror the consumerist subject critically. In effect, we see our economy of the art object as if from another culture (almost another planet); in this way a critical distance is created from within the very economy that seemed to foreclose it.

CRITICISM AND COMPLICITY

Simulation painting and commodity sculpture may have demonstrated the changed status of art in the political economy of the commodity-sign. But rather than treat this status in terms of a contradiction between an art economy that trades in commodities and a political economy that circulates signs, they tended to work both sides of the equation—to preserve the aesthetic categories and social distinctions of art even as they pointed to the structural implosion of high and low forms in this new order of exchange. To this extent they had it both ways: they played on the subsumption of painting as sign, but in the form of painting; they played on the collapse of the dialectic of art and commodity, but in the form of an art-commodity. Here, again, the difference in ambition between contemporary endgamings *in* art and modernist endings *of* art is clear.

Allan McCollum, *Perfect Vehicles*, 1986.

This is not to dismiss the "satiric literalizations" and "strategic inversions" performed in simulation painting and commodity sculpture as only opportunistic. Rather, they are best seen in terms of *cynical reason,* a paradoxical structure of thought explored by the German philosopher Peter Sloterdijk in a long critique published in 1983, or during the rise of simulation painting and commodity sculpture. According to Sloterdijk, cynical reason is "enlightened false consciousness."[28] The cynic knows his beliefs to be false or ideological, but he holds to them nonetheless for the sake of self-protection, as a way to negotiate the contradictory demands placed upon him. This duplicity recalls the ambivalence of the fetishist in Freud: a subject who recognizes the reality of castration or trauma (or, in my analogy here, of aesthetic conflict or political contradiction) but who disavows it. Yet the cynic does not disavow this reality so much as he ignores it, and this structure renders him almost impervious to ideology critique, for he is already demystified, already enlightened about his ideological relation to the world (this allows the cynic to feel superior to ideology critics as well). Thus ideological and enlightened at once, the cynic is "reflexively buffered": his very splitting armors him, his very ambivalence renders him immune. In this regard Sloterdijk describes cynical reason less as a toying with fetishism than as a "coquetting" with schizophrenia, a formulation that captures the subject-position of much contemporary art.[29]

I do not mean to suggest a zeitgeist of cynicism, but a specific cynical reason has developed within contemporary art, especially in the crisis of criticality that followed appropriation art. Already in 1982 one of the foremost practitioners of this art foresaw some of its dangers. In "'Taking' Pictures," a short text published in *Screen,* Barbara Kruger implied that appropriation art drew on both ideology critique and deconstruction (though she did not cite these methods by name).[30] On the one hand, like ideology critique, appropriation art was concerned to question stereotypes, to contradict "the surety of our initial readings," to expose the reality underneath the representation. On the other hand, like deconstruction, it was also concerned "to question ideas of competence, originality, authorship and property," to contradict the surety of *any* reading, to expose reality *as* a representation. Here Kruger offered two caveats. The first touched on the ideology-critical aspect of appropriation art: its negativity, she warned, "can merely serve to congratulate its viewers on their contemptuous acuity." The second touched on the deconstructive aspect of this art: its mimicry can turn into replication, its parody "subsumed by the power granted its 'original.'" These two cautions might be rewritten as follows: ideology critique can lapse into contempt, and deconstruction can slip into complicity. Much of the work that followed appropriation art stepped into one of these two traps.[31]

Yet a tension between ideology critique and deconstruction already existed *within* appropriation art. In the simplest forms of ideology critique the true dispels the false as science dispels ideology. Confident in knowledge, the ideology critic operates by exposure. This operation can be accusatory, even punitive, as it sees the world in terms of errors to be corrected. In this way it can also be dogmatic, even orthodox; or as Roland Barthes remarked as early as 1970: "denunciation, demystification (or demythification), has itself become discourse, stock of phrases, catechistic declaration."[32] Politically such truth telling is necessary, but it is also contingent, and when hardened into an abstract law ideology critique can be reductive in its rigor, not to mention in its *ressentiment*.[33]

If reductive ideology critique tends to be too presumptive about truth claims, extreme deconstruction tends to be too skeptical about them. Of course the investigations inspired by deconstruction—of the modernist artist as great original, of realist representation as documentary truth—are important. But they too must be seen as situated and polemical. Abstracted into general principles, the first critique tends to devalue artistic agency as such, and the second to question the very activity of representation. Such a facile account of both postmodernist art and poststructuralist theory encouraged the cynical conventionalism of much work that followed appropriation art. *To a great extent the aesthetic of cynical reason emerged not only as a reaction against the presumptive truth claims of ideology critique but also as an exaggeration of the epistemological skepticism of deconstruction.*[34]

If the aesthetic of cynical reason was prepared by a double slippage of ideology critique into contempt and deconstruction into complicity, what prepared this slippage? To be sure, there is antimodernist contempt in postmodernist art, especially in the critique of originality advanced in appropriation art. But, paradoxically perhaps, there is more antimodernist contempt in neomodernist art like neo-expressionism. For such mini-movements did not recover these modernist styles so much as burlesque them, and they did so *within* the traditional mediums. This siting in turn abetted the second slippage of deconstruction into complicity. Again, already in 1981 Thomas Lawson had argued that the critique of painting could only be continued within painting, as if deconstructively, with painting used as camouflage for its own subversion. This subversion was to shake the value structures of the art world, but much the opposite occurred: subversion was contained there, at the point of painting, and reversed into complicity. As Lawson feared, the deconstructive painter fell for the victim who was supposed to be seduced and abandoned (the language is his, and his test case was David Salle).[35] As we will see, this double bind is not new; here, however, it was *embraced*. Rather than a "last exit," then, such painting became the site of another "strategic inversion." And such inversions contributed to the making of an art world in which, without much irony, an art dealer could be presented as a master of deconstruction, a stockbroker could assume the mantle of Duchamp, and an investment banker could cite institution critique as his formative influence.[36]

Such inversions suggest more than another crisis in criticality; they point to a deep mortification of critique. In its history the avant-garde has produced several models of analysis, of course, but in a capitalist context none has proved more urgent than the attempt to turn its own compromised position into a critical purchase on the dominant culture. Even as the avant-garde was defined against the bourgeoisie, Greenberg argued in "Avant-Garde and Kitsch," it represented the self-critical elite of this class, to which it was also "attached by an umbilical cord of gold."[37] On the one hand, this "contradictory belonging-together-in-opposition of the avant-garde and its bourgeoisie" allowed critical purchase: the avant-garde could engage its patron-enemy behind the lines.[38] On the other hand, this compromised position also made for political ambiguity. This is why Marx presents bohemia as a site of complicity rather than contestation in *The Eighteenth Brumaire of Louis Bonaparte* (1852). In his virtuosic description, its denizens are double agents, not outside class lines but between them, positioned to serve not as saboteurs but as go-betweens, intermediaries of power.[39]

Perhaps this description prompted Benjamin to portray Baudelaire as "a secret agent" of his own class.[40] In any case Baudelaire acted out the double status of this avant-garde perhaps more hysterically than any artist before or since:

> I say "Long live the revolution!" as I would say "Long live destruc-
> tion! Long live penance! Long live chastisement! Long live death!"
> I would be happy not only as a victim; it would not displease me
> to play the hangman as well—so as to feel the revolution from both
> sides! All of us have the republican spirit in our blood as we have
> syphilis in our bones; we have a democratic and a syphilitic
> infection.[41]

In part this is the credo of the dandy, portrayed by Baudelaire in a famous sketch as a beautiful symptom of a historical interregnum: a figure who, pressured by democratic "leveling," elaborates aristocratic "distinction" into an artistic "cult of the self."[42] Yet Baudelaire was not only a dandy who reviled democracy; he was also a republican who celebrated it. And this political ambivalence has made him an object of identification for (petit-bourgeois) avant-gardists ever since— along with his great ability to turn this ambivalence into poetic art and critical intelligence.

Again, as Benjamin admits, this ambivalence often limits the politics of the Baudelairean avant-gardist to "the metaphysics of the *provocateur*," and it may be sadomasochistic at its core (the desire to be hangman and victim at once).[43] But this is not the only avant-gardist politic: opposite the dandy, for example, is the engagé; next to Baudelaire stands Courbet.[44] With certain com- plications this typology can be traced to our own day, with many hybrids along the way (André Breton is a prewar example, Marcel Broodthaers a postwar example). Indeed, the hybrid position is dominant in postwar art that aspires to criticality. Certainly there is a tension (or is it a compromise?) between commitment and dandyism through appropriation art at least. ("I appropriate these images," Levine remarked in an early statement, "to express my own simultaneous longing for the passion of engagement and the sublimity of aloofness.")[45] Yet this tension exists only as long as the political culture allows. As Reaganism spread in the early 1980s, the dandyish position became less ambiguous, more cynical, and the star of Warhol obscured all others.[46]

What, then, is the status of the critical ambiguity of the dandyish artist today? Are its discursive preconditions collapsed, or have they only shifted? Is its social space eclipsed, or has it simply moved? What might the aesthetic of cynical reason tell us in this regard? Of course, any narrative of a collapsed criticality is suspect, at least to the degree that it is projected as complete. Postwar art often mirrors the dominant culture: in some ways color-field painting reiterated the logic of corporate design, minimalism and pop the logic of differential consumption, conceptual art the logic of administered society, and so on.[47] As such these mirrorings prove little. Some engagement of the dominant culture is necessary for critique (which is no less mimetic than desire), and some identification with its patrons is essential to the avant-garde.

Yet precisely here the situation of simulation painting and commodity sculpture was different. Engagement of the dominant culture became a near embrace, and identification with patrons seemed all but total.[48] Artist and patron alike tended to regard art in terms of prestige signs and investment portfolios, and both tended to operate under a conventionalist ethos that treats almost everything as a commodity-sign for exchange. This political economy is overseen by a professional-managerial elite, "yuppies" as they were called in the middle 1980s, "symbolic analysts" as they were called in the early 1990s.[49] This elite directs the flow of commodity-signs in an electronic network in which market and media are all but symbiotic, with products transmuted into images and vice versa.[50] In the 1980s this elite powered the extraordinary boom in the art market (the name Saatchi may stand for this investment group), and naturally it rewarded practices that reflected its own conventionalist and posthistorical worldview. In this sense simulation painting and commodity sculpture were forms of salon portraiture, and when the market fell in 1987 and the collectors withdrew, these forms declined too.[51]

In this situation many artists turned on critical art as if it were the traitor, sometimes to question it, often to reverse it; thus was institution critique proclaimed a dead end. However, ambitious artists were not long satisfied with facile reversals. Faced with contradictory demands—to advance critical transformation in art *and* to demonstrate the historical futility of this project—some resorted to a "coquetting" with schizophrenia characteristic of cynical reason. This simulated schizophrenia was not new; in 1983 Craig Owens detected a similar posture among neo-expressionists, who were also confronted with contradictory demands to be avant-gardist ("as innovative and original as possible") *and* to be conformist ("to conform to established norms and conventions").[52] In both instances this simulated schizophrenia served as a mimetic defense against such double binds; it seemed to offer a way to suspend if not to escape them.

This defense has several precedents in modernism. Benjamin detected an "empathy with the commodity" at work in Baudelaire, a *homeopathic* procedure by which bits of commodity culture were used to innoculate poetry against complete infection by market capitalism (this defensive empathy can also be detected in Manet).[53] Sloterdijk saw "an irony of a bashed ego" at work in dada, a *hyperbolic* procedure by which "the degradation of the individual" under monopoly capitalism was pushed to the point of a parodic indictment (the best instances are Hugo Ball in writing and Max Ernst in art).[54] For Sloterdijk this "kynical irony" opposed cynical reason, but the two are not so distinct. For instance, did Warhol practice kynical irony or cynical reason? Certainly he simulated schizophrenia as a mimetic defense against the contradictory demands of the avant-gardist in the society of the spectacle, but it is difficult to distinguish his defense against spectacle from his identification with it. In simulation painting and commodity sculpture this distinction became almost impossible to draw, and in the pervasive practice of capitalist nihilism today it seems altogether blurred.

Faced with such impasses, many artists rejected the aesthetic of cynical reason, and in the next two chapters I follow two directions opened in the early 1990s. The first takes cynical reason to an extreme, pushes its pose of indifference to the point of disaffection, and challenges cynicism with abjection. Here the mimetic defense is no longer a simulated schizophrenia so much as a simulated imbecilism, infantilism, or autism—again, the paradoxical defense of the already damaged, defeated, or dead. The second confronts cynical reason, reclaims the figure of the engagé in opposition to the dandy, and turns from the involution of art-world endgames to the extroversion of quasi-ethnographic fieldwork. Yet, however different, the two directions converge on one point: both wish to break with the textualist model of the 1970s as well as with the conventionalist cynicism of the 1980s. In the wake of a crisis of the artistic sign (similar to the one discussed in chapter 3), these tendencies mark an emphatic turn to the bodily and the social, to the abject and the site-specific. From a conventionalist regime where nothing is real and the subject is superficial, much contemporary art presents reality in the form of trauma and the subject in the social depth of its own identity. After the apotheosis of the signifier and the symbolic, then, we are witness to a *turn to the real* on the one hand and a *turn to the referent* on the other. And with these turns come different returns—different genealogies of art and theory.

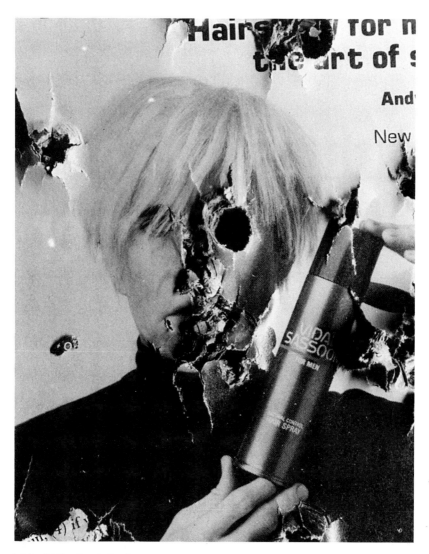

Richard Misrach, *Playboy #38 (Warhol),* 1989–91.

T H E   R E T U R N   O F   T H E   R E A L

In my reading of critical models in art and theory since 1960 I have stressed the minimalist genealogy of the neo-avant-garde. For the most part, artists and critics in this genealogy remained skeptical of realism and illusionism. In this way they continued the war of abstraction against representation by other means. As noted in chapter 2, minimalists like Donald Judd saw traces of realism in abstraction too, in the optical illusionism of its pictorial spaces, and expunged these last vestiges of the old order of idealist composition—an enthusiasm that led them to abandon painting altogether.[1] Significantly, this anti-illusionist posture was retained by many artists and critics involved in conceptual, institution-critical, body, performance, site-specific, feminist, and appropriation art. Even if realism and illusionism meant additional things in the 1970s and 1980s—the problematic pleasures of Hollywood cinema, for example, or the ideological blandishments of mass culture—they remained _bad_ things.

Yet another trajectory of art since 1960 was committed to realism and/or illusionism: some pop art, most superrealism (also known as photorealism), some appropriation art. Often displaced by the minimalist genealogy in the critical literature (if not in the marketplace), this pop genealogy takes on new interest today, for it complicates the reductive notions of realism and illusionism advanced by the minimalist genealogy—and in a way that illuminates contemporary reworkings of these categories as well. Our two basic models of representation miss the point of this pop genealogy almost entirely: that images are attached to referents, to iconographic themes or real things in the world, or, alternatively, that all images can do is represent other images, that all forms of representation (including realism) are auto-referential codes. Most accounts of postwar art based in photography divide somewhere along this line: the image as referential *or* as simulacral. This reductive either/or constrains such readings of this art, especially in the case of pop—a thesis that I will test initially against the "Death in America" images of Andy Warhol from the early 1960s, images that inaugurate the pop genealogy.[2]

It is no surprise that the *simulacral* reading of Warholian pop is advanced by critics associated with poststructuralism, for whom Warhol is pop and, more importantly, for whom the notion of the simulacral, crucial to the poststructuralist critique of representation, sometimes seems to depend on the example of Warhol as pop. "What pop art wants," Roland Barthes writes in "That Old Thing, Art" (1980), "is to desymbolize the object," to release the image from any deep meaning into simulacral surface.[3] In this process the author is also released: "The pop artist does not stand *behind* his work," Barthes continues, "and he himself has no depth: he is merely the surface of his pictures, no signified, no intention, anywhere."[4] With variations this simulacral reading of Warhol is performed by Michel Foucault, Gilles Deleuze, and Jean Baudrillard, for whom referential depth and subjective interiority are also victims of the sheer superficiality of pop. In "Pop—An Art of Consumption?" (1970), Baudrillard agrees that the object in pop "loses its symbolic meaning, its age-old anthropomorphic status"; but where Barthes and the others see an avant-gardist disruption of representation, Baudrillard sees an "end of subversion," a "total integration" of the art work into the political economy of the commodity-sign.[5]

The *referential* view of Warholian pop is advanced by critics and historians who tie the work to different themes: the worlds of fashion, celebrity, gay culture, the Warhol Factory, and so on. Its most intelligent version is presented by Thomas Crow, who, in "Saturday Disasters: Trace and Reference in Early War-

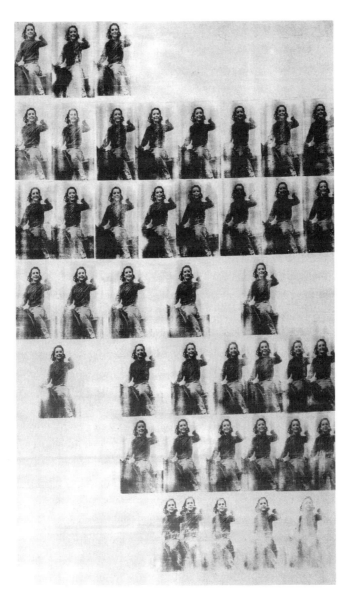

Andy Warhol, *National Velvet*, 1963.

hol" (1987), disputes the simulacral account of Warhol that the images are indiscriminate and the artist impassive. Underneath the glamorous surface of commodity fetishes and media stars Crow finds "the reality of suffering and death"; the tragedies of Marilyn, Liz, and Jackie in particular are said to prompt "straightforward expressions of feeling."[6] Here Crow finds not only a referential object *for* Warhol but an empathetic subject *in* Warhol, and here he locates the criticality *of* Warhol—not in an attack on "that old thing art" (as Barthes would have it) through an embrace of the simulacral commodity-sign (as Baudrillard would have it), but rather in an exposé of "complacent consumption" through "the brutal fact" of accident and mortality.[7] In this way Crow pushes Warhol beyond humanist sentiment to political engagement. "He was attracted to the open sores in American political life," Crow writes in a reading of the electric-chair images as agitprop against the death penalty and of the race-riot images as a testimonial for civil rights. "Far from a pure play of the signifier liberated from reference," Warhol belongs to the popular American tradition of "truth telling."[8]

This reading of Warhol as empathetic, even engagé, is a projection, but no more than the superficial, impassive Warhol, even though this projection was his own: "If you want to know all about Andy Warhol, just look at the surface of my paintings and films and me, and there I am. There's nothing behind it."[9] Both camps make the Warhol they need, or get the Warhol they deserve; no doubt we all do. And neither projection is wrong. I find them equally persuasive. But they cannot both be right . . . or can they? Can we read the "Death in America" images as referential *and* simulacral, connected *and* disconnected, affective *and* affectless, critical *and* complacent? I think we must, and we can if we read them in a third way, in terms of *traumatic realism*.[10]

TRAUMATIC REALISM

One way to develop this notion is through the famous motto of the Warholian persona: "I want to be a machine."[11] Usually this statement is taken to confirm the blankness of artist and art alike, but it may point less to a blank subject than to a shocked one, who takes on the nature of what shocks him as a mimetic defense against this shock: I am a machine too, I make (or consume) serial product-images too, I give as good (or as bad) as I get.[12] "Someone said my life has dominated me," Warhol told the critic Gene Swenson in a celebrated interview of 1963. "I liked that idea."[13] Here Warhol has just confessed to the same lunch every day for the past twenty years (what else but Campbell's soup?). In context, then, the two statements read as a preemptive embrace of the compulsion to repeat put into play by a society of serial production and consumption. If you can't beat it, Warhol suggests, join it. More, if you enter it totally, you might expose it; that is, you might reveal its automatism, even its autism, through your own excessive example. Used strategically in dada, this capitalist nihilism was performed ambiguously by Warhol, and, as we saw in chapter 4, many artists have played it out since.[14] (Of course this is a performance: there is a subject "behind" this figure of nonsubjectivity that presents it *as* a figure; otherwise the shocked subject is an oxymoron, for there is no subject self-present in shock, let alone in trauma. Yet the fascination of Warhol is that one is never certain about this subject behind: is anybody home, inside the automaton?)

These notions of shocked subjectivity and compulsive repetition reposition the role of *repetition* in the Warholian persona and images. "I like boring things" is another famous motto of this quasi-autistic persona. "I like things to be exactly the same over and over again."[15] In *POPism* (1980) Warhol glosses this embrace of boredom, repetition, domination: "I don't want it to be essentially the same—I want it to be *exactly* the same. Because the more you look at the same exact thing, the more the meaning goes away, and the better and emptier you feel."[16] Here repetition is both a draining of significance and a defending against affect, and this strategy guided Warhol as early as the 1963 interview: "When you see a gruesome picture over and over again, it doesn't really have any effect."[17] Clearly this is one function of repetition, at least as understood by Freud: to repeat a traumatic event (in actions, in dreams, in images) in order to integrate it into a psychic economy, a symbolic order. But the Warhol repetitions are not restorative in this way; they are not about a mastery of trauma. More than a patient release from the object in mourning, they suggest an obsessive fixation on the object in melancholy. Think of all the *Marilyns* alone, of the cropping, coloring, crimping of these images: as Warhol works over this image of love, a melancholic "wish-psychosis" seems in play.[18] But this analysis is not quite right either. For one thing the Warhol repetitions not only *re*produce traumatic effects; they also *produce* them. Somehow in these repetitions, then, several contradictory things occur at the same time: a warding away of traumatic significance *and* an opening out to it, a defending against traumatic affect *and* a producing of it.

Here I should make explicit the theoretical model I have implicated so far. In the early 1960s Jacques Lacan was concerned to define the real in terms of trauma. Titled "The Unconscious and Repetition," this seminar was roughly contemporaneous with the "Death in America" images (it ran in early 1964).[19] But unlike the theory of simulacra in Baudrillard and company, the theory of trauma in Lacan is not influenced by pop. It is, however, informed by surrealism, which here has its deferred effect on Lacan, an early associate of the surrealists, and below I will intimate that pop is related to surrealism as a traumatic realism (certainly my reading of Warhol is a surrealist one). In this seminar Lacan defines the traumatic as a missed encounter with the real. As missed, the real cannot be represented; it can only be repeated, indeed it *must* be repeated. "*Wiederholen*," Lacan writes in etymological reference to Freud on repetition, "is not *Reproduzieren*" (50); repetition is not reproduction. This can stand as an epitome of my argument too: repetition in Warhol is not reproduction in the sense of representation (of a referent) or simulation (of a pure image, a detached signifier). Rather, repetition serves to *screen* the real understood as traumatic. But this very need also *points* to the real, and at this point the real *ruptures* the screen of repetition. It is a rupture less in the world than in the subject—between the perception and the consciousness of a subject *touched* by an image. In an allusion to Aristotle on accidental causality, Lacan calls this traumatic point the *tuché;* in *Camera Lucida* (1980) Barthes calls it the *punctum*.[20] "It is this element which rises from the scene, shoots out of it like an arrow, and pierces me," Barthes writes. "It is what I add to the photograph and what is nonetheless

Andy Warhol, *White Burning Car III,* 1963.

already there." "It is acute yet muffled, it cries out in silence. Odd contradiction: a floating flash."[21] This confusion about the location of the rupture, *tuché,* or *punctum* is a confusion of subject and world, inside and outside. It is an aspect of trauma; indeed, it may be this confusion that *is* traumatic. ("Where is Your Rupture?," Warhol asks in a 1960 painting based on a newspaper advertisement, with several arrows aimed at the crotch of a female torso.)

In *Camera Lucida* Barthes is concerned with straight photographs, so he locates the *punctum* in details of content. This is rarely the case in Warhol. Yet there is a *punctum* for me (Barthes stipulates that it is a personal effect) in the indifference of the passerby in *White Burning Car III* (1963). This indifference to the crash victim impaled on the telephone pole is bad enough, but its repetition is *galling,* and this points to the general operation of the *punctum* in Warhol. It works less through content than through technique, especially through the "floating flashes" of the silkscreen process, the slipping and streaking, blanching and blanking, repeating and coloring of the images. To take another instance, a *punctum* arises for me not from the slumped woman in the top image in *Ambulance Disaster* (1963) but from the obscene tear that effaces her head in the bottom image. In both instances, just as the *punctum* in Gerhard Richter lies less in details than in the pervasive blurring of the image, so the *punctum* in Warhol lies less in details than in this repetitive "popping" of the image.[22]

These pops, such as a slipping of register or a washing in color, serve as visual equivalents of our missed encounters with the real. "What is repeated," Lacan writes, "is always something that occurs . . . *as if by chance*" (54). So it is with these pops: they seem accidental, but they also appear repetitive, automatic, even technological (the relation between accident and technology, crucial to the discourse of shock, is a great Warhol subject).[23] In this way he elaborates on our optical unconscious, a term introduced by Walter Benjamin to describe the subliminal effects of modern image technologies. Benjamin developed this notion in the early 1930s, in response to photography and film; Warhol updates it thirty years later, in response to the postwar society of the spectacle, of mass media and commodity-signs.[24] In these early images we see what it looks like to dream in the age of television, *Life,* and *Time*—or rather

Gerhard Richter, *Uncle Rudi*, 1965.

what it looks like to nightmare as shock victims who prepare for disasters that have already come, for Warhol selects moments when this spectacle cracks (the JFK assassination, the Monroe suicide, racist attacks, car wrecks), but cracks only to expand.

Thus the *punctum* in Warhol is not strictly private or public.[25] Nor is the content trivial: a white woman slumped from a wrecked ambulance, or a black man attacked by a police dog, is a shock. But, again, this first order of shock is screened by the repetition of the image, even though this repetition may also produce a second order of trauma, here at the level of technique, where the *punctum* breaks through the screen and allows the real to poke through.[26] The real, Lacan puns, is *trou*matic, and I noted that the tear in *Ambulance Disaster* is such a hole (*trou*) for me, though what loss is figured there I cannot say. Through these pokes or pops we seem almost to touch the real, which the repetition of the images at once distances and rushes toward us. (Sometimes the coloring of the images has this strange double effect as well.)[27]

In this way different kinds of repetition are in play in Warhol: repetitions that fix on the traumatic real, that screen it, that produce it. And this multiplicity makes for the paradox not only of images that are both affective and affectless, but also of viewers that are neither integrated (which is the ideal of most modern aesthetics: the subject composed in contemplation) nor dissolved (which is the effect of much popular culture: the subject given over to the schizo intensities of the commodity-sign). "I never fall apart," Warhol remarked in *The Philosophy of Andy Warhol* (1975), "because I never fall together."[28] Such is the subject-effect of his work as well, and it resonates in art that elaborates on pop: again, in some superrealism, some appropriation art, and some contemporary work involved in illusionism—a category, like realism, that it invites us to rethink.

TRAUMATIC ILLUSIONISM

In his 1964 seminar on the real Lacan distinguishes between *Wiederholung* and *Wiederkehr*. The first is the repetition of the repressed as symptom or signifier,

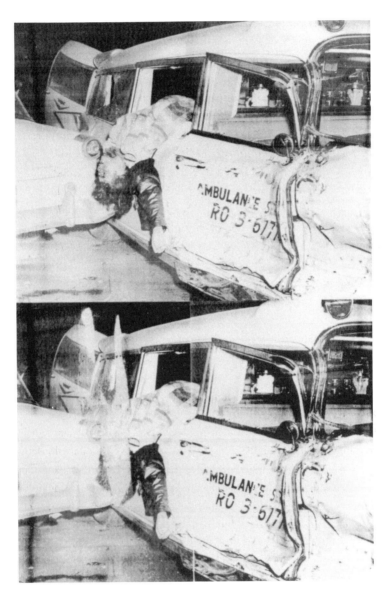

Andy Warhol, *Ambulance Disaster*, 1963.

which Lacan terms the *automaton,* also in allusion to Aristotle. The second is the return discussed above: the return of a traumatic encounter with the real, a thing that resists the symbolic, that is not a signifer at all, which again Lacan calls the *tuché.* The first, the repetition of the symptom, can contain or screen the second, the return of the traumatic real, which thus exists beyond the *automaton* of the symptoms, beyond "the insistence of the signs" (53–54), indeed beyond the pleasure principle.[29] Above I related these two kinds of recurrence to the two sorts of repetition in the Warholian image: a repeating of an image to screen a traumatic real, which is nonetheless returned, accidently and/or obliquely, in this very screening. Here I will venture a further analogy in relation to superrealist art: sometimes its illusionism is so excessive as to appear anxious—anxious to cover up a *troumatic* real—but this anxiety cannot help but indicate this real as well.[30] Such analogies between psychoanalytic discourse and visual art are worth little if nothing mediates the two, but here both the theory and the art relate repetition and the real to visuality and the gaze.

Roughly contemporaneous with the spread of pop and the rise of superrealism, the Lacan seminar on the gaze follows the seminar on the real; it is much cited but little understood. There may be a male gaze, and capitalist spectacle is oriented to a masculinist subject, but such arguments are not supported by *this* seminar of Lacan, for whom the gaze is not embodied in a subject, at least not in the first instance. To an extent like Jean-Paul Sartre, Lacan distinguishes between the look (or the eye) and the gaze, and to an extent like Maurice Merleau-Ponty, he locates this gaze *in the world.*[31] As with language in Lacan, then, so with the gaze: it *preexists* the subject, who, "looked at from all sides," is but a "stain" in "the spectacle of the world" (72, 75). Thus positioned, the subject tends to feel the gaze as a threat, as if it queried him or her; and so it is, according to Lacan, that "the gaze, *qua objet a,* may come to symbolize this central lack expressed in the phenomenon of castration" (77).

More than Sartre and Merleau-Ponty, then, Lacan challenges the old privilege of the subject in sight and self-consciousness (the *I see myself seeing myself* that grounds the phenomenological subject) as well as the old mastery of the subject in representation ("this *belong to me* aspect of representations, so reminiscent of property," that empowers the Cartesian subject [81]). Lacan mortifies this subject in the famous anecdote of the sardine can that, afloat on the sea and aglint in the sun, seems to look at the young Lacan in the fishing boat "at the level of the point of light, the point at which everything that looks at me is situated" (95). Thus seen as (s)he sees, pictured as (s)he pictures, the Lacanian subject is fixed in a double position, and this leads Lacan to superimpose on the usual cone of vision that emanates from the subject another cone that emanates *from the object,* at the point of light, which he calls the gaze.

The first cone is familiar from Renaissance treatises on perspective: the subject is addressed as the master of the object arrayed and focused as an image for him or her positioned at a geometral point of viewing. But, Lacan adds immediately, "I am not simply that punctiform being located at the geometral point from which the perspective is grasped. No doubt, in the depths of my eye, the picture is painted. The picture, certainly, is in my eye. But I, I am in the picture" (96).[32] That is, the subject is also under the regard of the object, photographed by its light, pictured by its gaze: thus the superimposition of the two cones, with the object also at the point of the light (the gaze), the subject also at the point of the picture, and the image also in line with the screen.

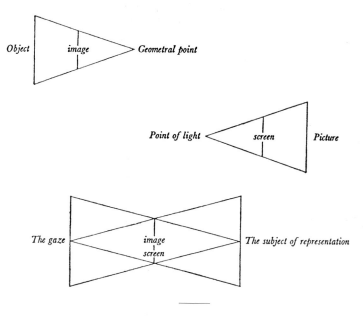

The meaning of this last term is obscure. I understand it to refer to the cultural reserve of which each image is one instance. Call it the conventions of art, the schemata of representation, the codes of visual culture, this screen *mediates* the object-gaze *for* the subject, but it also *protects* the subject *from* this object-gaze. That is, it captures the gaze, "pulsatile, dazzling and spread out" (89), and *tames* it in an image.[33] This last formulation is crucial. For Lacan animals are caught in the gaze of the world; they are only on display there. Humans are not so reduced to this "imaginary capture" (103), for we have access to the symbolic—in this case to the screen as the site of picture making and viewing, where we can manipulate and moderate the gaze. "Man, in effect, knows how to play with the mask as that beyond which there is the gaze," Lacan states. "The screen is here the locus of mediation" (107). In this way the screen allows the subject, at the point of the picture, to behold the object, at the point of light. Otherwise it would be impossible, for to see without this screen would be to be blinded by the gaze or touched by the real.

Thus, even as the gaze may trap the subject, the subject may tame the gaze. This is the function of the screen: to negotiate a *laying down* of the gaze as in a laying down of a weapon. Note the atavistic tropes of preying and taming, battling and negotiating; both gaze and subject are given strange agencies, and they are positioned in paranoid ways.[34] Indeed, Lacan imagines the gaze not only as maleficent but as violent, a force that can arrest, even kill, if it is not disarmed first.[35] Thus, when urgent, picture making is apotropaic: its gestures arrest this arresting of the gaze before the fact. When "Apollonian" (101), picture making is placating: its perfections pacify the gaze, "relax" the viewer from its grip (this Nietzschean term again projects the gaze as Dionysian, full of desire and death). Such is aesthetic contemplation according to Lacan: some art may attempt a *trompe-l'oeil,* a tricking of the eye, but all art aspires to a *dompte-regard,* a taming of the gaze.

Below I will suggest that some contemporary work refuses this age-old mandate to pacify the gaze, to unite the imaginary and the symbolic against the real. *It is as if this art wanted the gaze to shine, the object to stand, the real to exist, in all the glory (or the horror) of its pulsatile desire, or at least to evoke this sublime condition.*

To this end it moves not only to attack the image but to tear at the screen, or to suggest that it is already torn. For the moment, however, I want to remain with the categories of *trompe-l'oeil* and *dompte-regard,* for some post-pop art develops illusionist trickings and tamings in ways that are distinct from realism not only in the old referential sense but in the traumatic sense outlined above.[36]

In his seminar on the gaze Lacan retells the classical tale of the *trompe-l'oeil* contest between Zeuxis and Parrhasios. Zeuxis paints grapes in a way that lures birds, but Parrhasios paints a veil in a way that deceives Zeuxis, who asks to see what lies behind the veil and concedes the contest in embarrassment. For Lacan the story concerns the difference between the imaginary captures of *lured* animal and *deceived* human. Verisimilitude may have little to do with either capture: what looks like grapes to one species may not to another; the important thing is the appropriate sign for each. More significant here, the animal is lured in relation to the surface, whereas the human is deceived in relation to *what lies behind.* And behind the picture, for Lacan, is the gaze, the object, the real, with which "the painter as creator . . . sets up a dialogue" (112–13). Thus a perfect illusion is not possible, and, even if it were possible it would not answer the question of the real, which always remains, behind and beyond, to lure us. This is so because the real cannot be represented; indeed, it is defined as such, as the negative of the symbolic, a missed encounter, a lost object (the little bit of the subject lost to the subject, the *objet a*). "This other thing [behind the picture and beyond the pleasure principle] is the *petit a,* around which there revolves a combat of which *trompe-l'oeil* is the soul" (112).

As an art of the *trompe-l'oeil,* superrealism is also involved in this combat, but superrealism is more than a tricking of the eye. It is a subterfuge *against* the real, an art pledged not only to pacify the real but to seal it behind surfaces, to embalm it in appearances. (Of course this is not its self-understanding: superrealism seeks to deliver the reality of appearance. But to do so, I want to suggest, is to delay the real—or, again, to seal it.) Superrealism attempts this sealing in three ways at least. The first is to represent apparent reality as a coded *sign.* Often manifestly based on a photograph or a postcard, this superrealism shows the real as already absorbed into the symbolic (as in the early work of Malcolm

Morley). The second is to reproduce apparent reality as a fluid *surface*. More illusionist than the first, this superrealism *de*realizes the real with simulacral effects (related to the pop paintings of James Rosenquist, this category includes Audrey Flack and Don Eddy among others). The third is to represent apparent reality as a visual *conundrum* with reflections and refractions of many sorts. In this superrealism, which partakes of the first two, the structuring of the visual is strained to the point of implosion, of collapse onto the viewer. In front of these paintings one may feel under the gaze, looked at from many sides: thus the impossible double perspective that Richard Estes contrives in *Union Square* (1985), which converges *on* us more than extends *from* us, or his equally impossible *Double Self-Portrait* (1976), in which we look at a diner window in complete perplexity as to what is inside and what is outside, what is in front of us and what is behind. If *Union Square* pressures a Renaissance paradigm of linear perspective like *The Ideal City*, *Double Self-Portrait* pressures a baroque paradigm of pictorial reflexivity like *Las Meninas* (it is no surprise that, in the move to use lines and surfaces to tie up and smother the real, superrealists would turn to the baroque intricacies of such artists as Velazquez).

In these paintings Estes transports his historical models to a commercial strip and a storefront in New York; and indeed, as with pop, it is difficult to imagine superrealism apart from the tangled lines and lurid surfaces of capitalist spectacle: the narcissistic seduction of shop windows, the luscious sheen of sports cars—in short, the sex appeal of the commodity-sign, with the commodity feminized and the feminine commodified in a way that, even more than pop, superrealism celebrates rather than questions. As reproduced in this art, these lines and surfaces often distend, fold back, and so flatten pictorial depth. But do they have the same effect on *psychic* depth? In a comparison of pop and superrealism with surrealism Fredric Jameson has claimed as much:

> We need only juxtapose the mannequin, as a [surrealist] symbol, with the photographic objects of pop art, the Campbell's soup can, the pictures of Marilyn Monroe, or with the visual curiosities of op art; we need only exchange, for that environment of small work-

Richard Estes, *Double Self-Portrait,* 1976.

> shops and store counters, for the *marché aux puces* and the stalls in
> the streets, the gasoline stations along American superhighways, the
> glossy photographs in the magazines, or the cellophane paradise of
> an American drugstore, in order to realize that the objects of surre-
> alism are gone without a trace. Henceforth, in what we may now
> call postindustrial capitalism, the products with which we are fur-
> nished are utterly without depth: their plastic content is totally in-
> capable of serving as a conductor of psychic energy.[37]

Here Jameson marks a shift in production and consumption that affects art and subjectivity as well, but is it a "historical *break* of an unexpectedly absolute kind"?[38] These old objects may be displaced (already for the surrealists they were attractively outmoded), but they are not gone without a trace. Certainly the *subjects* related to these objects have not disappeared; the epochs of the sub-ject, let alone of the unconscious, are not so punctual.[39] In short, superrealism retains a subterranean connection to surrealism in the subjective register, and not only because both play on sexual and commodity fetishisms.

Georges Bataille once remarked that his kind of surrealism involved the *sub* more than the *sur,* the materialist low more than the idealist high (which he associated with André Breton).[40] My kind of surrealism involves the *sub* more than the *sur* too, but in the sense of the real that lies below, which this surrealism seeks to tap, to let erupt, as if by chance (which again is the mode of appearance of repetition).[41] Superrealism is also involved with this real that lies below, but as a *super*realism it is concerned to stay on top of it, to keep it down. Unlike surrealism, then, it wants to conceal more than to reveal this real; thus it lays down its layers of signs and surfaces drawn from the commodity world not only against representational depth but also against the traumatic real. Yet this anx-ious move to smooth over this real points to it nonetheless; superrealism remains an art of "the eye as made desperate by the gaze" (116), and the desperation shows. As a result its illusion fails not only as a tricking of the eye but as a taming of the gaze, a protecting against the traumatic real. That is, it fails *not* to remind us of the real, and in this way it is traumatic too: a *traumatic illusionism.*

The Return of the Real

If the real is repressed in superrealism, it also returns there, and this return disrupts the superrealist surface of signs. Yet as this disruption is inadvertent, so is the little disturbance of capitalist spectacle that it may effect. This disturbance is not so inadvertent in appropriation art, which, especially in the simulacral version associated with Richard Prince, can resemble superrealism with its surfeit of signs, fluidity of surfaces, and enveloping of the viewer. Yet the differences between the two are more important than the similarities. Both arts use photography, but superrealism exploits some photographic values (like illusionism) in the interests of painting and excludes others (like reproducibility) *not* in these interests, indeed that threaten such painterly values as the unique image. Appropriation art, on the other hand, uses photographic reproducibility in a questioning of painterly uniqueness, as in the early copies of modernist masters by Sherrie Levine. At the same time, it either pushes photographic illusionism to an implosive point, as in the early rephotographs of Prince, or turns round on this illusionism to question the documentary truth of the photograph, the referential value of representation, as in the early photo-texts of Barbara Kruger. Thus the vaunted critique of representation in this postmodernist art: a critique of artistic categories and documentary genres, of media myths and sexual stereotypes.

So, too, the two arts position the viewer differently: in its elaboration of illusion superrealism invites the viewer to revel almost schizophrenically in its surfaces, whereas in its exposure of illusion appropriation art asks the viewer to look through its surfaces critically. Yet sometimes the two cross here, as when appropriation art envelops the viewer in a superrealist way.[42] More importantly, the two approach one another in this respect: in superrealism reality is presented as overwhelmed by appearance, while in appropriation art it is presented as constructed in representation. (Thus, for instance, the Marlboro images of Prince picture the reality of North American nature through the myth of the cowboy West.) This constructionist vision of reality is the basic position of postmodernist art, at least in its poststructuralist guise, and it is paralleled by the basic position of feminist art, at least in its psychoanalytic guise: that the subject is dictated by the symbolic order. Taken together, these two positions have led many artists to focus on the image-screen (I refer again to the Lacanian diagram of visuality), often to the neglect of the real on the one side and sometimes to the neglect of the subject on the other. Thus, in the early copies of Levine for example, the image-screen is almost all there is; it is not much troubled by the real nor much altered by the subject (artist and viewer are given little agency in this work).

Yet the relation of appropriation art to the image-screen is not so simple: it can be critical of the screen, even hostile to it, and fascinated by it, almost enamored of it. And sometimes this ambivalence suggests the real; that is, as appropriation art works to expose the illusions of representation, it can poke through the image-screen. Consider the sunset images of Prince, which are rephotographs of vacation advertisements from magazines, familiar pictures of young lovers and cute kids on the beach, with the sun and the sea offered as so many commodities. Prince manipulates the superrealist look of these ads to the point that they are *de*realized in the sense of appearance but *realized* in the sense of desire. In several images a man thrusts a woman out of the water, but the flesh of each appears burned—as if in an erotic passion that is also a fatal irradiation. Here the *imaginary* pleasure of the vacation scenes goes bad, becomes obscene, displaced by a *real* ecstasy of desire shot through with death, a *jouissance* that lurks behind the pleasure principle of the ad image, indeed of the image-screen in general.[43]

This shift in conception—from reality as an effect of representation to the real as a thing of trauma—may be definitive in contemporary art, let alone in contemporary theory, fiction, and film. For with this shift in conception has come a shift in practice, which I want to graph here, again in relation to the Lacanian diagram of visuality, as a shift in focus from the image-screen to the object-gaze. This shift can be traced in the work of Cindy Sherman, who has done as much any artist to prepare it. Indeed, if we divide her work into three rough groups, it seems to move across the three main positions of the Lacanian diagram.

Richard Prince, *Untitled* (sunset), 1981.

Richard Prince, *Untitled* (cowboy), 1989.

In the early work of 1975–82, from the film stills through the rear projections to the centerfolds and the color tests, Sherman evokes the subject under the gaze, the subject-as-picture, which is also the principal site of other feminist work in early appropriation art. Her subjects see, of course, but they are much more *seen,* captured by the gaze. Often, in the film stills and the centerfolds, this gaze seems to come from another subject, with whom the viewer may be implicated; sometimes, in the rear projections, it seems to come from the spectacle of the world. Yet often, too, this gaze seems to come from within. Here Sherman shows her female subjects as self-surveyed, not in phenomenological immanence (*I see myself seeing myself*) but in psychological estrangement (*I am not what I imagined myself to be*). Thus in the distance between the made-up young woman and her mirrored face in *Untitled Film Still #2* (1977), Sherman captures the gap between imagined and actual body images that yawns in each of us, the gap of (mis)recognition where fashion and entertainment industries operate every day and night.

In the middle work of 1987–90, from the fashion photographs through the fairy-tale illustrations and the art-history portraits to the disaster pictures, Sherman moves to the image-screen, to its repertoire of representations. (I speak of focus only: she addresses the image-screen in the early work too, and the subject-as-picture hardly disappears in this middle work.) The fashion and art-history series take up two files from the image-screen that have affected self-fashionings, present and past, profoundly. Here Sherman parodies vanguard design with a long runway of fashion victims, and pillories art history with a long gallery of butt-ugly aristocrats (in ersatz Renaissance, baroque, rococo, and neoclassical types, with allusions to Raphael, Caravaggio, Fragonard, and Ingres). The play turns perverse when, in some fashion photographs, the gap between imagined and actual body images becomes psychotic (one or two sitters seem to have no ego awareness at all) and when, in some art-history photographs, deidealization is pushed to the point of desublimation: with scarred sacks for breasts and funky carbuncles for noses, these bodies break down the upright lines of proper representation, indeed of proper subjecthood.[44]

This turn to the grotesque is marked in the fairy-tale and disaster images, some of which show horrific accidents of birth and freaks of nature (a young woman with a pig snout, a doll with the head of a dirty old man). Here, as often in horror movies and bedtime stories alike, horror means, first and foremost, horror of maternity, of the maternal body made strange, even repulsive, in repression. This body is the primary site of the *abject* as well, a category of (non)being defined by Julia Kristeva as neither subject nor object, but before one is the former (before full separation from the mother) or after one is the latter (as a corpse given over to objecthood).[45] These extreme conditions are suggested by some disaster scenes, suffused as they are with signifers of menstrual blood and sexual discharge, vomit and shit, decay and death. Such images evoke the body turned inside out, the subject literally abjected, thrown out. But they also evoke the outside turned in, the subject-as-picture invaded by the object-gaze (e.g., *Untitled #153*). At this point some images pass beyond the abject, which is often tied to substances and meanings, not only toward the *informe,* a condition described by Bataille where significant form dissolves because the fundamental distinction between figure and ground, self and other, is lost, but also toward the *obscene,* where the object-gaze is presented *as if there were no scene to stage it, no frame of representation to contain it, no screen.*[46]

This is the domain of the work after 1991 as well, the civil war and sex pictures, which are punctuated by close-ups of simulated damaged and/or dead body parts and sexual and/or excretory body parts respectively. Sometimes the screen seems so torn that the object-gaze not only invades the subject-as-picture but overwhelms it. And in a few disaster and civil war images we sense what it is to occupy the impossible third position in the Lacanian diagram, to behold the pulsatile gaze, even to touch the obscene object, without a screen for protection. In one image (*Untitled #190*) Sherman gives this evil eye a horrific visage of its own.

In this scheme of things the impulse to erode the subject and to tear at the screen has driven Sherman from the early work, where the subject is caught in the gaze, through the middle work, where it is invaded by the gaze, to the recent work, where it is obliterated by the gaze, only to return as disjunct doll parts. But this double attack on subject and screen is not hers alone; it occurs

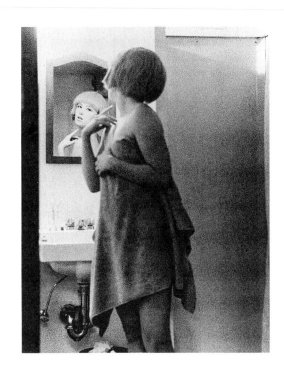

Cindy Sherman, *Untitled #2,* 1977.

Cindy Sherman, *Untitled #153,* 1985.

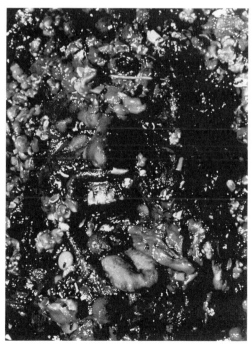

Cindy Sherman, *Untitled #183*, 1988.

Cindy Sherman, *Untitled #190,* 1989.

on several fronts in contemporary art, where it is waged, almost openly, in the service of the real.

This work evokes the real in different ways; I will begin with two approaches that bear on illusionism. The first involves an illusionism practiced less in pictures than with objects (if it looks back to superrealism, then, it is to the figures of Duane Hanson and John de Andrea). This art does intentionally what some superrealist and appropriation art did inadvertently, which is to push illusionism to the point of the real. Here illusionism is employed not to cover up the real with simulacral surfaces but to *un*cover it in uncanny things, which are often put into performances as well. To this end some artists estrange everyday objects related to the body (as with the sealed urinals and stretched sinks by Robert Gober, the table of still-life objects that refuse to be still by Charles Ray, and the quasi-athletic apparatuses developed as performance props by Matthew Barney). Other artists estrange childhood objects that return from the past, often distorted in scale or proportion, with a touch of the eerie (as in the little trucks or massive rats of Katarina Fritsch) or the pathetic (as in the Salvation Army stuffed animals of Mike Kelley), of the melancholic (as in the dead sparrows with knitted coats by Annette Messager) or the monstrous (as in the crib become a psychotic cage by Gober). Yet, however provocative, this illusionist approach to the real can lapse into a coded surrealism.

The second approach runs opposite to the first but to the same end: it rejects illusionism, indeed any sublimation of the object-gaze, in an attempt to evoke the real as such. This is the primary realm of abject art, which is drawn to the broken boundaries of the violated body. Often, as in the aggressive-depressive sculpture of Kiki Smith, this body is maternal, and it serves as the medium of an ambivalent child subject who damages and restores it in turn: in *Trough* (1990), for example, this body lies sectioned, an empty vessel, while in *Womb* (1986) it seems a solid object, almost autonomous, even autogenetic.[47] Often, too, the body appears as a direct double of the violated subject, whose parts are displayed as residues of violence and/or traces of trauma: the booted legs by Gober that extend, up or down, as if cut at the wall, sometimes with

the thighs planted with candles or the butt tattooed with music, are thus humili-
ated (often in a hilarious way). The strange ambition of this second approach is
to tease out the trauma of the subject, with the apparent calculation that, if its
lost *objet a* cannot be reclaimed, at least the wound that it left behind can be
probed (in the Greek *trauma* means "wound").[48] However, this approach has its
dangers too, for the probing of the wound can lapse into a coded expressionism
(as in the expressive desublimation of the diaristic art of Sue Williams and others) or a coded realism (as in the bohemian romance of the photography *verité*
of Larry Clark, Nan Goldin, Jack Pierson, and others). And yet this very problem can be provocative, for it raises the question, crucial to abject art, of the
possibility of an *obscene* representation—that is, of a representation *without* a
scene that stages the object for the viewer. Might this be one difference between
the *obscene,* where the object, without a scene, comes too close to the viewer,
and the *pornographic,* where the object is staged for the viewer who is thus dis-
tanced enough to be its voyeur?[49]

THE ARTIFICE OF ABJECTION

According to the canonical definition of Kristeva, the abject is what I must get
rid of *in order to be an I* (but what is this primordial I that expels in the first
place?). It is a fantasmatic substance not only alien to the subject but intimate
with it—too much so in fact, and this overproximity produces panic in the
subject. In this way the abject touches on the fragility of our boundaries, the
fragility of the spatial distinction between our insides and outsides as well as of
the temporal passage between the maternal body (again the privileged realm of
the abject) and the paternal law. Both spatially and temporally, then, abjection
is a condition in which subjecthood is troubled, "where meaning collapses";
hence its attraction for avant-garde artists who want to disturb these orderings
of subject and society alike.[50]

This only skims the surface of the abject, crucial as it is to the construction
of subjectivity, racist, homophobic, and otherwise.[51] Here I will note only the
ambiguities of the notion, for the cultural-political valence of abject art depends

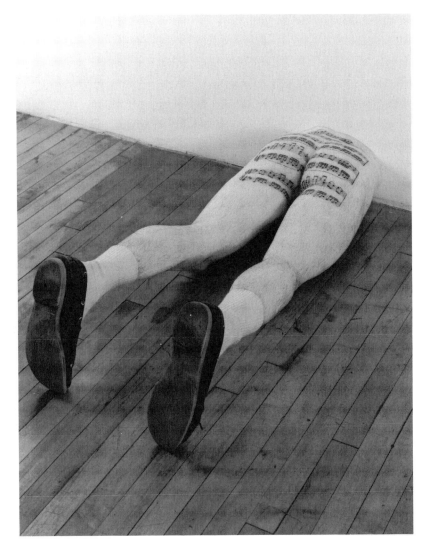

Robert Gober, *Untitled,* 1990.

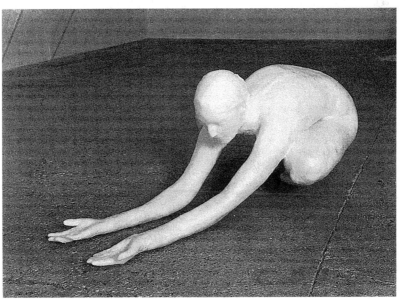

Robert Gober, *Slanted Playpen*, 1987.

Kiki Smith, *Untitled*, 1992.

on these ambiguities, on how they are decided (or not). Some are familiar by now. Can the abject be represented at all? If it is opposed *to* culture, can it be exposed *in* culture? If it is unconscious, can it made conscious and remain abject? In other words, can there be a *conscientious abjection,* or is this all there can be? Can abject art ever escape an instrumental, indeed moralistic, use of the abject? (In a sense this is the other part of the question: can there be an evocation of the obscene that is *not* pornographic?)

The crucial ambiguity in Kristeva is her slippage between the operation *to abject* and the condition *to be abject.* Again, to abject is to expel, to separate; to be abject, on the other hand, is to be repulsive, stuck, subject enough only to feel this subjecthood at risk.[52] For Kristeva the operation *to abject* is fundamental to the maintenance of subject and society alike, while the condition *to be abject* is corrosive of both formations. Is the abject, then, disruptive of subjective and social orders *or* somehow foundational of them, a crisis in these orders *or* somehow a confirmation of them? If a subject or a society abjects the alien within, is abjection not a regulatory operation? (In other words, might abjection be to regulation what transgression is to taboo? "Transgression does not deny the taboo," runs the famous formulation of Bataille, "but transcends and completes it.")[53] Or can the *condition* of abjection be mimed in a way that calls out, in order to disturb, the *operation* of abjection?

In modernist writing, Kristeva views abjection as conservative, even defensive. "Edged with the sublime," the abject tests the limits of sublimation, but even writers like Louis-Ferdinand Céline sublimate the abject, purify it. Whether or not one agrees with this account, Kristeva does intimate a cultural shift toward the present. "In a world in which the Other has collapsed," she states enigmatically, the task of the artist is no longer to sublimate the abject, to elevate it, but to plumb the abject, to fathom "the bottomless 'primacy' constituted by primal repression."[54] In a world in which the Other has collapsed: Kristeva implies a crisis in the paternal law that underwrites the social order.[55] In terms of the visuality outlined here, this implies a crisis in the image-screen as well, and some artists do attack it, whereas others, under the assumption that it is torn, probe behind it for the obscene object-gaze of the real. Meanwhile, in terms of the abject, still other artists explore the repressing of the maternal body said to underlie the symbolic order; that is, they exploit the disruptive effects of its material and/or metaphorical rem(a)inders.

Here the condition of image-screen and symbolic order alike is all-important; locally the valence of abject art depends on it. If it is deemed intact, the attack on the image-screen might retain a transgressive value. However, if it is deemed torn, such transgression might be beside the point, and this old vocation of the avant-garde might be at an end. But there is a third option as well, and that is to reformulate this vocation, *to rethink transgression not as a rupture produced by a heroic avant-garde outside the symbolic order but as a fracture traced by a strategic avant-garde within the order.*[56] In this view the goal of the avant-garde is not to break with this order absolutely (this old dream is dispelled), but to expose it in crisis, to register its points not only of break*down* but of break-*through,* the new possibilities that such a crisis might open up.

For the most part, however, abject art has tended in two other directions. As suggested, the first is to identify with the abject, to approach it somehow— to probe the wound of trauma, to touch the obscene object-gaze of the real. The second is to represent the condition of abjection in order to provoke its operation—to catch abjection in the act, to make it reflexive, even repellent in its own right. Yet this mimesis may also reconfirm a given abjection. Just as the old transgressive surrealist once called out for the priestly police, so an abject artist (like Andres Serrano) may call out for an evangelical senator (like Jesse Helms), who is allowed, in effect, to complete the work negatively. Moreover, as left and right may agree on the social representatives of the abject, they may shore each other up in a public exchange of disgust, and this spectacle may inadvertently support the normativity of image-screen and symbolic order alike.

These strategies in abject art are thus problematic, as they were over sixty years ago in surrealism. Surrealism was also drawn to the abject in a testing of sublimation; indeed, it claimed as its own the point where desublimatory im-pulses confront sublimatory imperatives.[57] Yet it was at this point too that surre-alism broke down, split into the two principal factions headed by Breton and Bataille. According to Breton, Bataille was an "excrement-philosopher" who

Andres Serrano, *Piss Christ*, 1987.

refused to rise above big toes, mere matter, sheer shit, to raise the low to the high.[58] For Bataille in turn, Breton was a "juvenile victim" involved in an Oedipal game, an "Icarian pose" assumed less to undo the law than to provoke its punishment: for all his confessions of desire, he was as committed to sublimation as the next aesthete.[59] Elsewhere Bataille termed this aesthetic *le jeu des transpositions* (the game of substitutions), and in a celebrated aphorism he dismissed it as no match for the power of perversions: "I defy any amateur of painting to love a picture as much as a fetishist loves a shoe."[60]

I recall this old opposition for its perspective on abject art. In a sense Breton and Bataille were both right, at least about each other. Often Breton and company did act like juvenile victims who provoked the paternal law *as if to ensure that it was still there*—at best in a neurotic plea for punishment, at worst in a paranoid demand for order. And this Icarian pose is assumed by contemporary artists and writers almost too eager to talk dirty in the museum, almost too ready to be tweaked by Hilton Kramer or spanked by Jesse Helms. On the other hand, the Bataillean ideal—to opt for the smelly shoe over the beautiful picture, to be fixed in perversion or stuck in abjection—is also adopted by contemporary artists and writers discontent not only with the refinements of sublimation but with the displacements of desire. Is this, then, the option that the artifice of abjection offers us—Oedipal naughtiness or infantile perversion? To act dirty with the secret wish to be spanked, or to wallow in shit with the secret faith that the most defiled might reverse into the most sacred, the most perverse into the most potent?

In the abject testing of the symbolic order a general division of labor has developed according to gender: the artists who probe the maternal body repressed by the paternal law tend to be women (e.g., Kiki Smith, Maureen Connor, Rona Pondick, Mona Hayt), while the artists who assume an infantilist position to mock the paternal law tend to be men (e.g., Mike Kelley, John Miller, Paul McCarthy, Nayland Blake).[61] This mimesis of regression is pronounced in contemporary art, but it has many precedents. Infantilist personae dominated dada and neo-dada: the anarchic child in Hugo Ball and Claes Oldenburg, for example, or the autistic subject in "Dadamax" Ernst and Warhol.[62]

Yet related figures appeared in reactionary art as well: all the clowns, puppets, and the like in neo-figurative painting of the late 1920s and early 1930s and in neo-expressionist painting of the late 1970s and early 1980s. Thus the political valence of this mimetic regression is not stable. In the terms of Peter Sloterdijk discussed in chapter 4, it can be *kynical,* whereby individual degradation is pushed to the point of social indictment, or *cynical,* whereby the subject accepts this degradation for protection and/or profit. The principal avatar of contemporary infantilism is the obscene clown that appears in Bruce Nauman, Kelley, McCarthy, Blake, and others; a hybrid figure, it seems both kynical and cynical, part psychotic inmate, part circus performer.

As these examples suggest, infantilist personae tend to perform at times of cultural-political reaction, as ciphers of alienation and reification.[63] Yet these figures of regression can also be figures of perversion, that is, of *père-version,* of a turning from the father that is a twisting of his law. In the early 1990s this defiance was manifested in a general flaunting of shit (or shit substitute: the real thing was rarely found). Of course Freud understood the disposition to order essential to civilization as a reaction against anal eroticism, and in *Civilization and its Discontents* (1930) he imagined an origin myth involving a related repression that turns on the erection of man from all fours to two feet. With this change in posture, according to Freud, came a revolution in sense: smell was degraded and sight privileged, the anal repressed and the genital pronounced. The rest is literally history: with his genitals exposed, man was retuned to a sexual frequency that was continuous, not periodic, and he learned shame; and this coming together of sex and shame impelled him to seek a wife, to form a family, to found a civilization, to boldly go where no man had gone before. Heterosexist as this zany tale is, it does reveal how civilization is conceived in normative terms—not only as a general renunciation and sublimation of instincts but as a specific reaction against anal eroticism that implies a specific abjection of homosexuality.[64]

In this light the shit movement in contemporary art may intend a symbolic reversal of this first step into civilization, of the repression of the anal and the olfactory. As such it may also intend a symbolic reversal of the phallic visuality of the erect body as the primary model of traditional painting and sculpture—the human figure as both subject and frame of representation in Western art. This double defiance of visual sublimation and vertical form is a strong subcurrent in twentieth-century art (which might be subtitled "Visuality and Its Discontents"),[65] and it is sometimes expressed in a flaunting of anal eroticism. "Anal eroticism finds a narcissistic application in the production of defiance," Freud wrote in his 1917 essay on the subject—in avant-gardist defiance too, one might add, from the chocolate grinders of Duchamp through the cans of *merde* of Piero Manzoni, to the mounds of shit substitute of John Miller.[66] These different gestures have different valences. In contemporary art anal-erotic defiance is often self-conscious, even self-parodic: not only does it test the anally repressive authority of traditional museum culture (which is in part an Oedipal projection), but it also mocks the anally erotic narcissism of the vanguard rebel-artist. "Let's Talk About Disobeying" reads one banner emblazoned with a cookie jar by Mike Kelley. "Pants-shitter and Proud of It" reads another that derides the self-congratulation of the institutionally incontinent. ("Jerk Off Too," this rebel-nerd adds, as if to complete his taunting of civilization according to Freud.)[67]

This defiance can be pathetic, but, again, it can also be perverse, a twisting of the paternal law of difference—sexual and generational, ethnic and social. This perversion is often performed through a mimetic regression to an anal world where given differences might be transformed.[68] Such is the fictive space that artists like Kelley and Miller set up for critical play. In *Dick/Jane* (1991) Miller stains a blonde, blue-eyed doll brown and buries her neck-deep in shit substitute. Familiar from the old primer, Dick and Jane taught several generations of North American kids how to read—and how to read sexual difference. However, in the Miller version the Jane is turned into a Dick, and the phallic composite is plunged into an anal mound. Like the stroke in the title, the difference between male and female is transgressed, erased and underscored at once, as is the difference between white and black. In short, Miller creates an anal world that tests the terms of symbolic difference.[69]

Kelley also places his creatures in an anal world. "We interconnect everything, set up a field," says the bunny to the teddy in *Theory, Garbage, Stuffed Animals, Christ* (1991), "so there is no longer any differentiation."[70] He too

John Miller, *Dick/Jane*, 1991.

Mike Kelley, *Nostalgic Depiction of the Innocence of Childhood*, 1990, detail.

explores this space where symbols are not stable, where "the concepts *faeces* (money, gift), *baby* and *penis* are ill-distinguished from one another and are easily interchangeable."[71] And he too does so less to celebrate mere indistinction than to trouble symbolic difference. *Lumpen,* the German word for "rag" that gives us *Lumpensammler* (the ragpicker that so interested Baudelaire) and *Lumpenprole-tariat* (the mass too ragged to form a class of its own that so interested Marx— "the scum, the leavings, the refuse of all classes"),[72] is a crucial word in the Kelley lexicon, which he develops as a third term, like the obscene, between the *informe* and the abject. In a sense he does what Bataille urges: he thinks materialism through "psychological or social facts."[73] The result is an art of lum-pen forms (dingy toy animals stitched together in ugly masses, dirty throw rugs laid over nasty shapes), lumpen subjects (pictures of dirt and trash), and lumpen personae (dysfunctional men that build weird devices ordered from obscure catalogues in basements and backyards). Most of these things resist formal shap-ing, let alone cultural sublimating or social redeeming. Insofar as it has a social referent then, the *Lumpen* of Kelley (unlike the *Lumpen* of Louis Bonaparte, Hitler, or Mussolini) resists molding, much less mobilizing. But does this in-difference constitute a politics?

Often in the cult of abjection to which abject art is related (the cult of slackers and losers, grunge and Generation X), this posture of indifference ex-pressed little more than a fatigue with the politics of difference (social, sexual, ethnic). Sometimes, however, it intimated a more fundamental fatigue: a strange drive to indistinction, a paradoxical desire to be desireless, to be done with it all, a call of regression beyond the infantile to the inorganic.[74] In a 1937 text crucial to the Lacanian discussion of the gaze, Roger Caillois, another associate of the Bataillean surrealists, considers this drive to indistinction in terms of vis-uality—specifically in terms of the assimilation of insects into space through mimicry.[75] Here, Caillois argues, there is no question of agency (like protective adaptation), let alone of subjecthood (these organisms are "dispossessed of [this] privilege"), a condition that he can only liken, in the human realm, to ex-treme schizophrenia:

To these dispossessed souls, space seems to be a devouring force. Space pursues them, encircles them, digests them in a gigantic phagocytosis [consumption of bacteria]. It ends by replacing them. Then the body separates itself from thought, the individual breaks the boundary of his skin and occupies the other side of his senses. He tries to look at himself from any point whatever in space. He feels himself becoming space, *dark space where things cannot be put*. He is similar, not similar to something, but just *similar*. And he invents spaces of which he is "the convulsive possession."[76]

The breaching of the body, the gaze devouring the subject, the subject becoming the space, the state of just similarity: these conditions are evoked in recent art—in images by Sherman and others, in objects by Smith and others. It recalls the perverse ideal of the beautiful, redefined in terms of the sublime, advanced in surrealism: a convulsive possession of the subject given over to a deathly *jouissance*.

If this convulsive possession can be related to contemporary culture, it must be split into its constituent parts: on the one hand an ecstasy in the imagined breakdown of the image-screen and/or the symbolic order; on the other hand a horror at this fantasmatic event followed by a despair about it. Some early definitions of postmodernism evoked this *ecstatic* structure of feeling, sometimes in analogy with schizophrenia. Indeed, for Fredric Jameson the primary symptom of postmodernism is a schizophrenic breakdown in language and temporality that provokes a compensatory investment in the image and the instant.[77] And many artists did explore simulacral intensities and ahistorical pastiches in the 1980s. In recent intimations of postmodernism, however, the *melancholic* structure of feeling dominates, and sometimes, as in Kristeva, it too is associated with a symbolic order in crisis. Here artists are drawn not to the highs of the simulacral image but to the lows of the depressive object. If some high modernists sought to transcend the referential figure and some early postmodernists to delight in the sheer image, some later postmodernists want to possess the real thing.

Today this bipolar postmodernism is pushed toward a qualitative change: many artists seem driven by an ambition to inhabit a place of total affect *and* to be drained of affect altogether, to possess the obscene vitality of the wound *and* to occupy the radical nihility of the corpse. This oscillation suggests the dynamic of psychic shock parried by protective shield that Freud developed in his discussion of the death drive and Walter Benjamin elaborated in his discussion of Baudelairean modernism—but now pushed well beyond the pleasure principle. Pure affect, no affect: *It hurts, I can't feel anything.*[78]

Why this fascination with trauma, this envy of abjection, today? To be sure, motives exist within art and theory. As suggested, there is dissatisfaction with the textualist model of culture as well as the conventionalist view of reality—as if the real, repressed in poststructuralist postmodernism, had returned as traumatic. Then, too, there is disillusionment with the celebration of desire as an open passport of a mobile subject—as if the real, dismissed by a performative postmodernism, were marshaled against the imaginary world of a fantasy captured by consumerism. But there are strong forces at work elsewhere as well: despair about the persistent AIDS crisis, invasive disease and death, systemic poverty and crime, the destroyed welfare state, indeed the broken social contract (as the rich opt out in revolution from the top and the poor are dropped out in immiseration from the bottom). The articulation of these different forces is difficult, yet together they drive the contemporary concern with trauma and abjection.

One result is this: for many in contemporary culture truth resides in the traumatic or abject subject, in the diseased or damaged body. To be sure, this body is the evidentiary basis of important witnessings to truth, of necessary testimonials against power. But there are dangers with this siting of truth, such as the restriction of our political imaginary to two camps, the abjectors and the abjected, and the assumption that in order not to be counted among sexists and racists one must become the phobic object of such subjects. If there is a subject of history for the cult of abjection at all, it is not the Worker, the Woman, or the Person of Color, but the Corpse. This is not only a politics of difference pushed to indifference; it is a politics of alterity pushed to nihility.[79] "Everything

Zoe Leonard, *Sewn Fruit (in memory of David W.),* 1993.

goes dead," says the Kelley teddy. "Like us," responds the bunny.[80] Yet is this point of nihility the epitome of impoverishment, where power cannot penetrate, or a place from which power emanates in a new form? Is abjection a refusal of power, its ruse, or its reinvention?[81] Finally, is abjection a space-time beyond redemption, or the fastest route for contemporary rogue-saints to grace?

Across artistic, theoretical, and popular cultures (in SoHo, at Yale, on *Oprah*) there is a tendency to redefine experience, individual and historical, in terms of trauma. On the one hand, in art and theory, trauma discourse continues the poststructuralist critique of the subject by other means, for again, in a psychoanalytic register, there is no subject of trauma; the position is evacuated, and in this sense the critique of the subject is most radical here. On the other hand, in popular culture, trauma is treated as an event that guarantees the subject, and in this psychologistic register the subject, however disturbed, rushes back as witness, testifier, survivor. Here is indeed a traumatic subject, and it has absolute authority, for one cannot challenge the trauma of another: one can only believe it, even identify with it, or not. *In trauma discourse, then, the subject is evacuated and elevated at once.* And in this way trauma discourse magically resolves two contradictory imperatives in culture today: deconstructive analyses and identity politics. This strange rebirth of the author, this paradoxical condition of absentee authority, is a significant turn in contemporary art, criticism, and cultural politics. Here the return of the real converges with the return of the referential, and to this point I now turn.[82]

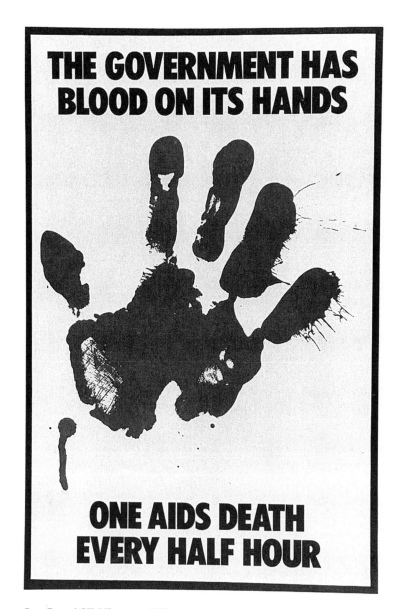

Gran Fury, ACT–UP poster, 1988.

The Artist as Ethnographer

One of the most important interventions in the relation between artistic authority and cultural politics is "The Author as Producer" by Walter Benjamin, first presented as a lecture in April 1934 at the Institute for the Study of Fascism in Paris. There, under the influence of the epic theater of Bertolt Brecht and the factographic experiments of Soviet writers like Sergei Tretiakov, Benjamin called on the artist on the left "to side with the proletariat."[1] In Paris in 1934 this call was not radical; the approach, however, was. For Benjamin urged the "advanced" artist to intervene, like the revolutionary worker, in the means of artistic production—to change the "technique" of traditional media, to transform the "apparatus" of bourgeois culture. A correct "tendency" was not enough; that was to assume a place "beside the proletariat." And "what kind of place is that?" Benjamin asked in lines that still scathe. "That of a benefactor, of an ideological patron—an impossible place."

Several oppositions govern this famous argument. Behind the privileging of "technique" over "theme" and "position" over "tendency" lies an implicit privileging of productivism over *proletkult,* two rival movements in the early Soviet Union. Productivism worked to develop a new proletarian culture through an extension of constructivist formal experiments into actual industrial production; in this way it sought to *overthrow* bourgeois art and culture altogether. No less committed politically, *proletkult* worked to develop a proletarian culture in the more traditional sense of the word; it sought to *surpass* bourgeois art and culture. For Benjamin this was not enough: again implicitly, he charged movements like *proletkult* with an ideological patronage that positioned the worker as passive other.[2] However difficult, the solidarity with producers that counted for Benjamin was solidarity in material practice, not in artistic theme or political attitude alone.

A glance at this text reveals that two oppositions that still plague the reception of art—aesthetic quality versus political relevance, form versus content—were "familiar and unfruitful" as long ago as 1934. Benjamin sought to overcome these oppositions in *representation* through the third term of *production,* but neither opposition has disappeared. In the early 1980s some artists and critics returned to "Author as Producer" to work through contemporary versions of these antitheses (e.g., theory versus activism).[3] This reading of Benjamin thus differed from his reception in the late 1970s; in a retracing of his own trajectory, allegorical disruptions of image and text were pushed toward cultural-political interventions. As Benjamin had responded to the aestheticization of politics under fascism, so these artists and critics responded to the capitalization of culture and privatization of society under Reagan, Thatcher, Kohl, and company—even as these transformations made such intervention more difficult. Indeed, when this intervention was not restricted to the art apparatus alone, its strategies were more situationist than productivist—that is, more concerned with reinscriptions of given representations.[4]

This is not to say that symbolic actions were not effective; many were, especially in the middle to late 1980s, around the AIDS crisis, abortion rights, and apartheid (I think of projects by ACT-UP artist groups, posters by Barbara Kruger, projections by Krzysztof Wodiczko). But they are not my subject here. Rather, I want to suggest that a new paradigm structurally similar to the old "Author as Producer" model has emerged in advanced art on the left: *the artist as ethnographer.*

THE CULTURAL POLITICS OF ALTERITY

In this new paradigm the object of contestation remains in large part the bourgeois-capitalist institution of art (the museum, the academy, the market, and the media), its exclusionary definitions of art and artist, identity and community. But the subject of association has changed: it is the cultural and/or ethnic other in whose name the committed artist most often struggles. However subtle it may seem, this shift from a subject defined in terms of *economic relation* to one defined in terms of *cultural identity* is significant, and I will comment further on it below. Here, however, the parallels between these two paradigms must be traced, for some assumptions of the old producer model persist, sometimes problematically, in the new ethnographer paradigm. First is the assumption that the site of political transformation is the site of artistic transformation as well, and that political vanguards *locate* artistic vanguards and, under certain circumstances, substitute for them. (This myth is basic to leftist accounts of modern art: it idealizes Jacques Louis David in the French Revolution, Gustave Courbet in the Paris Commune, Vladimir Tatlin in the Russian Revolution, and so on.)[5] Second is the assumption that this site is always *elsewhere,* in the field of the other—in the producer model, with the social other, the exploited proletariat; in the ethnographer paradigm, with the cultural other, the oppressed postcolonial, subaltern, or subcultural—and that this elsewhere, this outside, is the Archimedean point from which the dominant culture will be transformed or at least *subverted.* Third is the assumption that if the invoked artist is *not* perceived as socially and/or culturally other, he or she has but limited access to this transformative alterity, and that if he or she *is* perceived as other, he or she has automatic access to it. Taken together, these three assumptions may lead to a less desired point of connection with the Benjaminian account of the author as producer: the danger, for the artist as ethnographer, of "ideological patronage."[6]

This danger may stem from the assumed split in identity between the author and the worker or the artist and the other, but it may also arise in the very identification (or, to use the old language, commitment) undertaken to overcome this split. For example, the *proletkult* author might be a mere fellow traveler of the worker not because of any essential difference in identity but because identification with the worker alienates the worker, confirms rather than closes the gap between the two through a reductive, idealistic, or otherwise misbegotten representation. (This othering in identification, in representation, concerns Benjamin about *proletkult*.) A related othering may occur with the artist as ethnographer vis-à-vis the cultural other. Certainly the danger of ideological patronage is no less for the artist identified as other than for the author identified as proletarian. In fact this danger may deepen then, for the artist may be asked to assume the roles of native and informant as well as ethnographer. In short, identity is not the same as identification, and the apparent simplicities of the first should not be substituted for the actual complications of the second.

A strict Marxist might question the informant/ethnographer paradigm in art because it displaces the problematic of class and capitalist exploitation with that of race and colonialist oppression, or, more simply, because it displaces the social with the cultural or the anthropological. A strict poststructuralist might question this paradigm for the opposite reason: because it does not displace the producer problematic enough, because it tends to preserve its structure of the political—to retain the notion of a *subject* of history, to define this position in terms of *truth,* and to locate this truth in terms of *alterity* (again, this is the politics of the other, first projected, then appropriated, that interests me here).

From this poststructuralist perspective the ethnographer paradigm, like the producer model, fails to reflect on its *realist assumption:* that the other, here postcolonial, there proletarian, is somehow in reality, in truth, not in ideology, because he or she is socially oppressed, politically transformative, and/or materially productive. (For example, in 1957 Roland Barthes, who later became the foremost critic of the realist assumption, wrote: "There is therefore one language which is not mythical, it is the language of man as a producer: wherever man speaks in order to transform reality and no longer to preserve it as an image, wherever he links his language to the making of things, metalanguage is referred to a language-object, and myth is impossible. This is why revolutionary language proper cannot be mythical.")[7]) Often this realist assumption is compounded by a *primitivist fantasy:* that the other, usually assumed to be of color, has special access to primary psychic and social processes from which the white subject is somehow blocked—a fantasy that is as fundamental to primitivist modernisms as the realist assumption is to productivist modernisms.[8] In some contexts both myths are effective, even necessary: the realist assumption to claim the truth of one political position or the reality of one social oppression, and the primitivist fantasy to challenge repressive conventions of sexuality and aesthetics. Yet the automatic coding of apparent difference as manifest identity and of otherness as outsideness must be questioned. For not only might this coding essentialize identity, but it might also restrict the identification so important to cultural affiliation and political alliance (identification is not always ideological patronage).

There are two important precedents of the ethnographer paradigm in contemporary art where the primitivist fantasy is most active: the dissident surrealism associated with Georges Bataille and Michel Leiris in the late 1920s and early 1930s, and the *négritude* movement associated with Léopold Senghor and Aimé Césaire in the late 1940s and early 1950s. In different ways both movements connected the transgressive potential of the unconscious with the radical alterity of the cultural other. Thus Bataille related self-destructive drives in the unconscious to sacrificial expenditures in other cultures, while Senghor opposed an emotionality fundamental to African cultures to a rationality fundamental to European traditions.[9] However disruptive in context, these primitivist associations came to limit both movements. Dissident surrealism may have explored cultural otherness, but only in part to indulge in a ritual of self-othering (the classic instance is *L'Afrique fantôme,* the "self-ethnography" performed by Leiris on the French ethnographic-museological mission from Dakar to Djibouti in 1931).[10] So, too, the *négritude* movement may have revalued cultural otherness, but only in part to be constrained by this second nature, by its essentialist stereotypes of blackness, emotionality, African versus European, and so on (these problems were first articulated by Frantz Fanon and later developed by Wole Soyinka and others).[11]

Renée Green, *Import/Export Funk Office*, 1992, detail.

In quasi-anthropological art today the primitivist association of unconscious and other rarely exists in these ways. Sometimes the fantasy is taken up as such, critically, as in *Seen* (1990) by Renée Green, where the viewer is placed before two European fantasms of excessive African (American) female sexuality, the mid-nineteenth-century Hottentot Venus (represented by an autopsy) and the early-twentieth-century jazz dancer Josephine Baker (photographed in a famous nude pose), or in *Vanilla Nightmares* (1986) by Adrian Piper, where the racialist fantasms invoked in *New York Times* fashion advertisements become so many black specters to delight and terrify white consumers. Yet sometimes, too, the primitivist fantasy becomes absorbed into the realist assumption, so that now *the other* is held to be *dans le vrai*. This primitivist version of the realist assumption, this siting of political truth in a projected other or outside, has problematic effects beyond the automatic coding of identity vis-à-vis alterity noted above. First, this outside is not other in any simple sense. Second, this siting of politics as outside and other, as transcendental opposition, may distract from a politics of here and now, of immanent contestation.

First is the problem of the *projection* of this outside-other. In *Time and the Other: How Anthropology Makes its Object* (1983) Johannes Fabian argues that anthropology was founded on a mythical mapping of time onto space based on two presumptions: "1. Time is immanent to, hence coextensive with, the world (or nature, or the universe, depending on the argument); 2. Relationships between parts of the world (in the widest sense of both natural and sociocultural entities) can be understood as temporal relations. Dispersal in space reflects directly, which is not to say simply or in obvious ways, sequence in Time."[12] With space and time thus mapped onto one another, "over there" became "back then," and the most remote (as measured from some Greenwich Mean of European Civilization) became the most primitive. This mapping of the primitive was manifestly racist: in the Western white imaginary its site was always dark. It remains tenacious, however, because it is fundamental to narratives of history-as-development and civilization-as-hierarchy. These nineteenth-century narratives are residual in discourses like psychoanalysis and disciplines like art history, which still often assume a connection between the (ontogenetic) development

---

of the individual and the (phylogenetic) development of the species (as in human civilization, world art, and so on). In this association the primitive is first projected by the Western white subject as a primal stage in *cultural* history and then reabsorbed as a primal stage in *individual* history. (Thus in *Totem and Taboo* [1913], with its subtitle "Some Points of Agreement between the Mental Lives of Savages and Neurotics," Freud presents the primitive as "a well-preserved picture of an early stage of our own development.")[13] Again, this association of the primitive and the prehistoric and/or the pre-Oedipal, the other and the unconscious, *is* the primitivist fantasy. However revalued by Freud, where we neurotics may also be savage, or by Bataille and Leiris or Senghor and Césaire, where such otherness is the best part of us, this fantasy is not deconstructed. *And to the extent that the primitivist fantasy is not disarticulated, to the extent that the other remains conflated with the unconscious, explorations of alterity to this day will "other" the self in old ways in which the other remains the foil of the self (however troubled this self may be in the process) more than "selve" the other in new ways in which difference is allowed, even appreciated (perhaps through a recognition of an alterity in the self).* In this sense, too, the primitivist fantasy may live on in quasi-anthropological art.

Then there is the problem of the *politics* of this outside-other. Today in our global economy the assumption of a pure outside is almost impossible. This is not to totalize our world system prematurely, but to specify both resistance and innovation as immanent relations rather than transcendental events. Long ago Fanon saw an inadvertent confirmation of European culture in the oppositional logic of the *négritude* movement, but only recently have postcolonial artists and critics pushed practice and theory from binary structures of otherness to relational models of difference, from discrete space-times to mixed border zones.[14]

This move was difficult because it runs counter to the old politics of alterity. Basic to much modernism, this appropriation of the other persists in much postmodernism. In *The Myth of the Other* (1978) Italian philosopher Franco Rella argues that theorists as diverse as Lacan, Foucault, and Deleuze and Guattari idealize the other as the negation of the same—with deleterious effects on cultural politics. This work often assumes dominant definitions of the negative and/or the deviant even as it moves to revalue them.[15] So, too, it often allows rhetorical reversals of dominant definitions to stand for politics as such. More generally, this idealization of otherness tends to follow a temporal line in which one group is privileged as the new subject of history, only to be displaced by another, a chronology that may collapse not only different differences (social, ethnic, sexual, and so on) but also different positions within each difference.[16] The result is a politics that may *consume* its historical subjects before they become historically effective.

This Hegelianism of the other is not only active in modernism and post-modernism; it may be structural to the modern subject. In a celebrated passage in *The Order of Things* (1966) Michel Foucault argues that this subject, this modern man that emerges in the nineteenth century, differs from the classical subject of Cartesian and Kantian philosophies because he seeks his truth in the *un*thought—the unconscious and the other (this is the philosophical basis of the primitivist crossing of the two). "An unveiling of the nonconscious," Foucault writes, "is the truth of all the sciences of man," and this is why such unveilings as psychoanalysis and anthropology are the most privileged of modern discourses.[17] In this light the othering of the self, past and present, is only a partial challenge to the modern subject, for this othering also buttresses the self through romantic opposition, conserves the self through dialectical appropriation, extends the self through surrealist exploration, prolongs the self through poststructuralist troubling, and so on.[18] Just as the *elaboration* of psychoanalysis and anthropology was fundamental to modern discourses (modernist art included), so the *critique* of these human sciences is crucial to postmodern discourses (postmodernist art included); as I suggested in chapter 1, the two are in a relation of deferred action. Yet this critique, which is a critique of the subject, is still centered on the subject, and *it still centers the subject*.[19] In *The Savage Mind* (1962) Claude Lévi-Strauss predicts that man will be *dissolved* in the structural-linguistic refashioning of the human sciences.[20] At the end of *The Order of Things* Foucault reiterates this famous prediction with his bold image of man "erased like a face drawn in sand at the edge of the sea." Intentionally or not, might the psychoanalytic-anthropological turn in contemporary practice and theory work to *restore* this figure? Have we not slipped back into what Foucault calls "our anthropological sleep?"[21]

No doubt the othering of the self is crucial to critical practices in anthropology, art, and politics; at least in conjunctures such as the surrealist one, the use of anthropology as auto-analysis (as in Leiris) or social critique (as in Bataille) is culturally transgressive, even politically significant. But clearly too there are dangers. For then as now self-othering can flip into self-absorption, in which the project of an "ethnographic self-fashioning" becomes the practice of a narcissistic self-refurbishing.[22] To be sure, reflexivity can disturb automatic assumptions about subject-positions, but it can also promote a masquerade of this disturbance: a vogue for traumatic confessional in theory that is sometimes sensibility criticism come again, or a vogue for pseudo-ethnographic reports in art that are sometimes disguised travelogues from the world art market. Who in the academy or the art world has not witnessed these testimonies of the new empathetic intellectual or these *flâneries* of the new nomadic artist?[23]

ART AND THEORY IN THE AGE OF ANTHROPOLOGICAL STUDIES

What has happened here? What misrecognitions have passed between anthropology and art and other discourses? One can point to a virtual theater of projections and reflections over the last two decades at least. First some critics of anthropology developed a kind of artist envy (the enthusiasm of James Clifford for the intercultural collages of "ethnographic surrealism" is an influential instance).[24] In this envy the artist became a paragon of formal reflexivity, a self-aware reader of *culture understood as text*. But is the artist the exemplar here, or is this figure not a projection of an ideal ego of the anthropologist: the anthropologist as collagist, semiologist, avant-gardist?[25] In other words, might this artist envy be a self-idealization in which the anthropologist is remade as an artistic interpreter of the cultural text? Rarely does this projection stop there in the new anthropology or, for that matter, in cultural studies or in new historicism. Often it extends to the object of these studies, the cultural other, who is also reconfigured to reflect an ideal image of the anthropologist, critic, or historian.

This projection is hardly new to anthropology: some classics of the discipline presented entire cultures as collective artists or read them as aesthetic patterns of symbolic practices (*Patterns of Culture* by Ruth Benedict [1934] is only one example). But at least the old anthropology projected openly; the new anthropology persists in these projections, only it deems them critical, even deconstructive.

Of course the new anthropology understands culture differently, as text, which is to say that its projection onto other cultures is as textualist as it is aestheticist. This textual model is supposed to challenge "ethnographic authority" through "discursive paradigms of dialogue and polyphony."[26] However, long ago in *Outline of a Theory of Practice* (1972) Pierre Bourdieu questioned the structuralist version of this textual model because it reduced "social relations to communicative relations and, more precisely, to decoding operations" and so rendered the ethnographic reader *more* authoritative, not less.[27] Indeed, this "ideology of the text," this recoding of practice as discourse, persists in the new anthropology as well as in quasi-anthropological art, as it does in cultural studies and new historicism, despite the contextualist ambitions that also drive these methods.[28]

Recently the old artist envy among anthropologists has turned the other way: a new ethnographer envy consumes many artists and critics. If anthropologists wanted to exploit the textual model in cultural interpretation, these artists and critics aspire to fieldwork in which theory and practice seem to be reconciled. Often they draw indirectly on basic principles of the participant-observer tradition, among which Clifford notes a critical focus on a particular institution and a narrative tense that favors "the ethnographic present."[29] Yet these borrowings are only signs of the ethnographic turn in contemporary art and criticism. What *drives* it?

There are many engagements of the other in twentieth-century art, most of which are primitivist, bound up in the politics of alterity: in surrealism, where the other is figured expressly in terms of the unconscious; in the *art brut* of Jean Dubuffet, where the other represents a redemptive anti-civilizational resource; in abstract expressionism, where the other stands for the primal exemplar of all artists; and variously in art in the 1960s and 1970s (the allusion to prehistoric art in some earthworks, the art world as anthropological site in some conceptual and institution-critical art, the invention of archaeological sites and anthropological civilizations by Anne and Patrick Poirier, Charles Simonds, many others).[30] So what distinguishes the present turn, apart from its relative self-consciousness about ethnographic method? First, as we have seen, anthropology is prized as the science of *alterity;* in this regard it is, along with psychoanalysis, the lingua franca of artistic practice and critical discourse alike. Second, it is the discipline that takes *culture* as its object, and this expanded field of reference is the domain of postmodernist practice and theory (thus also the attraction to cultural studies and, to a lesser extent, new historicism). Third, ethnography is considered *contextual,* the often automatic demand for which contemporary artists and critics share with other practitioners today, many of whom aspire to fieldwork in the everyday. Fourth, anthropology is thought to arbitrate the *interdisciplinary,* another often rote value in contemporary art and criticism. Fifth, the recent *self-critique* of anthropology renders it attractive, for it promises a reflexivity of the ethnographer at the center even as it preserves a romanticism of the other at the margins. For all these reasons rogue investigations of anthropology, like queer critiques of psychoanalysis, possess vanguard status: it is along these lines that the critical edge is felt to cut most incisively.

Yet the ethnographic turn is clinched by another factor, which involves the double inheritance of anthropology. In *Culture and Practical Reason* (1976) Marshall Sahlins argues that two epistemologies have long divided the discipline: one stresses symbolic logic, with the social understood mostly in terms of exchange systems; the other privileges practical reason, with the social understood mostly in terms of material culture.[31] In this light anthropology *already* participates in the two contradictory models that dominate contemporary art and criticism: on the one hand, in the old ideology of the text, the linguistic turn in the 1960s that reconfigured the social as symbolic order and/or cultural system and advanced "the dissolution of man," "the death of the author," and so on; and, on the other hand, in the recent longing for the referent, the turn to context and identity that opposes the old text paradigms and subject critiques. *With a turn to this split discourse of anthropology, artists and critics can resolve these contradictory models magically: they can take up the guises of cultural semiologist and contextual fieldworker, they can continue and condemn critical theory, they can relativize and recenter the subject, all at the same time.* In our current state of artistic-theoretical ambivalences and cultural-political impasses, anthropology is the compromise discourse of choice.[32]

Again, this ethnographer envy is shared by many critics, especially in cultural studies and new historicism, who assume the role of ethnographer usually in disguised form: the cultural-studies ethnographer dressed down as a fellow fan (for reasons of political solidarity, but with great social anxiety); the new-historicist ethnographer dressed up as a master archivist (for reasons of scholarly respectability, but with great professional arrogance). First some anthropologists adapted textual methods from literary criticism in order to reformulate culture as text; then some literary critics adapted ethnographic methods in order to reformulate texts as cultures writ small. And these exchanges have accounted for much interdisciplinary work in the recent past.[33] But there are two problems with this theater of projections and reflections, the first methodological, the second ethical. If both textual and ethnographic turns depended on a single discourse, how truly *inter*disciplinary can the results be? If cultural studies and new historicism often smuggle in an ethnographic model (when not a sociological one), might it be "the *common theoretical ideology* that silently inhabits the 'consciousness' of all these specialists . . . oscillating between a vague spiritualism and a technocratic positivism"?[34] The second problem, broached above, is more serious. When the other is admired as playful in representation, subversive of gender, and so on, might it be a projection of the anthropologist, artist, critic, or historian? In this case an ideal practice might be projected onto the field of the other, which is then asked to reflect it as if it were not only authentically indigenous but innovatively political.

In part this is a projection of my own, and the application of new and old ethnographic methods has illuminated much. But it has also obliterated much in the field of the other, and in its name. This is the opposite of a critique of ethnographic authority, indeed the opposite of ethnographic method, at least as I understand them. And this "impossible place," as Benjamin called it long ago, is a common occupation of many anthropologists, artists, critics, and historians.

THE SITING OF CONTEMPORARY ART

The ethnographic turn in contemporary art is also driven by developments within the minimalist genealogy of art over the last thirty-five years. These developments constitute a sequence of investigations: first of the material constituents of the art medium, then of its spatial conditions of perception, and then of the corporeal bases of this perception—shifts marked in minimalist art in the early 1960s through conceptual, performance, body, and site-specific art in the early 1970s. Soon the institution of art could no longer be described only in spatial terms (studio, gallery, museum, and so on); it was also a discursive network of different practices and institutions, other subjectivities and communities. Nor could the observer of art be delimited only in phenomenological terms; he or she was also a social subject defined in language and marked by difference (economic, ethnic, sexual, and so on). Of course the breakdown of restrictive definitions of art and artist, identity and community, was also pressured by social movements (civil rights, various feminisms, queer politics, multiculturalism) as well as theoretical developments (the convergence of feminism, psychoanalysis, and film theory; the recovery of Antonio Gramsci and the development of cultural studies in Britain; the applications of Louis Althusser, Lacan, and Foucault, especially in the British journal *Screen;* the development of postcolonial discourse with Edward Said, Gayatri Spivak, Homi Bhabha, and others; and so on). Thus did art pass into the expanded field of culture that anthropology is thought to survey.

These developments also constitute a series of shifts in the *siting* of art: from the surface of the medium to the space of the museum, from institutional frames to discursive networks, to the point where many artists and critics treat conditions like desire or disease, AIDS or homelessness, as sites for art.[35] Along with this figure of siting has come the analogy of *mapping*. In an important moment Robert Smithson and others pushed this cartographic operation to a geological extreme that transformed the siting of art dramatically. Yet this siting had limits too: it could be recouped by gallery and museum, it played to the myth of the redemptive artist (a very traditional site), and so on. Otherwise mapping in recent art has tended toward the sociological and the anthropological, to the point where an ethnographic mapping of an institution or a community is a primary form of site-specific art today.

Sociological mapping is implicit in some conceptual art, sometimes in a parodic way, from the laconic recording of *Twenty-Six Gasoline Stations* by Ed Ruscha (1963) to the quixotic project of Douglas Huebler to photograph every human being (*Variable Piece: 70*). An important example here is *Homes for America* by Dan Graham, a report (published in a 1966–67 *Arts* magazine) of modular repetitions in a tract-housing development that reframes minimalist structures as found objects in a technocratic suburb. Sociological mapping is more explicit in much institutional critique, especially in the work of Hans Haacke, from the polls and profiles of gallery and museumgoers and the exposés of real-estate moguls in New York (1969–73) through the pedigrees of masterpiece collectors (1974–75) to the investigations of arrangements among museums, corporations, and governments. However, while this work questions social authority incisively, it does not reflect on sociological authority.

This is less true of work that examines the authority arrogated in documentary modes of representation. In a videotape like *Vital Statistics of a Citizen, Simply Obtained* (1976) and in a photo-text like *The Bowery in Two Inadequate Descriptive Systems* (1974–75), Martha Rosler belies the apparent objectivity of medical statistics regarding the female body and of sociological descriptions concerning the destitute alcoholic. Recently she has also pushed this critical use of documentary modes toward the geopolitical concerns that have long driven the work of Allan Sekula. In a cycle of three photo-text sequences in particular, Sekula traces the connections between German borders and Cold War politics (*Sketch for a Geography Lesson,* 1983), a mining industry and a financial institution (*Canadian Notes,* 1986), and maritime space and global economics (*Fish Story,*

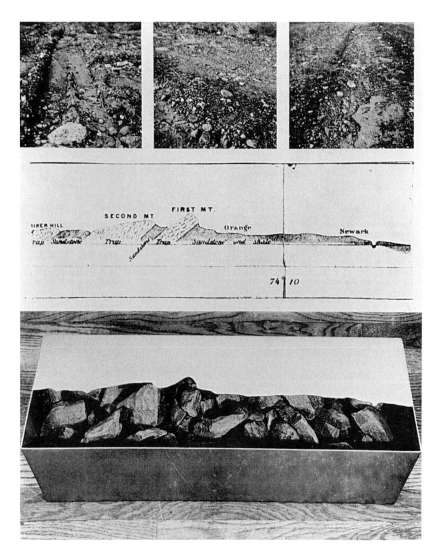

Robert Smithson, *Six Stops on a Section*, 1968, photo, map, bin.

Each block of houses is a self-contained sequence — there is no development — selected from the possible acceptable arrangements. As an example, if a section was to contain eight houses of which four model types were to be used, any of these permutational possibilities could be used:

AABBCCDD	ABCDABCD
AABBDDCC	ABDCABDC
AACCBBDD	ACBDACBD
AACCDDBB	ACDBACDB
AADDCCBB	ADBCADBC
AADDBBCC	ADCBADCB
BBAACCDD	BADCBADC
BBAADDCC	BACDBACD
BBCCAADD	BCADBCAD
BBCCDDAA	BCDABCDA
BBDDAACC	BDACBDAC
BBDDCCAA	BDCABDCA
CCAABBDD	CABDCABD
CCAADDBB	CADBCADB
CCBBDDAA	CBADCBAD
CCBBAADD	CBDACBDA
CCDDAABB	CDABCDAB
CCDDBBAA	CDBACDBA
DDAABBCC	DACBDACB
DDAACCBB	DABCDABC
DDBBAACC	DBACDBAC
DDBBCCAA	DBCADBCA
DDCCAABB	DCABDCAB
DDCCBBAA	DCBADCBA

The eight color variables were equally distributed among the house exteriors. The first buyers were more likely to have obtained their first choice in color. Family units had to make a choice based on the available colors which also took account of both husband and wife's likes and dislikes. Adult male and female color likes and dislikes were compared in a survey of the homeowners:

'LIKE'

Female	Male
Skyway Blue	Skyway Blue
Lawn Green	Colonial Red
Nickle	Patio White
Colonial Red	Yellow Chiffon
Yellow Chiffon	Lawn Green
Patio White	Nickle
Moonstone Grey	Fawn
Fawn	Moonstone Grey

'DISLIKE'

Female	Male
Patio White	Lawn Green
Fawn	Colonial Red
Colonial Red	Patio White
Moonstone Grey	Moonstone Grey
Yellow Chiffon	Fawn
Lawn Green	Yellow Chiffon
Skyway Blue	Nickle
Nickle	Skyway Blue

ground-level, 'Two Home Home', Jersey City, N. J.

uniform setbacks (front view), Bayonne, N. J.

Dan Graham, *Homes for America*, 1966, detail of layout.

```
     lush    wino    rubbydub
          inebriate
                alcoholic
     barrelhouse bum
```

Martha Rosler, *The Bowery in Two Inadequate Descriptive Systems*, 1975, detail.

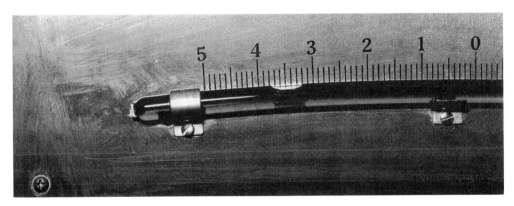

Allan Sekula, *Fish Story*, 1995, details of panorama and inclinometer in the mid-Atlantic.

1995). With these "imaginary and material geographies of the advanced capital- ist world," he sketches a "cognitive map" of our global order. Yet, with his perspectival shifts in narrative and image, Sekula is as reflexive as any new an- thropologist about the hubris of this ethnographic project.[36]

An awareness of sociological presumptions and anthropological compli- cations also guides the feminist mappings of artists like Mary Kelly and Silvia Kolbowski. Thus in *Interim* (1984–89) Kelly registers personal and political po- sitions within the feminist movement through a polyphonic mix of images and voices. In effect, she represents the movement as a kinship system in which she participates as an indigenous ethnographer of art, theory, teaching, activism, friendship, family, mentorship, aging. In various reframings of institutional definitions of art Kolbowski also takes up ethnographic mapping reflexively. In projects like *Enlarged from the Catalogue* (1987–88), she proposes a feminist ethnography of the cultural authority at work in art exhibitions, catalogues, reviews, and the like.[37]

Such reflexivity is essential, for, as Bourdieu warned, ethnographic map- ping is predisposed to a Cartesian opposition that leads the observer to abstract the culture of study. Such mapping may thus confirm rather than contest the authority of mapper over site in a way that reduces the desired exchange of dialogical fieldwork.[38] In his mappings of other cultures Lothar Baumgarten is sometimes charged with such arrogance. In several works over the last two decades he has inscribed the names of indigenous societies of North and South America, often imposed by explorers and ethnographers alike, in such settings as the neoclassical dome of the Museum Fredericianum in Kassel (Germany) in 1982 and the modernist spiral of the Guggenheim Museum in New York in 1993. Yet rather than ethnographic trophies, these names return, almost as dis- torted signs of the repressed, to challenge the mappings of the West: in the neoclassical dome as if to declare that the other face of Old World Enlighten- ment is New World Conquest, and in the Frank Lloyd Wright spiral as if to demand a new globe without narratives of modern and primitive or hierarchies of North and South, a different map in which the framer is also framed, plunged in a parallax in a way that complicates the old anthropological oppositions of an us-here-and-now versus a them-there-and-then.[39]

Yet the Baumgarten example points to another complication: these ethnographic mappings are often commissioned. Just as appropriation art in the 1980s became an aesthetic genre, even a media spectacle, so new site-specific work often seems a museum event in which the institution *imports* critique, whether as a show of tolerance or for the purpose of inoculation (against a critique undertaken by the institution, within the institution). Of course this position within the museum may be necessary to such ethnographic mappings, especially if they purport to be deconstructive: just as appropriation art, in order to engage media spectacle, had to participate in it, so new site-specific work, in order to remap the museum or to reconfigure its audience, must operate inside it. This argument holds for the most incisive of these projects, such as *Mining the Museum* by Fred Wilson and *Aren't They Lovely?* by Andrea Fraser (both 1992).

In *Mining the Museum,* sponsored by the Museum of Contemporary Art in Baltimore, Wilson acted as an archaeologist of the Maryland Historical Society. First he explored its collection (an initial "mining"). Then he reclaimed representations evocative of histories, mostly African-American, not often displayed as historical (a second "mining"). Finally he reframed still other representations that have long arrogated the right to history (for example, in an exhibit labeled "Metalwork 1793–1880," he placed a pair of slave manacles—a third "mining" that exploded the given representation). In so doing Wilson also served as an ethnographer of African-American communities lost, repressed, or otherwise displaced in such institutions. Andrea Fraser performed a different archaeology of museum archives and ethnography of museum cultures. In *Aren't They Lovely?* she reopened a private bequest to the art museum at the University of California at Berkeley in order to investigate how the heterogeneous domestic objects of a specific class member (from eyeglasses to Renoirs) are sublimated into the homogenous public culture of a general art museum. Here Fraser addressed institutional *sublimation,* whereas Wilson focused on institutional *repression*. Nonetheless, both artists play with museology first to expose and then to

Mary Kelly, *Historia*, 1989, detail of section III.

Silvia Kolbowski, *Enlarged from the Catalogue, February 1990*, detail.

Lothar Baumgarten, *America Invention,* 1993, detail, The Guggenheim Museum.

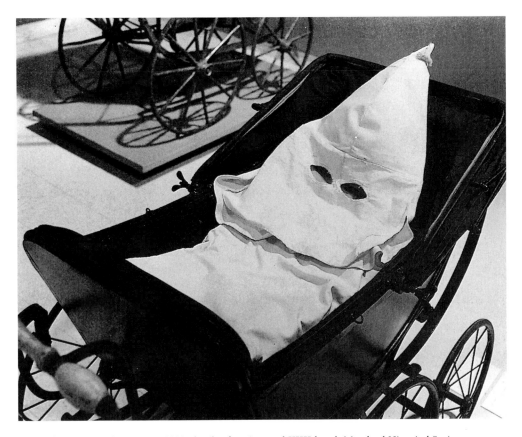

Fred Wilson, *Mining the Museum,* 1992, details of carriage and KKK hood, Maryland Historical Society.

reframe the institutional codings of art and artifacts—how objects are translated into historical evidence and/or cultural exempla, invested with value, and cathected by viewers.

However, for all the insight of such projects, the deconstructive-ethnographic approach can become a gambit, an insider game that renders the institution not more open and public but more hermetic and narcissistic, a place for initiates only where a contemptuous criticality is rehearsed. So, too, as we saw in chapter 4, the ambiguity of deconstructive positioning, at once inside and outside the institution, can lapse into the duplicity of cynical reason in which artist and institution have it both ways—retain the social status of art and entertain the moral purity of critique, the one a complement or compensation for the other.

These are dangers of site-specific work inside the institution; others arise when this work is sponsored outside the institution, often in collaboration with local groups. Consider the example of "Project Unité," a commission of forty or so installations for the Unité d'Habitation in Firminy (France) during the summer of 1993. Here the quasi-anthropological paradigm operated on two levels: first, indirectly, in that this dilapidated housing project designed by Le Corbusier was treated as an ethnographic site (has such modern architecture become exotic in this way?); and then, directly, in that its largely immigrant community was offered to the artists for ethnographic engagement. One project suggests the pitfalls of such an arrangement. Here the neo-conceptual team Clegg & Guttmann asked the Unité residents to contribute casettes for a disco-theque, which were then edited, compiled, and displayed according to apartment and floor in a model of the building as a whole. Lured by collaboration, the inhabitants loaned these cultural proxies, only to have them turned into anthropological exhibits. And the artists did not question the ethnographic authority, indeed the sociological condescension, involved in this facilitated self-representation.

This is typical of the quasi-anthropological scenario. Few principles of the ethnographic participant-observer are observed, let alone critiqued, and only limited engagement of the community is effected. Almost naturally the project strays from collaboration to self-fashioning, from a decentering of the artist as cultural authority to a remaking of the other in neo-primitivist guise. Of course this is not always the case: many artists have used these opportunities to collaborate with communities innovatively, to recover suppressed histories that are sited in particular ways, that are accessed by some more effectively than others. And symbolically this new site-specific work can reoccupy lost cultural spaces and propose historical counter-memories. (I think of the signs posted by Edgar Heap of Birds that reclaim Native American land in Oklahoma and elsewhere, and of the projects developed by collectives like Repo History that point to suppressed histories beneath official commemorations in New York and elsewhere.) Nevertheless, *the quasi-anthropological role set up for the artist can promote a presuming as much as a questioning of ethnographic authority, an evasion as often as an extension of institutional critique.*

At Firminy the ethnographic model was used to animate an old site, but it can also be used to develop a new one. The local and the everyday are thought to resist economic development, yet they can also attract it, for such development needs the local and the everyday even as it erodes these qualities, renders them siteless. In this case site-specific work can be exploited to make these nonspaces seem specific again, to redress them as grounded places, not abstract spaces, in historical and/or cultural terms.[40] Killed as culture, the local and the everyday can be revived as simulacrum, a "theme" for a park or a "history" in a mall, and site-specific work can be drawn into this zombification of the local and the everyday, this Disney version of the site-specific. Tabooed in postmodernist art, values like authenticity, originality, and singularity can return as properties of sites that artists are asked to define or to embellish. There is nothing wrong with this return per se, but sponsors may regard these properties precisely as sited values to develop.[41]

Art institutions may also use site-specific work for economic development, social outreach, and art tourism, and at a time of privatization this is assumed necessary, even natural. In "Culture in Action," a 1993 public art program of Sculpture Chicago, eight projects were sited throughout the city. Led by artists like Daniel Martinez, Mark Dion, and Kate Ericson and Mel Zeigler, these collaborations did serve "as an urban laboratory to involve diverse audiences in the creation of innovative public art projects."[42] But they could not but also serve as public-relations probes for the corporations and agencies that supported them. Another instance of this ambiguous public service is the yearly designation of a "Cultural Capital of Europe." In Antwerp, the capital for 1993, several site-specific works were again commissioned. Here the artists explored lost histories more than engaged present communities, in keeping with the motto of the show: "On taking a normal situation and retranslating it into overlapping and multiple readings of conditions past and present." Borrowed from Gordon Matta-Clark, a pioneer of site-specific work, this motto mixes the metaphors of site-mapping and situationist *détournement* (defined long ago by Guy Debord as "the reuse of preexisting artistic elements in a new ensemble").[43] Yet here again impressive site-specific projects were also turned into tourist sites, and situationist disruption was reconciled with cultural-political promotion.

In these cases the institution may shadow the work that it otherwise highlights: it becomes the spectacle, it collects the cultural capital, and the director-curator becomes the star. This is not a conspiracy, nor is it cooption pure and simple; nevertheless, it can detour the artist more than reconfigure the site.[44] Just as the *proletkult* author according to Benjamin sought to stand in the reality of the proletariat, only in part to sit in the place of the patron, so the ethnographic artist may collaborate with a sited community, only to have this work redirected to other ends. Often artist and community are linked through an identitarian reduction of both, the apparent authenticity of the one invoked to guarantee that of the other, in a way that threatens to collapse new site-specific work into identity politics *tout court*.[45] As the artist stands *in* the identity of a sited community, he or she may be asked to stand *for* this identity, to represent it institutionally. In this case the artist is primitivized, indeed anthropologized, in turn: here is your community, the institution says in effect, embodied in your artist, now on display.

For the most part the relevant artists are aware of these complications, and sometimes they foreground them. In many performances James Luna has acted out the stereotypes of the Native American in white culture (the ornamental warrior, the ritualistic shaman, the drunken Indian, the museum object). In so doing he invites these popular primitivisms to parody them, to force them back on his audience explosively. Jimmie Durham also pressures these primitivisms to the point of critical explosion, of utter bombast, especially in a work like *Self-Portrait* (1988), a figure that plays on the wooden chief of smoke-shop lore with an absurdist text of popular fantasies regarding the Indian male body. In his hybrid works Durham mixes ritualistic and found objects in a way that is preemptively auto-primitivist and wryly anti-categorical. These pseudo-primitive fetishes and pseudo-ethnographic artifacts resist further primitivizing and anthropologizing through a parodic "trickstering" of these very processes. All such strategies—a parody of primitivisms, a reversal of ethnographic roles, a preemptive playing-dead, a plurality of practices—disturb a dominant culture that depends on strict stereotypes, stable lines of authority, and humanist reanimations and museological resurrections of many sorts.[46]

DISCIPLINARY MEMORY AND CRITICAL DISTANCE

I want to elaborate two points in conclusion, the first to do with the siting of contemporary art, the second with the function of reflexivity within it. I suggested above that many artists treat conditions like desire or disease as sites for work. In this way they work *horizontally,* in a synchronic movement from social issue to issue, from political debate to debate, more than *vertically,* in a diachronic engagement with the disciplinary forms of a given genre or medium. Apart from the general shift (noted in chapter 2) from formalist "quality" to neo-avant-garde "interest," there are several markers of this move from medium-specific to discourse-specific practice. In "Other Criteria" (1968) Leo Steinberg saw a turn, in early Rauschenberg combines, from a vertical model of picture-as-window to the horizontal model of picture-as-text, from a "natural" paradigm of image as framed landscape to a "cultural" paradigm of image as informational network, which he regarded as inaugural of postmodernist art making.[47] Yet this shift from vertical to horizontal remained operational at best; its social dimension was not developed until pop. "Its acceptance

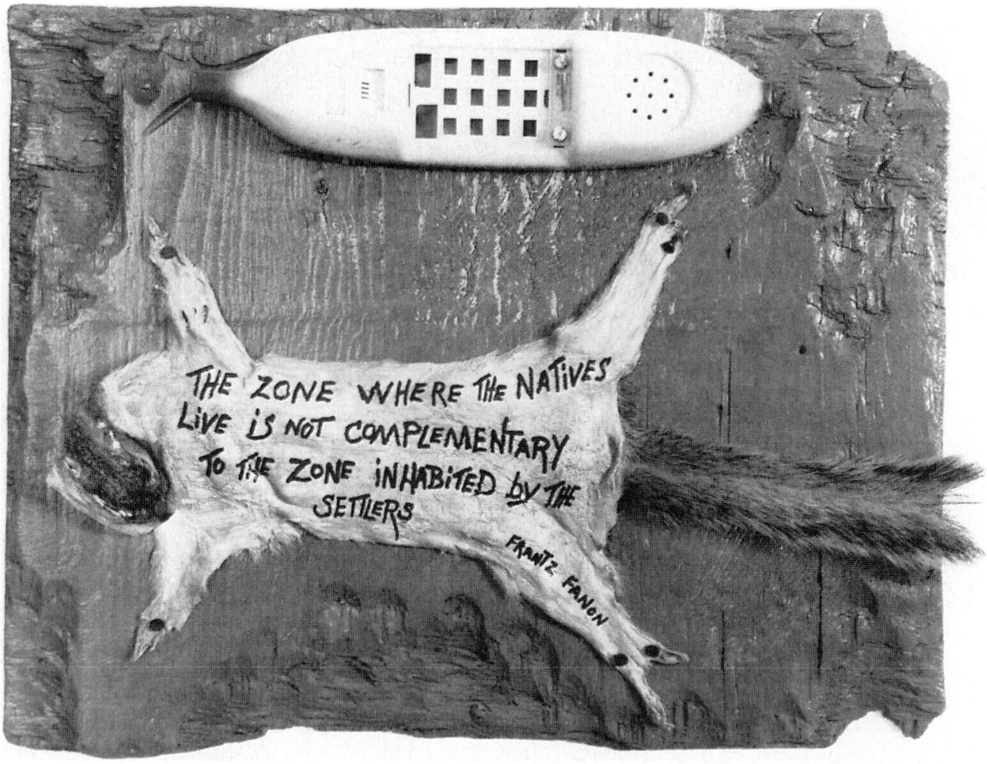
THE ZONE WHERE THE NATIVES
LIVE IS NOT COMPLEMENTARY
TO THE ZONE INHABITED BY THE
SETTLERS
FRANTZ FANON

Jimmie Durham, *Often Durham Employs . . .* , 1980s.

Edgar Heap of Birds, *Native Hosts,* 1988, detail, City Hall Park, New York.

of the mass media entails a shift in our notion of what culture is," Lawrence
Alloway predicted long ago in "The Long Front of Culture" (1958). "Rather
than frozen in layers in a pyramid," pop placed art "within a continuum" of
culture.[48] Thus, if Rauschenberg and company sought other criteria than the
formalist terms of medium-specific modernism, so pop repositioned the engagement with high art along the long front of culture. This horizontal expansion of artistic expression and cultural value is furthered, critically and not, in
quasi-anthropological art and cultural studies alike.

A few effects of this expansion might be stressed. First, the shift to a
horizontal way of working is consistent with the ethnographic turn in art and
criticism: one selects a site, enters its culture and learns its language, conceives
and presents a project, only to move to the next site where the cycle is repeated.
Second, this shift follows a spatial logic: one not only maps a site but also works
in terms of topics, frames, and so on (which may or may not point to a general
privileging of space over time in postmodern discourse).[49] Now in the postmodernist rupture, associated in chapter 1 with a return to the historical avant-garde,
the horizontal, spatial axis still intersected the vertical, temporal axis. In order
to extend aesthetic space, artists delved into historical time, and returned past
models to the present in a way that opened new sites for work. The two axes
were in tension, but it was a productive tension; ideally coordinated, the two
moved forward together, with past and present in parallax. Today, as artists follow horizontal lines of working, the vertical lines sometimes appear to be lost.

This horizontal way of working demands that artists and critics be familiar
not only with the structure of each culture well enough to map it, but also with
its history well enough to narrate it. Thus if one wishes to work on AIDS, one
must understand not only the discursive *breadth* but also the historical *depth* of
AIDS representations. To coordinate both axes of several such discourses is an
enormous burden. And here the traditionalist caution about the horizontal way
of working—that new discursive connections may blur old disciplinary memo-
ries—must be considered, if only to be countered. Implicit in the charge is that
this move has rendered contemporary art dangerously political. Indeed, this image of art is dominant in general culture, with all the calls to purify art of politics

altogether. These calls are obviously self-contradictory, yet they too must be considered in order to be countered.[50]

My second point concerns the reflexivity of contemporary art. I have stressed that reflexivity is needed to protect against an over-identification with the other (through commitment, self-othering, and so on) that may compromise this otherness. Paradoxically, as Benjamin implied long ago, this over-identification may alienate the other further if it does not allow for the othering already at work in representation. In the face of these dangers—of too little or too much distance—I have advocated parallactic work that attempts to frame the framer as he or she frames the other. This is one way to negotiate the contradictory status of otherness as given and constructed, real and fantasmatic.[51] This framing can be as simple as a caption to a photograph, as in The Bowery project by Rosler, or a reversal of a name, as in the signs of Heap of Birds or Baumgarten. Yet such reframing is not sufficient alone. Again, reflexivity can lead to a hermeticism, even a narcissism, in which the other is obscured, the self pronounced; it can also lead to a refusal of engagement altogether. *And what does critical distance guarantee?* Has this notion become somewhat mythical, *a*critical, a form of magical protection, a purity ritual of its own? Is such distance still desirable, let alone possible?

Perhaps not, but a reductive over-identification with the other is not desirable either. Far worse, however, is a murderous disidentification from the other. Today the cultural politics of left and right seem stuck at this impasse.[52] To a great extent the left over-identifies with the other as victim, which locks it into a hierarchy of suffering whereby the wretched can do little wrong. To a much greater extent the right disidentifies from the other, which it blames as victim, and exploits this disidentification to build political solidarity through fantasmatic fear and loathing. Faced with this impasse, critical distance might not be such a bad idea after all. It is to this question that I turn in the final chapter.

"The Truth about the Colonies," surrealist counter-exhibition, Paris, 1931.

Whatever Happened to Postmodernism?

Whatever happened to postmodernism? Not long ago it seemed a grand notion. For Jean-François Lyotard postmodernism marked an end to master narratives that made modernity appear synonymous with progress (the march of reason, the accumulation of wealth, the advance of technology, the emancipation of workers, and so on), while for Fredric Jameson postmodernism prompted a renewed Marxist narrative of different stages of modern culture related to different modes of capitalist production.[1] Meanwhile, for critics committed to advanced art, it signaled a move to break with an exhausted model of modernist art that focused on formal refinements to the neglect of historical determinations and social transformations alike.

Thus even within the left, especially within the left, postmodernism was a disputed notion. Yet not long ago there was a sense of a loose alliance, even a common project, particularly in opposition to rightist positions, which ranged from old attacks on modernism in toto as the source of all evil in our hedonistic society to new defenses of particular modernisms that had become official, indeed traditional, the modernisms of the museum and the academy.[2] For this position postmodernism was "the revenge of the philistines" (the happy phrase of Hilton Kramer), the vulgar kitsch of media hucksters, lower classes, and inferior peoples, a new barbarism to be shunned, like multiculturalism, at all costs.

I supported a postmodernism that contested this reactionary cultural politics and advocated artistic practices not only critical of institutional modernism but suggestive of alternative forms—of new ways to practice culture and politics. And we did not lose. In a sense a worse thing happened: treated as a fashion, postmodernism became *démodé*.

The notion was not only emptied by the media; again, it was disputed within the left, often with good reason. Despite its *adieu* to master narratives, the Lyotardian version of postmodernism was sometimes taken as the latest proper name of the West, now melancholically obsessed with its postcolonial decline (or the premature reports thereof). So, too, despite its focus on capitalist fragmentation, the Jamesonian version of postmodernism was sometimes considered too totalizing, not sensitive enough to cultural differences of many sorts. Finally, the art-critical version of postmodernism was sometimes seen to seal modernism in the formalist mold that we wanted to break. In the process the notion became incorrect as well as banal.

But should we surrender it? Apart from the fact that the left has already conceded too much in this war, the notion may still possess explanatory, even critical power. Consider the influential model of postmodernism developed by Jameson over the last decade. He adapts the long-wave theory of economic cycles elaborated by the economist Ernest Mandel, according to which the capitalist West has passed through four fifty-year periods since the late eighteenth century (roughly twenty-five years each of expansion and stagnation): the Industrial Revolution (until the political crises of 1848) marked by the spread of handcrafted steam engines, followed by three further technological epochs—the first (until the 1890s) marked by the spread of machined steam engines; the second (until World War II) marked by the spread of electric and combustion engines; and the third marked by the spread of machined electronic and nuclear systems.[3] Mandel relates these technological developments to economic stages: from market capitalism to monopoly capitalism around the last fin de siècle, to multinational capitalism in our millennial moment. Jameson in turn relates these economic stages to cultural paradigms: the worldview of much realist art and literature incited by the individualism encouraged by market capitalism; the abstraction of much high-modernist art and literature in response to the alien-ation of bureaucratic life under monopoly capitalism; and the pastiche of much postmodernist practice (in art, architecture, fiction, film, fashion, food) as a sign of the dispersed borders, the mixed spaces, of multinational capitalism. His model is not as mechanical as my précis makes it sound: Jameson stresses that these developments are uneven, that each period is a palimpsest of emergent and residual forms, that clean breaks do not occur. Nevertheless, his narrative is often condemned as too grand, as if capital were a great reaper that swept up everything in its path. For my purposes it is too spatial, not sensitive enough to the different speeds as well as the mixed spaces of postmodern society, to the deferred action as well as the incessant expansion of capitalist culture.[4]

As in chapter 1, I borrow the notion of deferred action (*Nachträglichkeit*) from Freud, for whom subjectivity, never set once and for all, is structured as a relay of anticipations and reconstructions of events that may become traumatic through this very relay. I believe modernism and postmodernism are constituted in an analogous way, in deferred action, as a continual process of anticipated futures and reconstructed pasts.[5] Each epoch dreams the next, as Walter Benja-min once remarked, but in so doing it revises the one before it. There is no simple *now*: every present is nonsynchronous, a mix of different times; thus there is no timely transition between the modern and the postmodern. In a sense each comes like sex(uality), too early or too late, and our consciousness of each is premature or after the fact.[6] In this regard modernism and postmod-ernism must be seen together, *in parallax* (technically, the angle of displacement of an object caused by the movement of its observer), by which I mean that our framings of the two depend on our position in the present *and* that this position is defined in such framings.

This notion is abstract, so let me apply it in one reading of the never-complete passage to the postmodern. Rather than adapt the cumbersome Man-delian scheme of four fifty-year periods, I will focus on three moments thirty years apart within the twentieth century: the middle 1930s, which I take to be the culmination of high modernism; the middle 1960s, which mark the full advent of postmodernism; and the middle 1990s. I will treat these moments in a discursive sense, to see how historical shifts may be registered in theoretical texts—which will thus serve as both objects and instruments of my history. This idiosyncratic narrative will not address art directly; instead, in addition to the relation of technology and culture (which tends to be privileged in these accounts), I will trace crucial shifts in Western conceptions of the individual subject and the cultural other.

My reason for this focus is simple. The quintessential question of modernity concerned identity: in the famous query of Paul Gauguin, *Where do we come from? Who are we? Where are we going?* As we saw in chapter 6, answers often came through an appeal to otherness, either to the unconscious or to the cultural other. Many high modernists felt truth was located there: hence the significance of psychoanalysis and the profusion of primitivisms throughout this century. Indeed, many high modernists conflated these two natural preserves, the unconscious and the cultural other, while some postmodernists argue that they are acculturated in advanced capitalism.[7] In short, the discourses of the unconscious and the cultural other, psychoanalysis and anthropology, are the privileged modern discourses because they speak to identity in these terms. In doing so they may also register more seismographically than any other discourses the epistemological changes that demarcate the postmodern.

Each moment at issue here represents a significant shift in discourses on the subject, the cultural other, and technology. In the middle 1930s Jacques Lacan was concerned with the formation of the ego, especially in the first version of "The Mirror Stage." Claude Lévi-Strauss was involved in the Brazilian fieldwork that revealed the mythological sophistication of "the savage mind." And Walter Benjamin was concerned with the cultural ramifications of modern technologies in "The Work of Art in the Age of Mechanical Reproduction." By the middle 1960s each of these discourses had changed dramatically. The death of the humanist subject, not its formation, was considered variously by Louis Althusser, Michel Foucault, Gilles Deleuze, Jacques Derrida, and Roland Barthes (whose signal texts on the topic swirl around the revolts of 1968). So, too, the cultural other, inspired by the liberation wars of the 1950s, had begun to talk back—to be heard for the first time—most incisively in the rewriting of master-slave dialectic in Hegel and Marx by Frantz Fanon, whose *The Wretched of the Earth* was published in 1961. Meanwhile, the penetration of media into psychic structures and social relations had reached a new level, which was seen in two complementary ways: fatalistically by Guy Debord as an intensity of reification in *The Society of the Spectacle* (1967) and ecstatically by Marshall McLuhan as an "extension of man" in *Understanding Media* (1964).

What has changed in these three discourses since then? In a sense the death of the subject is dead in turn: the subject has returned in the cultural politics of different subjectivities, sexualities, and ethnicities, sometimes in old humanist guise, often in contrary forms—fundamentalist, hybrid, or (as suggested in chapter 5) "traumatic." Meanwhile, at a time when first, second, and third worlds are no longer distinct (if they ever were), anthropology is critical of its protocols regarding the cultural other, and postcolonial imbrications have complicated anticolonial confrontations. Finally, even as our society remains one of spectacular images as outlined by Debord, it has become one of electronic discipline—or, if one prefers the technophilic version in the spirit of McLuhan, one of electronic freedom, of the new possibilities of cyberspace, virtual reality, and the like. My purpose is not to prove that one position is right, the other wrong, nor to assert that one moment is modern, the next postmodern, for again these events do not develop evenly or break cleanly. Instead each theory speaks of changes in its present, but only indirectly, in reconstruction of past moments when these changes are said to have begun, and in anticipation of future moments when these changes are projected to be complete: thus the deferred action, the double movement, of modern and postmodern times.[8]

VICISSITUDES OF THE SUBJECT

First I will consider the discourse on the subject over these three moments, and here as elsewhere I will cite only landmark texts. In "The Mirror Stage" Lacan argues that our ego is first formed in a primordial apprehension of our body in a mirror (though any reflection will do), an anticipatory image of corporeal unity that as infants we do not yet possess. This image founds our ego in this infantile moment as imaginary, that is, as locked in an identification that is also an alienation. For at the very moment that we see our self in the mirror we see this self as image, as other; moreover, it is usually confirmed by another other—the adult in whose presence the recognition is made. Importantly Lacan suggests that this imaginary unity of the mirror stage produces a retroactive fantasy of a prior stage when our body was still in pieces, a fantasy of a chaotic body, fragmentary and fluid, given over to drives that always threaten to overwhelm us, a fantasy that haunts us for the rest of our life—all those pressured moments when one feels about to *shatter.* In a sense our ego is pledged first and foremost against the return of this body in pieces; this threat turns the ego into an armor (a term Lacan uses) to be deployed aggressively against the chaotic world within *and* without—but especially without, against all others who seem to represent this chaos. (This is why Lacan questions the value of a strong ego, which most of us in ego culture take for granted.)[9]

Lacan does not specify his theory of the subject as historical, and certainly it is not limited to one period. However, this armored and aggressive subject is not just any being across history and culture: it is the modern subject as paranoid, even fascistic. Ghosted in his theory is a contemporary history of which fascism is the extreme symptom: a history of world war and military mutilation, of industrial discipline and mechanistic fragmentation, of mercenary murder and political terror. In relation to such events the modern subject becomes armored—against otherness within (sexuality, the unconscious) and otherness without (for the fascist this can mean Jews, Communists, gays, women), all figures of this fear of the body in pieces come again, of the body given over to the fragmentary and the fluid. Has this fascistic reaction returned? Did it ever go away? Does it rest within us all? (Is this why artists, then as now, resist it with an artifice of abjection?) Or is to ask such questions to repeat the error made by Lacan—that is, to render the fascistic subject too general, too *normal?*[10]

What happens to this theory in the 1960s when the death of the humanist subject is proclaimed? This is a moment of very different historical forces and intellectual imperatives. In Paris it is the twilight of structuralism, of the linguistic paradigm in which cultural activity (the myths of Indian groups for Lévi-Strauss, the structure of the unconscious for Lacan, the modes of Paris fashions for Barthes, and so on) is recoded as language. As noted in chapter 6, this linguistic recoding allows Foucault to announce in 1966 the erasure of man, the great riddle of modernity, "like a face drawn in sand at the edge of the sea."[11] This recoding also permits Barthes to declare in 1968 the toppling of the author, the great protagonist of humanist-modernist culture, into the play of signs of the text (which henceforth displaces the work as the paradigm of art). Yet the figure under attack here is not only the author-artist of humanist-modernist traditions; it is also the authoritarian personality of fascist structures, the paranoid figure who compels singular speech and forbids promiscuous signification (after all this is the 1960s, the days of rage against all such authoritarian institutions). It is an attack on the fascistic subject as indirectly imagined by Lacan, an attack also made with the very forces that this subject most fears: sexuality and the unconscious, desire and the drives, the *jouissance* (the privileged term of French theory during this time) that shatters the subject, that surrenders it to the fragmentary and the fluid.[12]

These forces were often celebrated, mostly in order to challenge the fascistic subject, a challenge made programmatic by Deleuze and Guattari in *Anti-Oedipus* (1972).[13] They appeal to schizophrenia not only to disrupt the armored fascistic subject but to exceed the rapacious capitalist one as well. Yet this appeal is dangerous, for if the fascistic subject is threatened by schizophrenic fragments and flows, the capitalist subject may thrive on such disruptions. Indeed, according to Deleuze and Guattari, only extreme schizophrenia is more schizophrenic than capital, more given over to decodings of fixed subjects and structures. In this light, what dispersed the subject in the 1960s, what disrupted its institutions, was a revolutionary force, indeed a whole congeries of conflictual forces (ex-colonial, civil-rights, feminist, student), but a revolutionary force released by capital—for what is more radical than capital when it comes to old subjects and structures that stand in its way?

However tendentiously, this argument might be extended to the recent return of the subject, by which I mean the partial recognition of new and ignored subjectivities in the 1990s. On the one hand, the *content* of this recognition reveals that the subject pronounced dead in the 1960s was a particular one that only pretended to be universal, only presumed to speak for everyone else. On the other hand, the *context* of this recognition, brazenly defined by George Bush as the New World Order, suggests that these different subjectivities must be seen in relation to the dynamic of capital, its reification and fragmentation of fixed positions. Thus, if we celebrate hybridity and heterogeneity, we must remember that they are also privileged terms of advanced capitalism, that social multiculturalism coexists with economic multinationalism. In the New World Order difference is an object of consumption too, as mega-corporations like Coca-Cola (We are the World) and Benetton (United Colors) know well.[14]

Such a vision does not totalize, for no order, capitalist or otherwise, can control all the forces that it releases. Rather, as Marx and Foucault variously suggest, a regime of power also prepares its resistance, calls it into being, in ways that cannot always be recouped. This is true too of the release of different subjectivities, sexual and ethnic, in the New World Order. Yet these forces need not be articulated progressively, and they may provoke reactive, even atavistic responses—though to blame these forces for such reactions is truly to blame the victims (an ethical position that, perversely, reactionary figures want to arrogate as well).

VISIONS OF THE OTHER

Let me shift now to the second discourse that may register the never-complete passage to the postmodern: the discourse on the cultural other. Here again I will highlight only three moments. The first, the middle 1930s in Western Europe, can be illuminated by a stark juxtaposition. In 1931 a massive exhibition concerning the French colonies was held in Paris, to which the surrealists (represented by Louis Aragon, Paul Eluard, and Yves Tanguy) responded with a little anti-imperialist show titled "The Truth about the Colonies." These artists not only appreciated tribal art for its formal and expressive values, as cubists and expressionists had done before them; they also attended to its political ramifications in the present. Indeed, they constructed a chiasmic identification with the modern legatees of this art who were made to disappear in its Western appropriation. On the one hand, the surrealists argued that these oppressed colonials were like exploited workers in the West, to be supported in similar ways (a placard at the show quoted Marx: "a people that oppresses others does not know to be free"). On the other hand, the surrealists announced that they too were primitives, that, as moderns given over to object desire, they too were fetishists (one exhibit of folkloric figurines was labeled "European fetishes"). In effect, they transvalued the revaluation of fetishism performed in the analyses of commodity and sexual fetishisms. If Marx and Freud used the perversion as a critique of modern European subjects, the surrealists took it as a compliment: they embraced the alterity of the fetishist for its disruptive potential, again through an association of the cultural other and the unconscious. (In this regard the surrealist subject is other to the fascistic subject as imagined by Lacan.)[15]

Yet, as noted in chapter 6, this association remained primitivist: that is, it depended on a racialist analogy between "primitive" peoples and primal stages of psychosexual life.[16] And it served a disastrous purpose in the very different cultural politics of the Nazis. By 1937 the Nazis had produced the infamous exhibitions on "degenerate" art, literature, and music that condemned all modernisms—but especially ones that connected the cultural other and the unconscious, here the arts of "the primitive," the child, and the insane, in order to deploy the disruptive alterity of these alien figures. An ideal to the surrealists, this primitivist fantasm threatened the Nazi subject, who also associated it with Jews and Communists, for this fantasm represented the degenerate forces that endangered its armored identity—again, both from within and from without. Thus, if the surrealists embraced the primitive, the fascists abjected it, aggressed against it. For the surrealists the primitive could not be close enough; for the fascists it was always too close. In the middle 1930s, then, a time of reaction at home and revolt in the colonies, the question of the other for the European, on the left as well as on the right, was one of *correct distance*.

I borrow this ambiguous term (with its hint of disdain) from the cultural critic Catherine Clément, who notes that, at the very moment that Lacan delivered the paper on the mirror stage near Nazi Germany, Lévi-Strauss was in the Amazon at work on "the ethnological equivalent of the mirror stage": "In both cases the question involved is one of correct distance."[17] What this means in the case of Lacan is fairly clear, for the mirror stage concerns the negotiation of a proper distance between the fledgling ego and its image as well as between the infant and its caretaker. Yet what might it mean for Lévi-Strauss? A first response is also fairly clear: it too concerns the negotiation of a proper distance, here a triangulation among the anthropological participant-observer, the home culture, and the culture of study.[18] But what might correct distance mean specifically for Lévi-Strauss in the middle 1930s, a friend (like Lacan) of the surrealists, a Jew who departed Europe on the verge of fascism? For this anthropologist, who has done much to critique the category of race, to reenvision "the savage mind" as logical and the modern mind as mythical, the fascist extreme of disidentification from the other was disastrous, but the surrealist tendency to over-identification might also be dangerous. For while the first destroyed difference brutally, the second was perhaps too eager to appropriate difference, to assume it, to become it somehow. A certain distance from the other was necessary. (Did Lévi-Strauss sense this danger not only in the psychological primitivisms of surrealist art, but also in the anthropological experiments of the Collège de Sociologie?)[19]

Twenty years later, with the publication of *Tristes Tropiques* (1955), his memoir of the time, Lévi-Strauss reframed this question of correct distance. The primary threat to the other was no longer from fascism but from "monoculture," that is, from the encroachment of the capitalist West on the rest of the world. (At one point he envisions entire Polynesian islands turned into aircraft carriers, and whole areas of Asia and Africa become dingy suburbs and shantytowns.)[20] This fatalistic vision of an exotic world on the wane, which locates its authenticity in a precontact past, is problematic, especially as this remorse about

Pamphlet for "Degenerate 'Art,'" Nazi exhibition of modernist art, 1937, with *The New Man* (1912) by Otto Freundlich on the cover.

the pure other lost over there can flip into a reaction against the dirty other found right here.[21] Yet it is consistent with the liberal discussion of the cultural other into the 1960s and beyond.

No doubt amid the liberation wars from Algeria to Vietnam, this discussion was a cruel farce to this other, belated in its concern after decades of colonialist violence. How could one speak, Frantz Fanon might ask, of correct distance when this violence was inscribed on the bodies and psyches of colonized and colonizer alike? Yet correct distance does concern Fanon in a text like "On National Culture," first delivered to the second Congress of Black Writers and Artists in Rome in 1959.[22] There, again in a rewriting of the master-slave dialectic, he distinguishes three phases in the renewal of national cultures. The first occurs when the native intellectual assimilates the culture of the colonial power. The second begins when this intellectual is called back to native traditions, which he or she tends to treat exotically (socially removed as he or she often is), as so many "mummified fragments" of a folklorish past. Finally, the third begins when this intellectual, now a participant in a popular struggle, helps to forge a new national identity in active resistance to the colonial power and in a contemporary recoding of the native traditions. Here, too, the question is one of correct distance, but it is reversed, asked by the other: how to negotiate a distance not only from the colonial power but from the nativist past? How to renew a national culture that is neither neocolonial nor auto-primitivist? How to leave behind "the obscene narcissism" of Europe "where they are never done talking of Man" and not fall into the triumphal separatism of racialist reaction?[23]

What has happened to this problematic of distance since then? To call our own world postcolonial is to mask the persistence of colonial and neocolonial relations; it is also to ignore that, just as there was always a first world in every third world, there was always a third world in every first world.[24] Yet the *recognition* of this lack of distance is postcolonial, indeed postmodern, at least to the degree that the modern world was often imagined in terms of spatial oppositions not only of culture and nature, city and country, but also of metropolitan core and imperial periphery, the West and the Rest. Today, at least in economies retooled as post-Fordist, these spaces do not orient much, and these poles have imploded somewhat—which is not to say that power hierarchies have folded, only that they are transformed. However, for my analysis here the question is: how are these worldly shifts registered in recent theory? Derridean deconstruction is pledged to the undoing of such oppositions as they inform Western thought, and Foucauldean archaeology is founded on the refusal of such foundations. Do these poststructuralisms elaborate the events of the postcolonial and the postmodern critically? Or do they serve as ruses whereby these events are sublimated, displaced, or otherwise defused? Or do they somehow do both?

In the modern world the cultural other, confronted in the course of empire, provoked a crisis in Western identity, which some avant-gardes addressed through the symbolic construct of primitivism, the fetishistic recognition-and-disavowal of this otherness. But this resolution was also a repression, and the other has returned at the very moment of its supposed eclipse: delayed by the moderns, its return has become the postmodern event. In a sense the modern incorporation of this otherness allowed for its postmodern eruption as *difference*. This may be what poststructuralism thinks, between the lines, as when Derrida proclaims the end of any "original or transcendental signified . . . outside a system of differences."[25] Yet this address remained precisely between the lines: for the most part poststructuralism failed to answer the Fanonian demand for recognition, and it continued to project the other as an outside, as a space of ideological escape from Western rationality. Thus all the epistemological exoticisms—neo-orientalist oases and neo-primitivist resorts—that appear in the poststructuralist landscape: the Chinese script in Derrida that "interrupts" Western logocentrism, the Chinese encyclopedia in Foucault that confounds the Western order of things, the Chinese women that lure Kristeva with alternative identifications, the Japan of Barthes that represents "the possibility of a difference, of a mutation, of a revolution in the propriety of symbolic systems,"[26] the other space of nomadism that for Deleuze and Guattari cuts across capitalist territoriality, the other society of symbolic exchange that for Baudrillard haunts our own order of commodity exchange, and so on. Yet if poststructuralism did not find a correct distance, at least it problematized the positing of difference as opposition, the opposing of inside to outside, subject to other. This critique

———

is extended in postcolonial discourse as well as in gay and lesbian studies, and poststructuralism has proved most productive there over the last decade (the work of Homi Bhabha on the deferral of modernity beyond the West is especially pertinent to my discussion).[27] In this regard poststructuralism cannot be dismissed as the latest proper name of the West any more than postmodernism can be.

FANTASIES OF TECHNOLOGY

I turn finally to the third discourse, the impact of technology on Western culture as thought in the middle 1930s, 1960s, and 1990s, and here again I will argue that, even as one moment leads to the next, this next comprehends the one before. Thus what Guy Debord sees in the spectacle of the 1960s are the technological transformations that Walter Benjamin anticipated in the 1930s; and what cyberpunk writers extrapolate in the 1990s are the cybernetic extensions that Marshall McLuhan predicted in the 1960s. In the discourse on technology the terms attached to these moments project an ideological totality: the age of mechanical reproduction in the 1930s, the age of cybernetic revolution in the 1960s, and the age of technoscience or technoculture in the 1990s (in which research and development, or culture and technology, cannot be separated). The same is true of the narratives that attend these terms, as in the supposed passage from an industrial or Fordist society to a postindustrial or post-Fordist one. For I agree with Mandel that the postindustrial signals not the supercession of industrialization so much as its extension, and I agree with Jameson that the postmodern announces not the end of modernization so much as its apogee.[28] Here, however, I will stay with the ideologeme of distance raised in the discourse on the cultural other, for it is central to the discourse on technology as well.

At the moment of "The Work of Art in the Age of Mechanical Reproduction" (1935–36) mechanical reproduction was a cultural dominant; indeed, given that radio was pervasive, sound film ascendant, and television conceived, "technical reproducibility" is the more accurate term (for the translation of the

———

title as well).[29] In this essay Benjamin argues that such reproducibility withers the aura of art, its uniqueness, authenticity, authority, *distance,* and that this withering "emancipates" art from its ritualistic bases, "brings things 'closer'" to the masses.[30] For Benjamin this eclipse of distance has liberatory potential, as it allows culture to become more collective. But it also has ideological potential, as it permits politics to become more spectacular. Socialism or fascism? Benjamin asks in the most dramatic ultimatum in modernist criticism. Yet by 1936 this alternative could not hold, that is, if the socialist referent includes the Soviet Union of Stalin, who had condemned avant-garde culture four years before and would conspire with Hitler (in the Nazi-Soviet nonaggression pact) three years later. In short, by 1936 the aestheticization of politics had overtaken the politicization of art. In 1944, in *Dialectic of Enlightenment,* Theodor Adorno and Max Horkheimer linked the total culture of Nazi Germany to the culture industry of the United States. And in 1967, in *The Society of the Spectacle,* Debord argued that the spectacle dominated the consumerist West. Finally, in 1988, in *Comments on the Society of the Spectacle,* published a year before the fall of the Berlin Wall, he pronounced the spectacle integrated West and East.

In Benjamin the withering of aura, the loss of distance, impacts on the body as well as on the image: the two cannot be separated. Here he makes a double analogy between the painter and the magician, and the cameraman and the surgeon: whereas the first two maintain a "natural distance" from the motif to paint or the body to heal, the second two "penetrate deeply into its web."[31] The new visual technologies are "surgical": they reveal the world in new representations, shock the observer into new perceptions. For Benjamin this "optical unconscious" renders the subject both more critical *and* more distracted (such is his great hope for cinema), and he insists on this paradox as a dialectic. Yet here again this dialectic was difficult to maintain. Already in 1931 Ernst Jünger had argued that technology was "intertwined with our nerves" in a way that subsumed criticality and distraction within "a second, colder consciousness."[32] And not much later, in 1947, Heidegger announced that distance and closeness were folded into "a uniformity in which everything is neither far nor near."[33]

By the middle 1960s the Benjaminian dialectic had split in such discourses on technology as Debord on spectacle and McLuhan on media. Implicitly, whereas Debord develops Benjamin on the image, McLuhan elaborates Benjamin on the body. However, both regard critical distance as doomed. For Debord spectacle subsumes criticality under distraction, and the dialectic of distance and closeness becomes an opposition of real separations concealed by imaginary unities (the modern myths according to Barthes: utopian images of the commodity, the middle class, the nation and so on).[34] On the one hand, external distance is eliminated in spectacle, as peripheral spectators are connected to central images. On the other hand, external distance is reproduced as internal distance, for this very connection to central images separates spectators serially—leaves them alone in spectacular fantasy.[35] This serial separation underwrites all the social separations of class, race, and gender (Debord is concerned only with the first).

Out of similar symptoms McLuhan arrives at a different diagnosis. As in the spectacle of Debord, so in "the global village" of McLuhan: distance, spatial as well as critical, is eclipsed. But rather than separation, McLuhan sees "retribalization," and rather than criticality lost, he sees distraction transvalued.[36] Oblivious to Benjamin, McLuhan develops related ideas, often only to invert them. For McLuhan new technologies do not penetrate the body "surgically" so much as they extend it "electrically." Yet like Benjamin he sees this operation as double: technology is both an excessive stimulus, a shock to the body, *and* a protective shield against such stimulus-shock, with the stimulus converted into the shield (which then invites more stimulus, and so on). Conceived by Freud in *Beyond the Pleasure Principle* (1920), this screening of shock is crucial to the Benjaminian dialectic of criticality and distraction. But in McLuhan this dialectic flies apart into an opposition impossible to reconcile. "We have put our central nervous systems outside us in electric technology," he remarks more than once.[37] Yet sometimes McLuhan sees this extension as an ecstatic body become electric, wired to the world, and sometimes as a "suicidal auto-amputation, as if the central nervous system could no longer depend on the physical organs to be protective buffers against the slings and arrows of outrageous mechanism."[38]

With these contradictory tropes of extension and amputation, McLuhan remains within *the logic of technology as prosthesis*—as a divine supplement to the body that threatens a demonic mutilation, or a glorious phallicization of the body that presupposes an horrific castration.[39] Operative in different modernisms, this logic presumes both a male body and a split subject, a subject in lack (indeed, in McLuhan the subject remains a Hamlet wounded by slings and arrows). The question here becomes: have we exceeded this logic today? The feminist model of the cyborg advanced by Donna Haraway attests that the interface of human and machine need not be imagined in terms of castration fears and fetish fantasies. "The cyborg is a creature in a postgender world," Haraway writes in "A Manifesto for Cyborgs" (1985), and it lives the human-machine interface as a condition of "fruitful couplings" rather than as a trauma of lost unity and present splitting.[40] But the question for the cyborg is: what remains of subjectivity, at least as defined by psychoanalysis? The marvelous cyborg is no less mythical than the Oedipal subject, and at least the Oedipal subject *is* a subject—a construct that helps one to understand fears and fantasies regarding technology (among other things).[41] These fears and fantasies have not diminished; on the contrary, they have become more extreme, *more effective,* in proportion to the dis/connection advanced in the logic of the prosthesis. Is our media world one of generous interaction, as benign as an ATM withdrawal or an Internet inquiry, or one of invasive discipline, each of us a "dividual" electronically tracked, genetically traced, not as a policy of a maleficent Big Brother but as a matter of quotidian administration?[42] Is our media world one of a cyberspace that renders bodies immaterial, or one in which bodies, not transcended at all, are marked, often violently, according to racial, sexual, and social differences?[43] Clearly it is both at once, and *this new intensity of dis/connection is postmodern.*

I can convey this postmodern dis/connection only anecdotally. With the sacrificed students in Beijing and the racial riots in Los Angeles, the murderous war in the Persian Gulf and the ethnic bloodbath in Bosnia, the bombing in Oklahoma City and the trial of O. J. Simpson, we have become *wired* to spectacular events. This wiring connects and disconnects us simultaneously, renders us both psychotechnologically immediate to events and geopolitically remote from them; in this way it subsumes both the imaginary effects of spectacle in Debord and the nervous networking of media in McLuhan. Such dis/connection is hardly new (think of the Kennedy assassinations, the Munich Terror Olympics, the Challenger explosion), but it has reached a new level of oxymoronic pain-and-pleasure. Such was the CNN Effect of the Gulf War for me: repelled by the politics, I was riveted by the images, by a psycho-techno-thrill that locked me in, as smart bomb and spectator are locked in as one. A thrill of techno-mastery (my mere human perception become a super machine vision, able to see what it destroys and to destroy what it sees), but also a thrill of an imaginary dispersal of my own body, of my own subjecthood.[44] Of course, when the screens of the smart bombs went dark, *my* body did not explode. On the contrary, it was bolstered: in a classic fascistic trope, my body, my subjecthood, was affirmed in the destruction of other bodies. In this techno-sublime, then, there is a partial return of a fascistic subjecthood, which occurs at the level of the mass too, for such events are massively mediated, and they produce a psychic collectivity—a psychic nation, as it were, that is also defined against cultural otherness both within and without.[45]

Questions of Distance

These are only some of the splittings that occur with a new intensity today: a spatiotemporal splitting, the paradox of immediacy produced through mediation; a moral splitting, the paradox of disgust undercut by fascination, or of sympathy undercut by sadism; and a splitting of the body image, the ecstasy of dispersal rescued by armoring, or the fantasy of disembodiment dispelled by abjection. If a postmodern subject can be posited at all, it is made and unmade in such splittings. Is it any wonder that this subject is often dysfunctional, suspended between obscene proximity and spectacular separation? Is it any wonder that when it does function it is often on automatic, given over to fetishistic responses, to partial recognitions syncopated with complete disavowals: I know about AIDS, but I cannot get it; I know sexists and racists, but I am not one; I know what the New World Order is, but my paranoia embraces it anyway. (Incidentally, paranoia informs all three discourses at issue here across all three moments—the middle 1930s, 1960s, and 1990s. Indeed, it might be the concept to connect them most effectively—if that is not too paranoid a claim!)[46]

As we saw in chapter 4, this fetishistic structure of recognition-and-disavowal (*I know but nevertheless*) is typical of cynical reason. Cynical reason does not cancel so much as relinquish agency—as if agency were a small price to pay for the shield that cynicism might provide, for the immunity that ambivalence might secure. Yet this is not a necessary condition, and the splittings of the subject need not render one politically dysfunctional. Consider again such spectacles of the last decade as the Clarence Thomas hearing, the Rodney King case, and the Simpson trial. These dramas involved extreme violations and difficult contradictions of difference—racial, sexual, and social. As such they were events of deep divisions, but they were also events around which impossible identifications became possible. Of course nothing guarantees these identifications: they can be negative, politically reactionary and socially destructive (in the 1990s rightist disidentifications have overwhelmed leftist overidentifications). Here too we confront the question of correct distance.

In different ways this question is the very riddle of the subject regarding its body image, its cultural others, and its technological prostheses. It is also the very riddle of the subject regarding its critical theory, which is usually thought to depend on an intellectual distance from its object. As we have seen in modernist and postmodernist narratives alike, this distance is often presented as lost or doomed. In *One-Way Street* (1928) Benjamin offers one version of this eclipse under the sign "This Space for Rent":

> Fools lament the decay of criticism. For its day is long past. Criticism is a matter of correct distancing. It was at home in a world where perspectives and prospects counted and where it was still possible to take a standpoint. Now things press too closely on human society.[47]

This is the topos of the loss of auratic distance developed in the Artwork essay (1935–36), for Benjamin locates this pressing in advertisements and films, which "abolish the space where contemplation moved."[48] Significant for me is the *visuality* of this problematic. In the Artwork essay Benjamin borrows an important opposition in art history between the optical and the tactile (developed by Alois Riegl in *The Late Roman Art Industry* [1901] and other works).[49] In Benjamin the value of these two terms is not fixed: in *One-Way Street* the tactile presses out critical distance, while in the Artwork essay the critical is reinvented in terms of tactile shock (both dada and cinema possess "a tacile quality" that "hits the spectator like a bullet").[50] Benjamin is no less ambivalent about the related value of distance: *One-Way Street* laments its loss, while the Artwork essay welcomes it. Yet, again, what interests me is the notion that "perspectives and prospects" underwrite critical distance.

This notion recalls a central text in art history, *Studies in Iconology* (1939), published by Erwin Panofsky three years after the Artwork essay. In his introduction Panofsky is concerned with the foundational question of the discipline, the renaissance of classical antiquity, and he too posits correct perspective as the precondition of critical history:

> For the medieval mind, classical antiquity was too far removed and at the same time too strongly present to be conceived as an historical phenomenon. . . . Just as it was impossible for the Middle Ages to elaborate the modern system of perspective, which is based on the realization of a fixed distance between the eye and the object, and thus enables the artist to build up comprehensive and consistent images of visible things; just as impossible was it for them to evolve the modern idea of history, which is based on the realization of an intellectual distance between the present and the past, and thus enables the scholar to build up comprehensive and consistent concepts of bygone periods.[51]

Too far, too close; the imperative of proper perspective; the analogy between pictorial and spatial constructs: Benjamin rejects this epistemology as historicist a year later in "Theses on the Philosophy of History" (1940).[52] One can justify Panofsky: he offered a different (almost Benjaminian) rendering of perspective fifteen years before in *Perspective as Symbolic Form* (1924–25); he is concerned here with a pedagogical methodology capable of academic confirmation and replication; and so on. Nevertheless, he does present perspective as a true seeing, and he does figure history as a scientific retrospect.

Today this epistemology is impossible to retain, but the questions of correct distance and critical history have hardly disappeared. This book began with a question about critical history: what allows for a critical recovery of a past practice? How can we understand the insistence of these historical returns? Panofsky answered with "an intellectual distance between the present and the past." I have advanced a model of deferred action, a relay of anticipation and reconstruction. This book concludes here with a question about correct distance. Panofsky responded with a claim of perspectival truth. I have advanced a model of parallactic framing that attempts to keep our present projections in view as well. "A historian who takes this as his point of departure stops telling the sequence of events like the beads of a rosary," Benjamin wrote at the end of his life. "Instead, he grasps the constellation which his own era has formed with a definite earlier one."[53]

Critical distance cannot be foregone *and* it must be rethought; it does little good to lament or to celebrate its putative passing. Often the lamenters project a mythical moment of true criticality, while the celebrants see critical distance as instrumental mastery in disguise.[54] However, this suspicion of distance does touch critical theory at a sensitive point, which is the relation between critical distance and social distinction.[55] In *The Genealogy of Morals* (1887) Nietzsche intimates that two contrary impulses are at work in all critical judgment: a "noble" will to distinction or a "base" reflex of resentment. At one point he asserts that the difference between the noble and the base (in ethical-political terms) depends on the distance between the high and the low (in social-spatial terms): "It was only this *pathos of distance* that authorized them [the noble] to create values and name them—what was utility to them?"[56] In effect, Nietzsche poses the question of whether criticism can ever be free of distinctions on the noble side and resentments on the base side.[57]

———

Etymologically, to criticize is to judge or to decide, and I doubt if any artist, critic, theorist, or historian can ever escape value judgments. We can, however, make value judgments that, in Nietzschean terms, are not only reactive but active—and, in non-Nietzschean terms, not only distinctive but useful. Otherwise critical theory may come to deserve the bad name with which it is often branded today.

NOTES

INTRODUCTION

1

See Alois Riegl, "Late Roman or Oriental?" (1902) in Gert Schiff, ed., *German Essays on Art History* (New York: Continuum, 1988), 187; and Heinrich Wölfflin, *Principles of Art History: The Problem of the Development of Style in Later Art* (1915), trans. M. D. Hottinger (New York: Dover, 1950), 234.

2

Clement Greenberg, "Modernist Painting," *Art and Literature* (Spring 1965; original version 1961), 199; and Michael Fried, *Three American Painters: Kenneth Noland, Jules Olitski, Frank Stella* (Cambridge: Fogg Art Museum, 1965), 9.

3

Greenberg, "Modernist Painting," 193, 201.

4

Peter Bürger, *Theory of the Avant-Garde* (1974), trans. Michael Shaw (Minneapolis: University of Minnesota Press, 1984), 64. I discuss his influential thesis in chapters 1 and 2.

5

This ethnographic dimension is not new to art history; it runs throughout the writings of Riegl, Aby Warburg, and others, where it is often in tension with the Hegelian imperative of the discipline. This dimension is again pronounced in studies of visual culture (let alone in cultural studies and new historicism); indeed, the presence of "culture" in this rubric suggests that the guardian discourse of this emergent field may be anthropology more than history. On this question see *October* 77 (Summer 1996).

6

The 1960s saw the most important theoretical elaborations of such ruptures, as in the "paradigm shift" advanced by Thomas Kuhn in *The Structure of Scientific Revolutions* (1962) and the "epistemological break" developed by Louis Althusser and Michel Foucault (from Gaston Bachelard and Georges Canguilhem). Some artists and critics aspired to such epistemological reflexivity—to think in terms of paradigms rather than teleologies. Yet artistic innovation and scientific revolution are hardly analogous. And though I refer to shifts and breaks, the transformations traced here are not so abrupt or total. Instead this book attempts a double movement of turns and returns, of genealogies and deferred actions. The Mekons provide the best lyrics for this retroaction: "Your dead are buried ours are reborn/you clean up the ashes we light the fire/they're queuing up to dance on socialism's grave/this is my testimony a dinosaur's confession/how can something really be dead when it hasn't even happened?" ("The Funeral," *The Curse of the Mekons* [U.K.: Blast First/Mute Record Ltd., 1991]).

7

Even resistance to contemporary practices can be productive. Erwin Panofsky wrote brilliantly on perspective and proportion in the early 1920s—precisely when they had become irrelevant to innovative art—and his iconographic model appeared in the 1930s in the face of a modernist abstraction that defied it. Perhaps art history is always late in this way, but it ought not be a place of refuge, of melancholic denial of present loss. Resistance can be productive; blockage is not.

8

I do address feminist art, but not in a separate chapter, because I see its most effective work in relation to a genealogy of other practices—a genealogy that it redirects, to be sure, but immanently, from within. I also do not include separate discussions of conceptual art, process art, performance art, and so on. My primal scene came with minimalism, and I tend to see these practices through its prism.

9

Just as art invokes different critics, so criticism fashions different subjects. (Such self-fashioning is one motif of this book, especially where it addresses critical distance.) Anglo-American formalism is self-aware in this regard, committed as it is to "life as few are inclined to live it: in a state of continuous intellectual and moral alertness" (Fried, *Three American Painters*, 9). As

I note in chapter 2, this model asks that art compel conviction, that it promote a subject at once enlightened and devoted. Other models ask other things of the subject—like critical doubt.

10

This is not a territorial claim; it is only a request that visual culture not be treated as a new colony. Art and literary studies often share models: the notion of the *work* in new criticism, or that of the *text* in postmodernist theory. In chapter 6 I argue an ethnographic turn in art and theory; this is the "cultural" side of the field of visual culture. But there is also a "visual" side, and it is accessed through the *image*. Just as "culture" is governed by anthropological assumptions, so "image" is governed by psychoanalytic projections, and both have licensed work that is less interdisciplinary than nondisciplinary.

11

The alternative call in the academy, an administrative meltdown of disciplines into programs, should also be met with suspicion.

12

See Michael Bérubé, *Public Access: Literary Theory and American Cultural Politics* (New York: Verso, 1994). On the other hand, the rightist reaction has invested art and academy alike with a political prominence that neither has had since the 1960s, and this symbolic significance might be turned to advantage.

13

I address a further reciprocity between leftist provocations and rightist prohibitions in chapter 5. As this work of (dis)articulation proceeds, the neoconservative strategy of the last two decades comes into focus. Its essence is twofold: first, to denounce vanguard and popular cultures as hedonistic, and then to blame this bad culture for the social ravages incurred from a capitalism that *is* hedonistic; second, to celebrate traditional and authoritarian cultures as ethical, and then to use this good culture (of family values and the rest) to buy votes for this rapacious capitalism (that, never mindful of the working class, is evermore heedless of the middle class as well). It is a clever trick, but why do so many people fall for it even as they see through it? This is where the work of (dis)articulation comes into play (let alone the critique of cynical reason).

14

Often speculative, this book retains the influence of near-totalistic accounts of capitalist culture advanced in the Reaganomic 1980s. The limits of these accounts are clear (they allow little agency), but it remains necessary to comprehend this cultural logic nonetheless. Too many critics today make a fetish of historical specificity—as though, once context is tracked down, the contingent truth of a given problem will come out with its hands up.

Parts of chapter 1 have appeared in "What's Neo about the Neo-Avant-Garde?," *October* 70 (Fall 1994); of chapter 2 in "The Crux of Minimalism," in Howard Singerman, ed., *Individuals* (Los Angeles: Museum of Contemporary Art, 1986); of chapter 3 in "Wild Signs," in Andrew Ross, ed., *Universal Abandon? The Politics of Postmodernism* (Minneapolis: University of Minnesota Press, 1989); and of chapter 7 in "Postmodernism in Parallax," *October* 63 (Winter 1993).

1

Who's Afraid of the Neo-Avant-Garde?

1

Peter Bürger poses the question of the neo-avant-garde in *Theory of the Avant-Garde* (1974), more on which below; but Benjamin Buchloh has specified its paradigm repetitions in several texts over the last fifteen years. This chapter is written in dialogue with his criticism, and I try to clarify my debts as well as my differences as I go along.

2

Michel Foucault, *Language, Counter-Memory, Practice,* ed. Donald F. Bouchard (Ithaca: Cornell University Press, 1977), 113–38.

3

Lacan details this connection in "The Agency of the Letter in the Unconscious" (1957), and in "The Meaning of the Phallus" (1958) he deems it fundamental to his return to Freud: "It is on the basis of such a wager—laid down by me as the principle of a commentary of Freud's work which I have been pursuing for seven years—that I have been led to certain conclusions: above all, to argue, as necessary to any articulation of analytic phenomena, for the notion of the signifier, in the sense in which it is opposed to that of the signified in modern linguistic analysis. The latter, born since Freud, could not be taken into account by him, but it is my contention that Freud's discovery stands out precisely for having had to anticipate its formulas, even while setting out from a domain in which one could hardly expect to recognise its sway. Conversely, it is Freud's discovery that gives to the opposition of signifier to signified the full weight which it should imply: namely, that the signifier has an active function in determining the effects in which the signifiable appears as submitting to its mark, becoming through that passion the signified" (*Feminine Sexuality,* ed. Juliet Mitchell and Jacqueline Rose [New York: W. W. Norton, 1985], 78).

A similar strategy of historical connection has transformed modernist studies. In a deferred recognition some critics have linked Saussurean linguistics to high-modernist re-formulations of the artistic sign: in primitivist cubism (Yve-Alain Bois, "Kahnweiler's Lesson," *Representations* 18 [Spring 1987]); in cubist collage (Rosalind Krauss, "The Motivation of the Sign," in Lynn Zelevansky, ed., *Picasso and Braque: A Symposium* [New York: Museum of Modern Art, 1992]; in the Duchampian readymade (Benjamin Buchloh in various texts). On another axis T. J. Clark has juxtaposed the fantasmatic figures of the late Cézanne with the sexual theories of the early Freud in "Freud's Cézanne" (*Representations* [Winter 1996]); and in *Compulsive Beauty* (Cambridge: MIT Press, 1993) I connect surrealism with the contemporaneous theory of the death drive.

4

Foucault, "What is an Author?", 135.

5

Of course these discourses are not lost and found, nor did they disappear. There was continuous work on Marx and Freud, just as there was on the historical avant-garde; indeed, continuity with the neo-avant-garde exists in the person of Duchamp alone.

6

See Benjamin Buchloh, "Constructing (the History of) Sculpture," in Serge Guilbaut, ed., *Reconstructing Modernism* (Cambridge: MIT Press, 1989), and my "Some Uses and Abuses of Russian Constructivism," in Richard Andrews, ed., *Art into Life: Russian Constructivism 1914–1932* (New York: Rizzoli, 1990).

7

This trumping, which I discuss further in chapter 2, is not unique to Judd; all minimalists and conceptualists confronted the "painterly peripety" posed by Frank Stella and others (see Benjamin Buchloh, "Formalism and Historicity: Changing Concepts in American and European Art since 1945," in Anne Rorimer, ed., *Europe in the Seventies* [Chicago: Art Institute of Chicago, 1977], 101). Neither is the method of contradictory combination specific to North American art; its master may well be Marcel Broodthaers, who draws on Mallarmé, Duchamp, Magritte, Manzoni, George Segal. . . .

8

Obviously both formulations require qualification. Not all readymades are everyday objects; and though I disagree with aestheticist readings of the readymades, not all are indifferent. As for constructivism, its industrial ambitions were foiled at many levels—materials, training, factory integration, cultural policy.

9

I do not discuss feminist practices specifically, for they postdate the initial neo-avant-garde at issue here. In this moment the Duchampian urinal returned, but mostly for men. In a later moment, however, feminist artists put the readymade device to critical use—a development traced in chapter 2.

10

Theory of the Avant-Garde provoked much debate in Germany, which is resumed in W. M. Lüdke, ed., *"Theorie der Avant-garde." Antworten auf Peter Bürgers Bestimmung von Kunst und bürgerlicher Gesellschaft* (Frankfurt: Suhrkamp Verlag, 1976). Bürger responded in a 1979 essay that introduces the English translation of his book (Minneapolis: University of Minnesota Press, 1984; all subsequent references appear in the text). There are many responses in English; the most pointed one—Benjamin Buchloh, "Theorizing the Avant-Garde," *Art in America* (November 1984)—informs some points I make below.

11

"What makes Bürger so important," Jochen Schulte-Sasse writes in his Foreword to *Theory of the Avant-Garde,* "is that his theory reflects the conditions of its own possibilities" (xxxiv). This is not true of its artistic conditions. As Buchloh notes in his review, Bürger is oblivious to that neo-avant-garde which does what he says it cannot do: develop the critique of the institution of art.

12

On the ramifications of this premise for the formation of art history as a discipline, see M. M. Bahktin/P. M. Medvedev, "The Formal Method in European Art Scholarship," in *The Formal Method in Literary Scholarship* (1928), trans. Albert J. Wehrle (Baltimore: Johns Hopkins University Press, 1978), 41–53.

13

A productivist demand may also be implicit in some readymades, even in the anarchistic formula of the reciprocal readymades: "Use a Rembrandt as an ironing board" (Duchamp, "The Green Box" [1934], in *The Essential Writings of Marcel Duchamp,* ed. Michel Sanouillet and Elmer Peterson [London: Thames & Hudson, 1975], 32). On this point also see chapter 4.

14

Karl Marx, *Grundrisse,* trans. Martin Nicolaus (New York: Vintage Books, 1973), 105.

15

If Hegel and Kant preside over the discipline of art history, one cannot escape historicism by a turn from the former to the latter. Formalism can be historicist too, as in the Greenbergian argument that artistic innovation proceeds through formal self-criticism.

16

Robert Smithson, *The Writings of Robert Smithson,* ed. Nancy Holt (New York: New York University Press, 1979), 216. "A new generation of Dadaists has emerged today," Richard Hamilton wrote in 1961, "but Son of Dada is accepted" ("For the Finest Art, Try Pop," *Gazette,* no. 1 [1961]). In this pop "affirmation" Hamilton registers the shift from the transgression value of the avant-garde *object* to the spectacle value of the neo-avant-garde *celebrity.*

17

On the latter point see Benjamin Buchloh, "Marcel Broodthaers: Allegories of the Avant-Garde," *Artforum* (May 1980): 56.

18

This is similar to the charge made by Greenberg, a great enemy of avant-gardism, against minimalism in particular. See his "Recentness of Sculpture" (1967), in Gregory Battcock, ed., *Minimal Art* (New York: Dutton, 1968). Also see chapter 2.

19

This model of tragedy and farce need not produce posthistorical effects. Moreover, in Marx the first term is ironized, not heroicized, by the second term: the moment of farce tunnels back and digs under the moment of tragedy. In this way the great original—in his case Napoleon, in our case the historical avant-garde—may be undermined. In "'Well Grubbed, Old Mole': Marx, *Hamlet,* and the (Un)fixing of Representation," Peter Stallybrass, to whom I am indebted for this point, comments: "Marx thus pursues a double strategy in *The Eighteenth Brumaire.* Through the first strategy, history is represented as a catastrophic decline from Napoleon to Louis Bonaparte. But in the second strategy, the effect of this 'debased' repetition is to unsettle the status of the origin. Napoleon I can now only be read back through his nephew: his ghost is awakened but as a caricature" (lecture at Cornell University, March 1994). In this way if the evolutionist analogy in Marx is beyond critical salvage, this rhetorical model may not be. On repetition in Marx see Jeffrey Mehlman, *Revolution and Repetition: Marx/Hugo/Balzac* (Berkeley: University of California Press, 1977) as well as Jacques Derrida, *Spectres of Marx* (London: Verso, 1995); on rhetoricity in Marx see Hayden White, *Metahistory* (Baltimore: Johns Hopkins University Press, 1973). On the notion of the posthistorical see

Lutz Niethammer, *Posthistoire: Has History Come to an End?,* trans. Patrick Camiller (London: Verso, 1992).

20

Although no less a projection than the present, this past is obscure: what is this lost object of the melancholic critic? For Bürger it is not the historical avant-garde alone, even though he does castigate it like a melancholic betrayed by a love object. Most critics of modernism and/or postmodernism harbor a lost ideal against which the bad object of the present is judged, and often, as in the Freudian formula of melancholia, this ideal is not quite conscious.

21

Some comparison of Bürger and Buchloh is useful at this point. Buchloh also regards avant-garde practice as punctual and final (e.g., in "Michael Asher and the Conclusion of Modernist Sculpture" he deems traditional sculpture "definitely abolished by 1913" with the Tatlin constructions and the Duchamp readymades [in Chantal Pontbriand, ed., *Performance, Text(e)s & Documents* (Montreal: Parachute, 1981), 56]). Yet he draws an opposite conclusion from Bürger: the avant-garde does not advance arbitrariness but counters it; rather than a relativism of means, it imposes a necessity of analysis, the slackening of which (as in the various *rappels à l'ordre* of the 1920s) threatens to undo modernism as such (see "Figures of Authority, Ciphers of Regression" [*October* 16 (Spring 1981)]). "The meaning of the break in the history of art that the historical avant-garde movements provoked," Bürger writes, "does not consist in the destruction of art as an institution, but in the destruction of the possibility of positing esthetic norms as valid ones" (87). "The conclusion," Buchloh responds in his review, "that, because the one practice that set out to dismantle the institution of art in bourgeois society failed to do so, all practices become equally valid, is not logically compelling at all" (21). For Buchloh this "aesthetic passivism" promotes "a vulgarized notion of postmodernism" even as it condemns it.

   Bürger and Buchloh also agree on the failure of the avant-garde, but not on its ramifications. For Buchloh avant-garde practice addresses social contradictions that it cannot resolve; in this structural sense *it can only fail.* Yet if the work of art can register such contradictions, its very failure is recouped. "The failure of that attempt," Buchloh writes of the welded sculpture of Julio Gonzalez, Picasso, and David Smith, which evokes the contradiction between collective industrial production and individual preindustrial art, "inasmuch as it becomes evident in the work itself, is then the work's *historic and aesthetic* authenticity" ("Michael Asher," 59). According to this same dialectic of failure, Buchloh regards repetition as the authentic appearance of the neo-avant-garde. This dialectic is seductive, but it tends to limit the possibilities of the neo-avant-garde before the fact—a paradox in the work of this important advocate of its practices. Moreover, even if Buchloh (or any of us) gauges these limits precisely, from what purchase does he (do we) do so?

22

Adorno criticizes Benjamin on a related count in his famous response to "The Work of Art in the Age of Mechanical Reproduction": "It would border on anarchism to revoke the reification of a great work of art in the spirit of immediate use values" (letter, March 16, 1936, in *Aesthetics and Politics* [London: New Left Books, 1977], 123). For instances of the dadaist ideology of immediacy see almost any relevant text by Tristan Tzara, Richard Hülsenbeck, etc.

23

Jürgen Habermas, "Modernity—An Incomplete Project," in Hal Foster, ed., *The Anti-Aesthetic: Essays on Postmodern Culture* (Seattle: Bay Press, 1983), 11. A complementary critique argues that the avant-garde *succeeded*—but only at cost to us all; that it penetrated other aspects of social life—but only to desublimate them, to open them up to violent aggressions. For a contemporary version of this Lukàscian critique (which is sometimes difficult to distinguish from the neoconservative condemnation of avant-gardism *tout court*), see Russell A. Berman, *Modern Culture and Critical Theory* (Madison: University of Wisconsin Press, 1989).

24

B. Lindner, "Aufhebung der Kunst in der Lebenspraxis? Über die Aktualität der Auseinandersetzung mit den historischen Avantgardebewegungen," in Lüdke, ed., *Antworten*, 83.

25

Rauschenberg quoted in John Cage, "On Rauschenberg, Artist, and His Work" (1961), in *Silence* (Middletown: Wesleyan University Press, 1969), 105.

26

See Allan Kaprow, *Assemblages, Environments and Happenings* (New York: Abrams, 1966). The first serious intimation of postmodernism in art draws on this avant-garde project to challenge the modernism advanced by Greenberg. In "Other Criteria" (1968/1972) Leo Steinberg plays on the classic definition of modernist self-criticism: rather than define its medium in order to "entrench it more firmly in its area of competence" (Greenberg in "Modernist Painting" [1961/1965]), Steinberg calls on art to "redefine the area of its competence by testing its limits" (*Other Criteria* [London: Oxford University Press, 1972], 77). The dominant axis of much neo-avant-garde art was vertical, traced in time; it researched past practices in order to return them, transformed, to the present. The dominant axis of much contemporary art is

———

horizontal, arrayed across space; it moves from debate to debate as so many sites for work—a reorientation that I discuss in chapter 5.

27

Alexander Rodchenko, "Working with Mayakowsky," in *From Painting to Design: Russian Constructivist Art of the Twenties* (Cologne: Galerie Gmurzyska, 1981), 191. How are we to read the retrospective aspect of this statement? How retroactive is it? For a different account see Buchloh, "The Primary Colors for the Second Time: A Paradigm Repetition of the Neo-Avant-Garde," *October* 37 (Summer 1986): 43–45.

28

But can one distinguish this work from its rejection? It can also be argued that the policy of the Society exhibition—to include all comers in alphabetical order—was more transgressive than *Fountain* (despite the fact that its rejection belied this policy). In any case *Fountain* poses the question of the *unpresentable:* not shown, then lost, later replicated, only to enter the discourse of modern art retroactively as a foundational act. (*Monument to the Third International* is a different instance of a work turned into a fetish that covers its own absence, a process that I think below in terms of trauma.) The unpresentable is its own avant-garde paradigm, indeed its own tradition, from the Salon des Refusés through the Secession movements onward. It should be distinguished from the *unrepresentable,* the modernist concern with the sublime, as well as from the *unexhibited.* This last distinction might point again to the heuristic difference between convention critique and institution critique.

29

The *Musée d'art moderne* of Marcel Broodthaers is a "masterpiece" of this analysis, but let me offer two later examples. In 1979 Michael Asher conceived a project for a group show at the Art Institute of Chicago in which a statue of George Washington (a copy of the celebrated one by Jean Antoine Houdon) was moved from the central front of the museum, where it performed a commemorative and decorative role, to an eighteenth-century period gallery, where its aesthetic and art-historical functions were foregrounded. These functions of the statue became clear in the simple act of its displacement—as did the fact that in neither position did the statue become historical. Here Asher elaborates the readymade paradigm into a situational aesthetics in which certain limitations of the art museum as a place of historical memory are underscored. ("In this work I was the author of the *situation,* not of the elements," Asher comments in *Writings 1973–1983 on Works 1969–1979* [Halifax: The Press of the Nova Scotia College of Art and Design, 1983], 209.)

My other example also elaborates the readymade paradigm but in order to trace extrinsic affiliations. *MetroMobilitan* (1985) by Hans Haacke consists of a miniature facade of the

Metropolitan Museum of Art inset with a statement from the museum to corporations concerning the "many public relations opportunities" of museum sponsorship. It is also decorated with the usual banners, one of which announces a show of ancient treasures from Nigeria. The other banners, however, are not usual: they quote policy statements of Mobil, sponsor of the Nigeria show, about its involvement with the apartheid regime of South Africa. This work makes the co-duplicity of museum and corporation patent, again through the effective use of the assisted readymade.

30

Bürger acknowledges this "false elimination of the distance between art and life" and draws two conclusions: "the contradictoriness of the avant-gardiste undertaking" (50) and the necessity of some autonomy for art (54). Buchloh is more dismissive. "The primary function of the neo-avant-garde," he writes in "Primary Colors," "was not to examine this historical body of aesthetic knowledge [i.e., the paradigm of the monochrome], but to provide models of cultural identity and legitimation for the reconstructed (or newly constituted) liberal bourgeois audience of the postwar period. This audience sought a reconstruction of the avant-garde that would fulfill its own needs, and the demystification of aesthetic practice was certainly not among those needs. Neither was the integration of art into social practice, but rather the opposite: the association of art with spectacle. It is in the spectacle that the neo-avant-garde finds its place as the provider of a mythical semblance of radicality, and it is in the spectacle that it can imbue the repetition of its obsolete modernist strategies with the appearance of credibility" (51). I do not question the truth of this specific statement (made in relation to Yves Klein) so much as its finality as a general pronouncement upon the neo-avant-garde.

31

Obviously this singling out is artificial: Rauschenberg cannot be detached from a Cage milieu any more than Kaprow can be dissociated from a Fluxus ethos, and Broodthaers and Buren emerge in spaces vectored by different artistic and theoretical forces. Other historical examples would also generate other theoretical emphases.

32

Again Buchloh has led the way: "I want to argue, against Bürger, that the positing of a moment of historical originality in the relationship between the historical avant-garde and the neo-avant-garde does not allow for an adequate understanding of the complexity of that relationship, for we are confronted here with practices of repetition that cannot be discussed in terms of influences, imitation, and authenticity alone. A model of repetition that might better describe this relationship is the Freudian concept of repetition that originates in repression and disavowal" ("Primary Colors," 43).

33

I return to this strategy in chapters 4 and 5. In paired poems in *Pense-Bête* (1963–64), "La Moule" and "La Méduse", Broodthaers offers two complementary totems of this tactic. The first, on the mussel, reads: "This clever thing has avoided society's mold./ She's cast herself in her very own./ Other look-alikes share with her the anti-sea./ She's perfect." And the second, on the jellyfish: "It's perfect/ No mold/ Nothing but body" (translated by Paul Schmidt in *October* 42). Also see Buchloh, "Marcel Broodthaers: Allegories of the Avant-Garde," where he notes that Broodthaers was influenced by Lucien Goldmann, who in turn studied with Georg Lukács, the great theorist of reification. Broodthaers was also influenced along these lines by Manzoni.

34

Benjamin Buchloh, "Conceptual Art 1962–1969," *October* 55 (Winter 1990): 137–38. As Buchloh remarks, Buren directs his critique less at Duchamp than at his neo-avant-garde disciples (the phrase "petit-bourgeois anarchist radicality" is Buchloh's). But, as we will see, Buren is not immune to this charge either. Moreover, as his stripes are now his signature, it could be argued that they reinforce more than expose these parameters.

35

Again, one might note here the concomitant shift to a horizontal, synchronic, social axis of operation.

36

Daniel Buren, as quoted in Lucy Lippard, *Six Years: The Dematerialization of the Art Object from 1966 to 1972* (New York: Praeger, 1973), 41.

37

Daniel Buren, "The Function of the Studio," *October* 10 (Fall 1979): 58; and *Reboundings*, trans. Philippe Hunt (Brussels: Daled & Gevaert, 1977), 73. This language informs influential theory of the time too, as in this trumping of ideology critique by Barthes, also in 1971: "It is no longer the myths which need to be unmasked (the doxa now takes care of that), it is the sign itself which must be shaken" ("Change the Object Itself," in *Image-Music-Text,* trans. Stephen Heath [New York: Hill and Wang, 1977], 167). How are we to relate institution critique in art and theory to other political forms of intervention and occupation around 1968? For me this question is riddled by a photo-document of an April 1968 project by Buren, which consisted of two hundred striped panels posted around Paris—to test the legibility of painting beyond the limits of the museum. In this one instance the panel is posted over various advertisements on a bright orange billboard, but it also obscures a handwritten announcement of a student meeting at Vincennes (again, this is April 1968). Was the placement inadvertent? How are we to mediate these image-events?

38

I practice this continuation of the subject by other means in chapter 7; both here and there it is meant only as a model. In part this turn is driven by the need to think the atavistic aspects of contemporary nationalisms and neofascisms in a psychoanalytic frame (the work of Mikkel Borch-Jacobsen on identification and Slavoj Žižek on fantasy is important in this regard). It is also driven by the sense of a traumatic core in historical experience. This application has dangers, such as an invitation to immediate identification with the traumatized victim—a point at which popular culture and academic vanguard converge (sometimes the model of both seems to be *Oprah,* and the motto "Enjoy your symptom!"). Today innovative work in the humanities appears reconfigured less as cultural studies than as *trauma studies.* Repressed by various poststructuralisms, the real has returned, but as the traumatic real—a problem that I take up in chapter 5.

39

Jean Laplanche, *New Foundations of Psychanalysis,* trans. David Macey (London: Basil Black-well, 1989), 88. Also see his *Seduction, Translation, the Drives,* ed. John Fletcher and Martin Stanton (London: Institute for Contemporary Art, 1992).

40

The classic discussion of deferred action occurs in the Wolf-Man case history, "From the History of an Infantile Neurosis" (1914/1918). Above I said "comprehended" rather than "constituted," but the two processes are imbricated, especially in my analogy if the avant-garde artist-critic assumes the position of both analyst and analysand. This slippage between comprehended and constituted is not only my vacillation; it operates in the concept of deferred action, where the traumatic scene is ambiguous: is it actual, fantasmatic, and/or analytically constructed?

There are other problems with my model (besides the very problem of analogy). This deferral might not comprehend other delays and differences across other cultural space-times. So, too, even as it complicates the canonical avant-garde, it might obscure other innovative practices. It might also retain a normative logic whereby the good neo-avant-garde, like the good subject, is a self-aware one that recognizes repression and works through trauma.

41

T. J. Clark pointed to this need over twenty years ago in *Image of the People* (London: Thames & Hudson, 1973): "As for the public, we could make an analogy with Freudian theory. . . . The public, like the unconscious, is present only where it ceases; yet it determines the structure of private discourse; it is key to what cannot be said, and no subject is more important" (12).

42

"The crucial point here," Žižek writes in his Lacanian gloss, "is the changed status of an event: when it erupts for the first time it is experienced as a contingent trauma, as an intrusion of a certain nonsymbolized Real; only through repetition is this event recognized in its symbolic necessity—it finds its place in the symbolic network; it is realized in the symbolic order" (*The Sublime Object of Ideology* [London: Verso, 1989], 61). In this formulation repetition appears restorative, even redemptive, which is unusual for Žižek, who privileges the intransigence of the traumatic real. Thus formulated in relation to the avant-garde, the discourse of trauma is no great improvement on the old discourse of shock, where repetition is little more than absorption, as here in Bürger: "As a result of repetition, it changes fundamentally: there is such a thing as expected shock. . . . The shock is 'consumed'" (81). The difference between shock and trauma is important to retain; it points to a crucial distinction between modernist and postmodernist discourses.

43

See Žižek, *The Sublime Object of Ideology,* 55. We hardly need another magical key to Duchamp, but it is extraordinary how he built recursion and retroactivity into his art—as if he not only allowed for deferred action but took it as his subject. The language of suspended delays, missed encounters, *infra-mince* causalities, repetition, resistance, and reception, is everywhere in his work, which is, like trauma, like the avant-garde, definitively unfinished but always inscribed. Consider the specifications for the readymades in "The Green Box": "By planning for a moment to come (on such a day, such a date such a minute), 'to *inscribe* a readymade'—The readymade can later be looked for.—(with all kinds of delays). *The important thing then is just* this matter of timing, this snapshot effect, like a speech delivered on no matter what occasion but *at such and such an hour.* It is a kind of rendezvous" (*Essential Writings,* 32).

44

In a sense the very discovery of *Nachträglichkeit* is deferred. However operative in such texts as the Wolf-Man case history, it was left to readers like Lacan and Laplanche to develop its theoretical implications. Moreover, Freud was not aware that his own thought developed in *nachträglich* fashion: e.g., not only the return of trauma in his work but also the double temporality through which trauma is conceived there—the diphastic onset of sexuality, the fear of castration (that requires both a traumatic sighting and a paternal injunction), and so on.

45

In the essay devoted to this notion, perhaps the crucial one in the shift from a structuralist to a poststructuralist problematic, Derrida writes: "*Différance* is neither a *word* nor a *concept*. In it, however, we shall see the juncture—rather than the summation—of what has been most decisively inscribed in the thought of what is conveniently called our 'epoch': the difference of forces in Nietzsche, Saussure's principle of semiological difference, difference as the possibility of [neurone] facilitation, impression and delayed effect in Freud, difference as the irreducibility of the trace of the other in Levinas, and the ontic-ontological difference in Heidegger" (*Speech and Phenomena,* trans. David B. Allison [Evanston: Northwestern University Press, 1973, 130]).

46

Derrida, *Writing and Difference,* trans. Allan Bass (Chicago: University of Chicago Press, 1978), 202, 203.

2

THE CRUX OF MINIMALISM

1

Like 1848 for its subsequent generations, 1968 remains a prime cultural-political stake, and current interest in the art of the 1960s is part of its contestation.

2

The epigraphs of the four sections that follow are drawn from Donald Judd (1 and 3) in Bruce Glaser, "Questions to Stella and Judd," *ArtNews* (September 1966), reprinted in Gregory Battcock, ed., *Minimal Art* (New York: Dutton, 1968), 159, 157; Tony Smith (2) in Samuel Wagstaff, "Talking with Tony Smith," *Artforum* (December 1966): 19; and Gilles Deleuze (4), *Difference and Repetition* (1968), trans. Paul Patton (New York: Columbia University Press, 1994), 293.

3

Donald Judd, "Specific Objects," *Arts Year Book* 8 (1965), reprinted in *Complete Writings* (New York and Halifax: The Press of the Nova Scotia School of Art and Design, 1975), 184. Unless otherwise stated, all subsequent Judd quotations are from this text (181–89).

4

See Rosalind Krauss, "LeWitt in Progress," in *The Originality of the Avant-Garde and Other Modernist Myths* (Cambridge: MIT Press, 1984). Although few critics listened, LeWitt insisted on the illogic of his art in statements like "Sentences on Conceptual Art" (*Art-Language* [May 1969]).

5

Frank Stella in Glaser, "Questions to Stella and Judd," 158.

6

Clement Greenberg, "Recentness of Sculpture," in *American Sculpture of the Sixties* (Los Angeles: Los Angeles County Museum of Art, 1967), reprinted in Battcock, ed., *Minimal Art,* 183. All subsequent Greenberg quotations are from this text (180–86).

7

John Cage, *Silence* (Middleton: Wesleyan University Press, 1961), 76.

8

For example, Yvonne Rainer compared the factory fabrication, unitary forms, and literal aspect of minimalist art to the found movement, equal parts, and tasklike activity of Judson Church dance; see her "A Quasi Survey of Some 'Minimalist' Tendencies in the Quantitatively Minimal Dance Activity Midst the Plethora, or an Analysis of Trio A," in Battcock, ed., *Minimal Art.*

9

Richard Wollheim, "Minimal Art," *Arts* (January 1965), reprinted in Battcock, ed., *Minimal Art,* 399.

10

Judd in Glaser, "Questions to Stella and Judd," reprinted in Battcock, ed., *Minimal Art,* 156. Judd ascribes this a priori quality to European modern art as such, which is typical of the absolutist judgments of the time. This definition also opposes minimalist art to conceptual art in which the system is often a priori. Whether the precedence of the concept devalues the authorial subjectivity of the artist (as LeWitt claims in "Paragraphs on Conceptual Art" [*Artforum,* Summer 1967], "the idea becomes the machine that makes the art") or inflates this subjectivity (as occurs in most idealist versions) is a crucial ambiguity in conceptual art. How it is decided will determine its status in relation to minimalism—whether conceptual art elaborates "the crux of minimalism" or recoups it. But then this ambiguity may be undecidable, and this undecidablity may be fundamental to conceptual art.

11

Among the antecedents of minimalism both positivist and avant-gardist tendencies appear in Johns (a case can be made for Ad Reinhardt as well).

12

See Rosalind Krauss, "Sense and Sensibility—Reflections on Post '60s Sculpture," *Artforum* (November 1973).

13

See Michael Fried, "Art and Objecthood," *Artforum* (June 1967). I discuss this text at length below.

14

Rosalind Krauss, *Passages in Modern Sculpture* (Cambridge: MIT Press, 1977), 292–93. The ultimate move comes with work that follows directly on minimalism, such as Robert Smithson's *Spiral Jetty* (1970), Serra's *Shift* (1970–72), and Bruce Nauman's video *Corridor* (1968–70). In this history Krauss favors sculpture that, like minimalism, is materialist (its meaning opaque, carried on the surface) as opposed to idealist (its meaning transparent to its structure), but this very opposition is idealist.

15

See, for example, "Sculpture in the Expanded Field," *October* 13 (Spring 1979).

16

Krauss, *Passages in Modern Sculpture,* 3–4.

17

The reception of phenomenology was mediated by Maurice Merleau-Ponty, especially his *Phenomenology of Perception,* which was translated in 1962. The reception of structural linguistics was mediated by Claude Lévi-Strauss, Roland Barthes and others, some of whose work was read by some North American artists in the middle 1960s.

18

"Notes on Sculpture, Parts 1 and 2" were published in *Artforum* (February and October 1966); Morris published "Part 3" in *Artforum* (June 1967), the same issue in which "Art and Objecthood" appeared, and "Part 4" appears in his collection *Continuous Project Altered Daily* (Cambridge: MIT Press, 1993). The Morris and Fried texts are reprinted in Battcock, ed., *Minimal Art,* from which the quotations here are drawn.

19

See Greenberg, "'American-Type' Painting" (1955/1958), in *Art and Culture* (Boston: Beacon Press, 1961).

20

Perhaps "interest" does not displace "quality" so much as provide the first term of its normative scheme. In this light Judd ascended to the pantheon of quality, which he defended passionately. (As Howard Singerman suggested to me, Judd implies as much in "A long discussion not about master-pieces but why there are so few of them," *Art in America* [September and October 1984].) Moreover, it was his consistency that allowed minimalism to become a style. Finally, in his obsession with (anti)illusionism he remained bound to painting.

21

The remark is a response to questions about a six-foot steel cube titled *Die* (1962). Morris quotes Smith as follows:

Q: Why didn't you make it larger so that it would loom over the observer?

A: I was not making a monument.

Q: Then why didn't you make it smaller so that the observer could see over the top?

A: I was not making an object.

22

Even late-modernist sculpture such as Anthony Caro's suspends its objecthood, Fried argues, by its emphasis on opticality and "the efficacy of gesture."

23

Tony Smith in Wagstaff, "Talking with Tony Smith," 19. Smith mentions other "abandoned" sites that artists like Smithson soon entered, but one of his examples might qualify the avant-gardist value of this "expanded field": the Nazi drill ground in Nuremberg designed by Albert Speer. In short, on the other side of traditional forms also lies mass spectacle, and the desublimation of these forms can also abet a regression of the subject.

24

This is also the heretical stake of its avant-garde predecessors, with this difference argued in chapter 1: whereas avant-garde artists like Rodchenko mistook the conventionality of art for its end, neo-avant-garde artists like Smith imagined its end in the very limits of its conventionality.

25

In his subsequent historical work, Fried reads these principles into the origins of modern art.

26

For a critique of the notion of presentness see Rosalind Krauss, "The Blink of an Eye," in David Carroll, ed. *The States of "Theory"* (New York: Columbia University Press, 1990). Also see the exchange between Fried and Krauss in Hal Foster, ed., *Discussions in Contemporary Culture* (Seattle: Bay Press, 1987).

27

Ultimately the stake of Anglo-American formalism is the autonomous art object *only to the degree that it supports the autonomous art subject,* defined in aesthetic judgment and refined through aesthetic taste. This ethical imperative is strong in Fried, as manifest in the value of "conviction" and the fear of "corruption." (In this regard "theatre" may represent the threat not only of avant-gardism but of mass culture—its perversion of the moral subject as formed through modernist art. Certainly this is the case for Greenberg in "Modernist Painting.") In *Three American Painters: Kenneth Noland, Jules Olitski, Frank Stella,* Fried is explicit about the morality of autonomy: "While modernist painting has increasingly divorced itself from the concerns of the society in which it precariously flourishes, the actual dialectic by which it is made has taken on more and more of the denseness, structure and complexity of moral experience—that is, of life itself, but life as few are inclined to live it: in a state of continuous intellectual and moral alertness" ([Cambridge: Fogg Art Museum, 1965], 9). But this autonomy might also be undermined by conviction in this sense: conviction suggests dependence on the art object, indeed devotion to it, which might render the object less a mirror of the subject than a support that the subject requires. In any case the subject presumed by this criticism is quite different from the dominant models of my generation, which insisted not on conviction but on demystification and deconstruction. (On this point see my exchange with Fried in *Discussions in Contemporary Culture* as well as my remarks in chapter 4.)

28

Clement Greenberg, "After Abstract Expressionism," *Art International* (October 25, 1962): 30.

29

For example, minimalism pushes the "empirico-transcendental" analytic of modernist art, its double concern with the material and the spiritual, the immanent and the transcendental, to the point where this analytic is transformed—in the institution critique central to postmodernist art, its creative analysis of the discursive conditions of art. (On the "empirico-transcendental" analytic see Michel Foucault, *The Order of Things* [New York: Vintage Books, 1970], 318–22.)

30

That is, when it did not present the avant-garde as an expression of capitalist freedom—a use discussed by Serge Guilbaut in *How New York Stole the Idea of Modern Art* (Chicago: University of Chicago Press, 1983).

———

31

Another factor in the delayed reception of the historical avant-garde was the immaturity of North American institutions of high art, which had to be established before they could be embattled. In this establishment, however, modernist art was enshrined, and this, along with the wartime presence of European modernists in North America, allowed for a rapid recognition of this art as a discourse, then as an institution, and now as a period.

32

Peter Bürger, *Theory of the Avant-Garde,* trans. Michael Shaw (Minneapolis: University of Minnesota Press, 1984), 53.

33

Ibid., 87. As suggested in chapter 1, Bürger intimates a posthistorical condition—that artists, critics, and historians are now, in a period *after* art, in the position of mere technocratic custodians *of* art. I see very different consequences.

34

See Douglas Crimp, "Pictures," *October* 8 (Spring 1978), and Craig Owens, "Earthwords," *October* 10 (Fall 1979).

35

Fried suggests as much in *Discussions in Contemporary Culture,* 56. The reversal of the opposition of presence and presentness was only one example of failed deconstruction. Another instance crucial to theories of postmodernism was the reversal of the oppositions of aura and reproduction, originality and repetition, developed by Walter Benjamin in "The Work of Art in the Age of Mechanical Reproduction" (1936). Too often this text was taken as a weapon to wither art suspected of aura; hence the attack on the original and the unique and the embrace of the photographic and the textual. Granted, this attack was provoked by a forced resurrection of aura—the various Frankenstein monsters, produced in the laboratory of market and academy, of neo-expressionism, postmodern architecture, art photography, and the like. Nonetheless, the postmodernist reading of Benjamin tended to collapse his dialectic of mechanical reproduction and auratic experience. In so doing it also tended to void the critical potential of each term—as long as they are held in tension.

36

Especially as its signal artists like Judd begin to die. In an excellent new introduction to the Battcock anthology on minimalism (Berkeley: University of California Press, 1995), Anne M. Wagner draws on Foucault to define this status of minimalism: the "privileged region of the archive is neither past nor present: at once close to us, and different from our present existence, it is the border of time that surrounds our presence, which overhangs it, and which indicates it in its otherness; it is that which, outside ourselves, delimits us" (*The Archaeology of Knowledge and the Discourse on Language*, trans. A. M. Sheridan Smith [New York: Harper and Row, 1976], 130). This problematizes the objectivity of the minimalist crux: is it liminal as such—or only for us now?

37

There are also thematic femmings and queerings of minimalism. As represented by the exhibition *Sense and Sensibility*, curated by Lynn Zelevansky at the Museum of Modern Art in 1994, this femmed minimalist art is posed against the psychoanalytic feminist art of the 1970s and 1980s, which it regards as oppressive. There is also a critical version of this position, as represented by Anna C. Chave in "Minimalism and the Rhetoric of Power" (*Arts* [January 1990]), which attacks minimalism for macho iconography. Minimalism worked to avoid the authority of iconographic meaning; it is thus counterproductive to reassert this authority when it is this authority that is in question. Moreover, both reactions—artistic and critical—condemn minimalism in a way that forecloses a historical basis of feminist art. For again, however circumscribed, minimalism did put the question of the subject in play, and in this respect feminist art begins where minimalism ends.

38

The two main positions in independent film in the 1960s—the North American cinema represented by Michael Snow, Hollis Frampton, and Paul Sharits, and the French cinema represented by Jean-Luc Godard—are analogous. To Annette Michelson both respond to the "trauma of dissociation" suffered by cinema in the course of its industrial division of labor and Hollywood separation into genres. While Godard and company collide these genres as readymades in a critical montage, the North American independents refuse them and, in a modernist reflection on the medium, seek to reassert its totality as an art. See Michelson, "Film and the Radical Aspiration," in Gerald Mast and Marshall Cohen, eds., *Film Theory and Criticism* (New York: Oxford University Press, 1974).

39

Fredric Jameson, "Periodizing the 60s," in Sohnya Sayres et al., eds., *The Sixties without Apology* (Minneapolis: University of Minnesota Press, 1984), 195.

40

For an analysis of this ambiguous status of minimalism (which draws on the original version of the present chapter), see Rosalind Krauss, "The Cultural Logic of the Late Capitalist Museum," *October* 54 (Fall 1990).

41

See Krauss, *Passages,* 250.

42

Jean Baudrillard, *For a Critique of the Political Economy of the Sign,* trans. Charles Levin (St. Louis: Telos Press, 1981), 104.

43

Ibid., 109. Baudrillard continues: "It is this serial and differential organization, with its own temporality punctuated by fashion and the recurrence of behavior models, to which art currently testifies." This testimony is ambiguous, but at least seriality is not sublimated in minimalism and pop, as it often is in conceptual art. Here again it is not clear to me whether conceptual art elaborates or recoups the minimalist crux.

44

Paradoxically, this severing is performed in superrealist painting to the degree that its referent is another image, a photograph, more on which in chapter 5.

45

I develop this point further in chapter 4. For a related history of musical paradigms see Jacques Attali, *Noise,* trans. Brian Massumi (Minneapolis: University of Minnesota Press, 1985).

46

Benjamin Buchloh, "Michael Asher and the Conclusion of Modernist Sculpture," in Chantal Pontbriand, ed., *Performance, Text(e)s & Documents* (Montreal: Parachute), 58.

47

Ernest Mandel, *Late Capital* (London: Verso, 1978), 387.

48

Baudrillard: "The sign object is neither given nor exchanged: it is appropriated, withheld and manipulated by individual subjects as a sign, that is, as coded difference. Here lies the object of consumption" (*For a Critique of the Political Economy of the Sign,* 65).

49

Deleuze, *Difference and Repetition,* 293. In Chapter 5 I return to the appearance of "destruction and death," especially in pop.

50

See Jameson, "Periodizing the 60s," for a very impressive attempt.

———

3

The Passion of the Sign

1

This third way is associated with the work of Fredric Jameson. See his *Postmodernism, or the Cultural Logic of Late Capitalism* (Durham: Duke University Press, 1991). I return to these debates in Chapter 7.

2

See my "(Post)Modern Polemics," in *Recodings: Art, Spectacle, Cultural Politics* (Seattle: Bay Press, 1985).

3

See Jameson, *Postmodernism*, 95–96.

4

See Roland Barthes, *S/Z* (New York: Hill and Wang, 1974). My reading of this text is indebted to Dana Polan, "Brief Encounters: Mass Culture and the Evacuation of Sense," in Tania Modleski, ed., *Studies in Entertainment* (Bloomington: Indiana University Press, 1986).

5

Ibid., 40.

6

Jacques Derrida, *Writing and Difference*, trans. Alan Bass (Chicago: University of Chicago Press, 1978), 280.

7

Rosalind Krauss, *The Originality of the Avant-Garde and Other Modernist Myths* (Cambridge: MIT Press, 1984), 34. Also see chapter 1, note 3.

8

Derrida, *Writing and Difference*, 280. "Always already" suggests the complex temporality of deferred action.

9

The shift from index to sign as outlined by Barthes suggests another passage in what Jean-Joseph Goux calls "symbolic economies": a partial shift in the economy of the subject from the classical capitalist regime of *repression* meted out by the phallic power of the father to the advanced-capitalist regime of *investment* in which flows of desires are released in order to be

---

channeled more productively. (See Goux, *Symbolic Economies: After Marx and Freud,* trans. Jennifer Curtiss Gage [Ithaca: Cornell University Press, 1990].) If we relate this shift to the discourse of postmodernism, we can demystify its pervasive ideologeme of *loss*—the loss of historical narratives, political legitimation, artistic mastery, and so on. Not only is this loss registered mostly by authorities of patriarchy, but it is hardly real: it is but a reformation of social regime, a redeployment of productive bodies. As Polan writes: "Power doesn't always take shape as the power of the Symbolic Father, and the overthrow of a centered, authoritative Symbolic may simply mean that other forms of power-relations—often more subtle than the model of feudal power focused on a lordly figure—have come into dominance. Thus, for Goux, the overthrow of the Law of the Father in the overthrow of gold not only brings about the emergence of a free-floating economic sign, but also ties this emergence to the parallel emergence of a new law that finds its force in the transnational monopoly—the new corporation whose micropolitical channels of control are so widespread and dispersed that no single authoritative father-figure is necessary to put the machine in operation" ("Brief Encounters," 177–78). This shift in the orders of subjectivity and power is related to the shift remarked by Derrida from a centered structure to a "system of differences." As Derrida implies, this rupture, produced in monopoly capitalism and registered in high modernism, is still with us, as monopoly capitalism is still with us, now raised to a new level of totality in advanced capitalism. This suggests that his "system of differences" is not without a referent too—the system of advanced capitalism, a centerless system that, if not global as a regime, is nonetheless total as a differential order that governs relations throughout the world market. In this system, with its multinational deployment of capital and its international division of labor, center and periphery are indeed deconstructed.

10

Jean Baudrillard, "The Precession of Simulacra," *Art & Text* 11 (Spring 1983): 28. Capital is sometimes seen by Baudrillard and Jameson as *the* subject of history. This capitalogical view shares in the commodity fetishism (that is, in the endowment of inhuman things with human attributes) that it critiques. Nevertheless, it was very seductive in the middle 1980s (when the original version of this chapter was written).

11

Jameson, "Periodizing the 60s," in *The 60s Without Apology,* ed. Sohnya Sayres et al. (Minneapolis: University of Minnesota Press, 1984), 200.

12

On depicted and literal shape see Michael Fried, "Shape as Form: Frank Stella's New Paintings," *Artforum* (November 1966). As we saw in chapter 2, Fried advocated shape as a means to control the optical illusionism of late-modernist painting, for this illusionism threatened to dissolve the material flatness of the painting. At the same time shape was a way to make literal objecthood over into pictorial form and so to defend painting against the minimalist incursion. Thus Fried also sees a crisis at work in this art, but he frames it in terms very different from mine.

13

As Rosalind Krauss wrote of this work in 1973, "The logic of the deductive structure is . . . shown to be inseparable from the logic of the sign" ("Sense and Sensibility: Reflections on Post '60s Sculpture," *Artforum* [November 1973]: 47). In the star paintings it is also inseparable from the logo of the celebrated Stella.

14

However, in the historical crux of minimalism Stella occupied a crucial position, as both formalists and minimalists claimed him. "In a sense," Fried remarked in retrospect, "Carl Andre and I were fighting for his soul" (in Hal Foster, ed., *Discussions in Contemporary Culture* [Seattle: Bay Press, 1987], 79).

15

In a sense these are old options for the avant-garde in capitalist society. If, as Clement Greenberg remarked in "Avant-Garde and Kitsch" (1939/1961), its task is "to keep culture *moving* in the midst of ideological confusion and violence," some avant-gardes have worked either to resolve this ideological confusion in aesthetic form or to escape it altogether, while others have sought to exploit it for critical purposes. However, in our time these options appear overwhelmed. Indeed, Stella marks a point at which the avant-garde loses its critical purchase on this ideological confusion. In retrospect, however resistant to the commodity status of the art object, the aforementioned strategies of the 1960s and 1970s partake in the passion of the sign under discussion here. They may even prepare the fetishism of the signifier rampant in art and theory in the 1980s (more on which in chapter 4).

16

Krauss, *The Originality of the Avant-Garde*, 196–219. Subsequent references to this essay appear in the text.

17

That Duchamp might preside over indexicality too demonstrates the sheer multivalence of "Duchamp" since the early 1960s at least.

18

For some artists and critics this turn to physical presence marked a *transformation* in art; for others it threatened an *end* to art. As we saw in chapter 2, to submit to mundane presence is, for Michael Fried, to fall from aesthetic grace, and he was not alone in this estimation.

19

Krauss is clear about her focus (which she has held for a long time): "I am not so much concerned here with the genesis of this condition within the arts, its historical process, as I am with its internal structure as one now confronts it in a variety of work" (210).

20

Craig Owens, "Earthwords," *October* 10 (Fall 1979): 120–30.

21

Owens, "The Allegorical Impulse: Toward a Theory of Postmodernism," *October* 12 and 13 (Spring and Summer 1980); reprinted in Brian Wallis, ed., *Art After Modernism: Rethinking Representation* (Boston and New York: David R. Godine/New Museum of Contemporary Art, 1984), 209. Subsequent references to this essay appear in the text.

22

Charles Baudelaire, *The Painter of Modern Life and Other Essays,* trans. Jonathan Mayne (London: Phaidon, 1964), 13.

23

See Thomas Crow, "Modernism and Mass Culture in the Visual Arts," in Benjamin Buchloh, Serge Guilbault, and David Solkin, eds., *Modernism and Modernity* (Halifax: The Press of the Nova Scotia College of Art and Design, 1983), 257. Also see Michael Newman, "Revising Modernism, Representing Postmodernism: Critical Discourses of the Visual Arts," in *Postmodernism,* ICA Documents 5 (London: Institute of Contemporary Art, 1986), 42–45.

24

Walter Benjamin, "Central Park" (1939), *New German Critique* 34 (Winter 1985): 34.

25

Benjamin H.D. Buchloh, "Allegorical Procedures: Appropriation and Montage in Contemporary Art," *Artforum* (September 1982): 44. Subsequent references to this essay appear in the text.

26

See my "The Art of Spectacle" in *Recodings.* As Buchloh noted, even the allegorical aspects of this art, such as its aesthetic contemplation of history and its rhetorical confusion of time and space, "were discussed in 1923 by Georg Lukàcs [in *History and Class Consciousness*] as the essential features of the collective condition of reification" (56), a condition only more intensive in the spectacular world of advanced capitalism.

———

27

See Jean Baudrillard, *For a Critique of the Political Economy of the Sign,* trans. Charles Levin (Saint Louis: Telos Press, 1981), passim. In this account the poststructuralist position that the signified is another signifier may mark a further station in the capitalist passion of the sign. On some of these points see my *Recodings,* 173–75.

28

Benjamin, "Central Park," 52. Baudrillard is critical of conventionalism, yet conventionalist artists like Peter Halley adopted him as a guide—a role Baudrillard politely refused.

29

Roland Barthes, *Mythologies* (New York: Hill and Wang, 1972), 135. Also see my *Recodings,* 166–79.

30

See Douglas Crimp, "Appropriating Appropriation," in Janet Kardon, ed., *Image Scavengers* (Philadelphia: Institute of Contemporary Art, 1983).

31

See Barthes, "Change the Object Itself," in *Image-Music-Text,* trans. Stephen Heath (New York: Hill & Wang, 1977).

32

Baudrillard, *For a Critique of the Political Economy of the Sign,* 92.

4

THE ART OF CYNICAL REASON

1

Ross Bleckner, "Failure, Theft, Love, Plague," in *Philip Taaffe* (New York: Pat Hearn Gallery, 1986), 5.

2

Bleckner, as quoted in Jeanne Siegel, "Geometry Desurfacing," *Arts* (March 1986): 28. Neo-geo might be termed "necro-geo"; indeed, most neo-styles betray a necrophilic aspect. For these zombie movements the first term (expressionism, geometric abstraction, conceptual art, whatever) must die as a practice so that it might be reborn as a sign in the second. This is the opposite of the critical renaissance sketched in chapter 1.

3

David Diao moved to the pathetic within the very terms of neo-geo: through citations of modernist abstraction, he has presented his own painting, in a strange gesture of triumphal resentment, as belated, failed.

4

Taaffe insists that his painting is sublime, but it is ridiculous. The tension between profundity and superficiality is more sustained in Bleckner, but, given his subject matter (e.g., the AIDS crisis), it is also more dangerous. When these poles implode, pathos turns to bathos.

5

See Thomas Lawson, "Last Exit: Painting," *Artforum* (October 1981).

6

Ashley Bickerton, exhibition statement (New York: Cable Art Gallery, 1986).

7

Ibid.

8

Ibid. This question is answered by artists who elaborate institution critique creatively.

9

Bickerton quoted in David Robbins, ed., "From Criticism to Complicity," *Flash Art* 129 (Summer 1986): 46–49.

10

For a related argument regarding fiction see Fredric Jameson, "Beyond the Cave: Demystifying the Ideology of Modernism" (1975), in *The Ideologies of Theory,* vol. 2 (Minneapolis: University of Minnesota Press, 1988).

11

Gilles Deleuze, "Plato and the Simulacrum," trans. Rosalind Krauss, *October* 27 (Winter 1983): 5. This text is an appendix to *The Logic of Sense* (1969), trans. Mark Lester (New York: Columbia University Press, 1990).

12

It might also disturb our basic accounts of postmodernism. The copy produces the original as model: contrary to myriad readings of "The Work of Art in the Age of Mechanical Reproduction," the copy does not trouble originality or authenticity; it defines them as such, even affirms them as values. Benjamin suggests as much: "At the time of its origin a medieval picture of the Madonna could not yet be said to be 'authentic.' It became 'authentic' only during the succeeding centuries and perhaps most strikingly so during the last one" (*Illumina-*

tions, ed. Hannah Arendt, trans. Harry Zohn [New York: Schocken Books, 1968], 243). The simulacrum, on the other hand, does disturb these categories.

13

For a prewar example, surrealism is less a return to representation than a turn to simulation—in this case the simulacral scenes of fantasy. See Michel Foucault, *This is Not a Pipe* (1963), trans. Richard Miller (Berkeley: University of California Press, 1984), and my *Compulsive Beauty* (Cambridge: MIT Press, 1993), 95–98. In chapter 5 I rethink the pop genealogy of simulacral art.

14

Bickerton, exhibition statement (New York: Cable Art Gallery, 1986).

15

The relation among these constructs—surveillance in Foucault, spectacle in Guy Debord, and simulation in Baudrillard—is a complex subject in its own right.

16

Jean Baudrillard, "The Precession of the Simulacra," *Art & Text* 11 (September 1983): 8.

17

See Fredric Jameson, *Postmodernism* (Durham: Duke University Press, 1991), passim.

18

Fredric Jameson, "On Diva," *Social Text* 5 (1982), 118.

19

Of course this difference is also governed by political possibilities: it is one thing for Rodchenko to announce the end of painting in revolutionary Russia, quite another for neo-geo artists in Reaganomic New York. For a different account of ends and endgames in twentieth-century painting, see Yve-Alain Bois, "Painting: The Task of Mourning," in David Joselit and Elisabeth Sussman, ed., *Endgame: Reference and Simulation in Recent Painting and Sculpture* (Boston: Institute of Contemporary Art, 1986).

20

See Clement Greenberg, *Art and Culture* (Boston: Beacon Press, 1961) and Theodor Adorno, letter to Walter Benjamin, March 18, 1936, in Rodney Livingstone et al., eds., *Aesthetics and Politics* (London: New Left Books, 1977), 123.

21

Jean Baudrillard, *For a Critique of the Political Economy of the Sign,* trans. Charles Levin (St. Louis: Telos Press, 1981), 92. Elsewhere Baudrillard argues: "An object is not an object of consumption unless it is released from its psychic determinations as *symbol;* from its functional determinations as *instrument;* from its commercial determinations as *product;* and is thus *liberated as a sign* to be recaptured by the formal logic of fashion, i.e., by the logic of differentiation" (67).

22

I doubt Duchamp intended this last reading. Critics on the left tend to project an almost Brechtian aspect on this dandyish practice (especially in relation to Warhol). For Benjamin on exhibition value see "The Work of Art in the Age of Mechanical Reproduction" (1936), in *Illuminations,* 224–25.

23

Marcel Duchamp, "The Green Box" (1934), in *The Essential Writings of Marcel Duchamp,* ed. Michel Sanouillet and Elmer Peterson (London: Thames and Hudson, 1975), 32. My formulation is indebted to Benjamin Buchloh, "Parody and Appropriation in Francis Picabia, Pop and Sigmar Polke," *Artforum* (March 1982).

24

Benjamin, "The Work of Art in the Age of Mechanical Reproduction," 231.

25

Andy Warhol, *The Philosophy of Andy Warhol* (New York: Harcourt Brace Jovanovich, 1975), 77. I return to this philosophy in chapter 5.

26

Baudrillard argues that modernisms such as the Bauhaus and de Stijl rendered art not more functional as an object but more commutable as a sign—that they advanced a conventionalist equivalence of social signs in the guise of a productivist transformation of art forms (*For a Critique of the Political Economy of the Sign,* 185–203). Yet this economy also provoked a counter-discourse, for such rationalization is never complete—it always leaves a remainder or a repressed. Thus the Bauhausian object calls out for the surrealist object, just as rational design calls out for absurd kitsch. Are these dialectics also collapsed—or at least transformed? Steinbach suggests as much.

27

Walter Benjamin, "Central Park" (1939), *New German Critique* 34 (Winter 1985): 34.

28

Peter Sloterdijk, *Critique of Cynical Reason,* trans. Michael Eldred (Minneapolis: University of Minnesota Press, 1987), 5.

29

Ibid., 5, 118. I return to this armoring through splitting, this immunity of ambivalence, in chapter 7.

———

30

Barbara Kruger, "'Taking' Pictures," *Screen* 23, no. 2 (July–August 1982); 90. Subsequent references in this paragraph are from this source.

31

In another early statement Kruger described this line between critical and cynical reason as "a doubled address, a coupling of the ingratiation of wishful thinking and the criticality of knowing better" ("Pictures and Promises" [New York: The Kitchen, 1981]).

32

Roland Barthes, "Change the Object Itself," in *Image-Music-Text,* trans. Stephen Heath (New York: Hill and Wang, 1977), 166.

33

My purpose is not to correct "politically correct" art, or to complain about a "culture of complaint." These reactions are symptoms of the disease that they presume to cure. On the other hand, *ressentiment* in critique may be irreducible—a problem to which I return in chapter 7.

34

This is evident from a May 1986 discussion among principal practitioners of simulation painting and commodity sculpture (Levine, Halley, Bickerton, Taaffe, Koons, and Steinbach) moderated by Peter Nagy. Titled "From Criticism to Complicity," the text (see note 9) reads as a primer in the aesthetic of cynical reason. First, in its posthistorical attitude, which is the effect of an epistemological skepticism taken to a defeatist extreme: "Along with reality," Halley remarks, "politics is sort of an outdated notion. We are now in a post-political situation." Second, in its move to recoup this epistemological skepticism as an aesthetic advance: if appropriation art was concerned with "the process of the corruption of truth," Bickerton claims, simulation painting and commodity sculpture are interested in "that process of corruption as a poetic form" (or, as he states succinctly in his 1986 exhibition statement, in "epistemology as gimmick"). All that remains is to place the aesthetic of cynical reason within a "tradition of endgame art" in which a dandyish savoir faire is the ultimate value: "The thing," Levine warns her interlocutors, "is not to lose your sense of humor, because it's only art."

35

This strategy of complicity can be provocative, and it does foreground the role of desire in the economy of contemporary art, at least more than art strictly pledged to ideology critique or deconstruction. ("There is a stronger sense of being complicit with the production of desire," Steinbach remarks in "From Criticism to Complicity." "In this sense the idea of criticality in art is also changing.")

36

The dealer is Mary Boone as presented by Lawson in "The Dark Side of the Bright Light," *Artforum* (November 1982). The stockbroker is Koons. The banker is Jeffrey Deitch: "In the mid 1970s I became involved with Daniel Buren and Hans Haacke, and was very influenced by their exploration of how the context of a work of art shapes its meaning" ("Mythologies: Art and the Market. Jeffrey Deitch Interviewed by Matthew Collings," *Artscribe* 57 [April/May 1986]: 22).

37

Greenberg, *Art and Culture,* 5.

38

T. J. Clark, "Clement Greenberg's Theory of Art," *Critical Inquiry* (September 1982): 144. This text remains the most perceptive analysis of this aspect of Greenberg.

39

"Alongside decayed roués of doubtful origin and uncertain means of subsistence, alongside ruined and adventurous scions of the bourgeoisie, there were vagabonds, discharged soldiers, discharged criminals, escaped galley slaves, swindlers, confidence tricksters, *lazzaroni,* pick-pockets, sleight-of-hand experts, gamblers, *maquereaux,* brothel-keepers, porters, pen-pushers, organ-grinders, rag-and-bone merchants, knife-grinders, tinkers, and beggars, in short, the whole indeterminate fragmented mass, tossed backwards and forwards, which the French call *la bohème*" (*The Eighteenth Brumaire of Louis Bonaparte,* in *Surveys from Exile,* ed. David Fernbach [New York: Vintage Books, 1974], 197). According to Marx, this lumpenproletariat provided Bonaparte with "an unconditional basis."

40

Walter Benjamin, "Addendum to 'The Paris of the Second Empire in Baudelaire'," in *Charles Baudelaire: A Lyric Poet in the Era of High Capitalism,* trans. Harry Zohn (London: New Left Books, 1973), 104. "The secret" here was also the "discontent of his class with its own rule."

41

Baudelaire as quoted in Benjamin, *Charles Baudelaire,* 14.

42

Charles Baudelaire, "The Painter of Modern Life" (1860/1863), in *The Painter of Modern Life and Other Essays,* trans. and ed. Jonathan Mayne (London: Phaidon Press, 1964), 27.

43

Benjamin, *Charles Baudelaire,* 14.

44

In a 1981 preface to *Image of the People* and *The Absolute Bourgeois* (1973), a double study of art and politics in France in the era of the 1848 revolution (Princeton: Princeton University Press, 1982), T. J. Clark counterposes the committed Courbet to the ambivalent Baudelaire in these terms.

45

Sherrie Levine (c. 1980) quoted in Benjamin Buchloh, "Allegorical Procedures: Appropriation and Montage in Contemporary Art," *Artforum* (September 1982). This combination of passion and aloofness may make for melancholy, the psychological humor of the allegorist discussed in chapter 3 as both critical and contemplative.

46

In 1981, even as Clark held out for Courbet "as an alternative model, more difficult to emulate," he admitted that Baudelaire was "the only possible hero of my story": "How could we fail to warm in the present circumstances to a strategy of *déclassement* and duplicity, of hiding, self-regard and self-destruction?" (*Image of the People,* 7). Such is the trajectory of many artists from the early 1980s through the early 1990s—from duplicity to self-regard and self-destruction (or, in contemporary parlance, to abjection, more on which in chapter 5).

47

On color-field painting see Leo Steinberg, "Other Criteria," in *Other Criteria* (New York: Oxford University Press, 1972). On conceptual art see Benjamin Buchloh, "Conceptual Art 1962–1969: From the Aesthetics of Administration to the Critique of Institutions," *October* 55 (Winter 1990).

48

To update Clark in note 46, *déclassement* and hiding are exchanged for *arrivisme* and scene making. As Koons remarked in 1987: "The people who are collecting and supporting my work are the ones that are in the same political direction that I am" (Giancarlo Politi, "Luxury and Desire: An Interview with Jeff Koons," *Flash Art* [February/March 1987]: 76).

49

See Robert Reich, *The Work of Nations* (New York: Alfred A. Knopf, 1991).

50

See Jameson, *Postmodernism,* 275–78. Baudrillard provides the long view here: "In the economic order it is the mastery of *accumulation,* of the appropriation of surplus value, which is essential. In the order of signs (of culture), it is mastery of *expenditure* that is decisive, that is, a mastery of the transubstantiation of economic exchange value into sign exchange value based on a monopoly of the code. Dominant classes have always either assured their domination over sign values from the outset (archaic and traditional societies) or endeavored (in the capitalist bourgeois order) to surpass, to transcend and to consecrate their economic privilege because this later stage represents the ultimate stage of domination. This logic, which comes to relay class logic and which is no longer defined by ownership of the means of production but by the mastery of the process of signification . . . activates a mode of production radically different from that of material production" (*For a Critique of the Political Economy of the Sign,* 115–16).

51

If the art world in the middle 1980s was akin to Wall Street, in the early 1990s it was akin to the fashion world. The emblematic artist in the middle 1980s was a former stockbroker; the emblematic artist in the early 1990s was a former model.

52

Craig Owens, "Honor, Power, and the Love of Women," *Art in America* (January 1983).

53

Benjamin, *Charles Baudelaire,* 58–59. For Benjamin the use of shock in Baudelaire is also homeopathic in this sense.

54

Sloterdijk, *Critique of Cynical Reason,* 441, 443. On Hugo Ball in this regard see *Flight from Time* (1927), trans. Ann Raimes (New York: Viking, 1974), and on Ernst see my "Amor Fou," *October* 56 (Spring 1991).

5

THE RETURN OF THE REAL

1

In a sense this critique of illusionism continues the old story of Western art as the pursuit of the perfect representation, as told from Pliny through Vasari and John Ruskin to Ernst Gombrich (who wrote in opposition to abstract art), only here the goal is reversed: to abolish rather than to achieve this representation. Nonetheless, this reversal carries on the structure of the old story—its terms, values, and so on.

2

"Death in America" was the title of a projected show in Paris of "the electric-chair pictures and the dogs in Birmingham and car wrecks and some suicide pictures" (Warhol, as quoted in Gene Swenson, "What is Pop Art? Answers from 8 Painters, Part I," *ArtNews* 62 [November 1963]: 26).

In chapters 2 and 4 I complicated the art-historical opposition of representation and abstraction with the third term of the simulacral. Below I complicate the representational opposition of reference and simulation in a similar way, with the third term of the traumatic.

3

Roland Barthes, "That Old Thing, Art," in Paul Taylor, ed., *Post-Pop* (Cambridge: MIT Press, 1989), 25–26. By deep meaning Barthes means both metaphorical associations and metonymic connections.

4

Ibid., 26.

5

Jean Baudrillard, "Pop—An Art of Consumption?", in *Post-Pop,* 33, 35. (This text is extracted from *La société de consommation: ses mythes, ses structures* [Paris: Gallimard, 1970], 174–85.)

6

Thomas Crow, "Saturday Disasters: Trace and Reference in Early Warhol," in Serge Guilbaut, ed., *Reconstructing Modernism* (Cambridge: MIT Press, 1990), 313, 317. This is the second version; the first appeared in *Art in America* (May 1987).

7

Ibid., 322.

8

Ibid., 324.

9

Gretchen Berg, "Andy: My True Story," *Los Angeles Free Press,* March 17, 1963, 3. Warhol continues: "There was no profound reason for doing a death series, no victims of their time; there was no reason for doing it at all, just a surface reason." Of course, this insistence could be read as a denial, as a signal that there is a "profound reason." This shuttling between surface and depth is unstoppable in pop, and it may be characteristic of (its) traumatic realism.

What, by the way, renders Warhol such a site for projection? He posed as a blank screen, to be sure, but Warhol was very aware of these projections, indeed very aware of identification *as* projection; it is one of his great subjects.

10

For reasons that will become clear, there can be no traumatic realism as such. Nonetheless, it is useful as a heuristic notion—if only as one way out of the stalemated oppositions of new

—————

art history (semiotic versus social-historical methods, text versus context) and cultural criticism (signifier versus referent, constructivist subject versus naturalist body).

11

Swenson, "What is Pop Art?," 26.

12

I hesitate between "product" and "image" and "make" and "consume" because Warhol seems to occupy a liminal position between orders of production and consumption; at least the two operations blur in his work. This liminal position also bears on my hesitation between "shock," a discourse that develops around accidents in industrial production, and "trauma," a discourse in which shock is rethought through psychic effectivity and imaginary fantasy— and so a discourse perhaps more pertinent to a consumerist subject.

13

Swenson, "What is Pop Art?," 26.

14

For capitalist nihilism in dada see my "Armor Fou," *October* 56 (Spring 1991); in Warhol see Benjamin Buchloh, "The Andy Warhol Line," in Gary Garrels, ed., *The Work of Andy Warhol* (Seattle: Bay Press, 1989). Today, I suggest below, this nihilism often assumes an infantilist aspect, as if "acting out" were the same as "performing."

15

Undated statement by Warhol, as read by Nicholas Love at the Memorial Mass for Andy Warhol, St. Patrick's Cathedral, New York, April 1, 1987, and as cited in Kynaston McShine, ed., *Andy Warhol: A Retrospective* (New York: Museum of Modern Art, 1989), 457.

16

Andy Warhol and Pat Hackett, *POPism: The Warhol '60s* (New York: Harcourt Brace Jovanovich, 1980), 50.

17

Swenson, "What Is Pop Art?," 60. That is, it has an effect, but not *really*. I use "affect" not to reinstate a referential experience but, on the contrary, to suggest an experience that cannot be located precisely.

18

Sigmund Freud, "Mourning and Melancholia" (1917), in *General Psychological Theory,* ed. Philip Rieff (New York: Collier Books, 1963), 166. Crow is especially good on the Warhol memorial to Marilyn, but he reads it in terms of mourning rather than melancholy.

19

See Jacques Lacan, *The Four Fundamental Concepts of Psychoanalysis,* trans. Alan Sheridan (New York: W. W. Norton, 1978), 17–64; other references will be included in the text. The seminar on the gaze, "Of the Gaze as *Objet Petit a*," has received more attention than the seminar on the real, but the latter has as much relevance to contemporary art as the former (in any case the two must be read together). For a provocative application of the seminar on the real to contemporary writing, see Susan Stewart, "Coda: Reverse Trompe L'Oeil / The Eruption of the Real," in *Crimes of Writing* (New York: Oxford University Press), 273–90.

20

"I am trying here to grasp how the *tuché* is represented in visual apprehension," Lacan states. "I shall show that it is at the level that I call the stain that the tychic point in the scopic function is found" (77). This tychic point, then, is in the subject, but the subject as an effect, a shadow or a "stain" cast by the gaze of the world.

21

Roland Barthes, *Camera Lucida,* trans. Richard Howard (New York: Hill and Wang, 1981), 26, 55, 53.

22

Yet another instance of this popping is the blanking of the image (which often occurs in the diptychs—e.g., a monochrome next to a panel of a crash or an electric chair), as though it were a correlative of a blackout.

23

For that matter, it is a great modernist subject from Baudelaire to surrealism and beyond. See Walter Benjamin, "On Some Motifs in Baudelaire" (1939), in *Illuminations,* trans. Harry Zohn (New York: Schocken Books, 1969), as well as Wolfgang Schivelbusch, *The Railway Journey* (Berkeley: University of California Press, 1986). As I note in chapter 7, this shock is tactile in Benjamin, as it is differently in Warhol: "I see everything that way, the surface of things, a kind of mental Braille, I just pass my hands over the surface of things" (Berg, "Andy: My True Story," 3).

24

In fact Benjamin only touches on the notion in "A Short History of Photography" (1931), in Alan Trachtenberg, ed., *Classic Essays on Photography* (New Haven: Leete's Island Books, 1980) and "The Work of Art in the Age of Mechanical Reproduction" (1936), in *Illuminations.*

25

This is also true of Richter, especially in his 1988 suite of paintings, *October 18, 1977,* concerning the Baader-Meinhof group. The *punctum* of these paintings, which are based on photographs of group members, prison cells, corpses, and funerals, is not a private affair, but neither is it explained by a public code (or *studium* in the Barthesian lexicon). This too speaks to a traumatic confusion of private and public.

26

Shock may exist in the world, but *trauma* develops only in the subject. As noted in chapters 1 and 7, it takes two traumas to make a trauma: for a shock to be turned into a trauma, it must be recoded by a later event; this is what Freud means by deferred (*nachträglich*) action. In relation to Warhol this suggests that the shock of the JFK assassination or the Monroe suicide becomes a trauma only later, *après-coup,* for us.

27

This coloring might recall the hysterical red that Marnie sees in the eponymous Hitchcock film (1964). But this red is too coded, safely symbolic. The Warhol colors are arbitrary, acrid, *effective* (especially in the electric-chair images).

28

Warhol, *The Philosophy of Andy Warhol,* 81. In "Andy Warhol's One-Dimensional Art: 1956–1966," Benjamin Buchloh argues that "consumers . . . can celebrate in Warhol's work their proper status of having been erased as subjects" (in McShine, ed., *Andy Warhol: A Retrospective,* 57). This is opposite the Crow position that Warhol exposes "complacent consumption." Again, rather than choose between the two, we must think them together.

29

The symptom hauls us back to the same point (Lacan puns on the etymology of *Wiederholen,* to haul again), but at least this repetition offers us a consistency, even a pleasure. The real, on the other hand, returns violently into the symbolic (again, it cannot be assimilated there) to break us down. As a rupture, it is both ecstatic and deadly, precisely beyond the pleasure principle, and it must be bound somehow—by the symptom if nothing else.

30

As we will see, this *trou*matic point may be associated with the vanishing point in linear perspective from which the depicted world gazes back at the viewer. Perspectival painting has different ways to sublimate this hole: in religious painting the point often represents the infinity of God (in the Leonardo *Last Supper* it pierces the halo of Christ), in landscape painting the infinity of nature (there are many nineteenth-century American examples), and so on.

Superrealist painting, I will suggest, seals or smears this point with surfaces, while much contemporary art seeks to present it as such—or at least to counter its traditional sublimations.

31

Lacan draws on the Sartre of *Being and Nothingness* (1943) and the Merleau-Ponty of *The Phenomenology of Perception* (1945) in particular.

32

Curiously the Sheridan translation adds a "not" ("But I am not in the picture") where the original reads "Mais moi, je suis dans le tableau" (*Le Seminaire de Jacques Lacan, Livre XI* [Paris: Editions du Seuil, 1973], 89). This addition has abetted the mistaking of the place of the subject mentioned in the next note. Lacan is clear enough on this point; e.g.: "the first [triangular system] is that which, in the geometral field, puts in our place the subject of representation, and the second is that which turns *me* into a picture" (105).

33

Some readers place the subject in the position of the screen, perhaps on the basis of this statement: "And if I am anything in the picture, it is always in the form of the screen, which I earlier called the stain, the spot" (97). The subject is a screen in the sense that, looked at from all sides, (s)he blocks the light of the world, casts a shadow, is a "stain" (paradoxically this screening is what permits the subject to see at all). But this screen is different from the image-screen, and to place the subject only there contradicts the superimposition of the two cones wherein the subject is both viewer and picture. The subject is an agent of the image-screen, not one with it.

In my reading the gaze is not already semiotic, as it is for Norman Bryson (see *Tradition and Desire: From David to Delacroix* [Cambridge: Cambridge University Press, 1984], 64–70). In some respects he improves on Lacan, who, through Merleau-Ponty, renders the gaze almost animistic. On the other hand, to read the gaze as already semiotic is to tame it before the fact. For Bryson, however, the gaze is benign, "a luminous plenitude," and the screen "mortifies" rather than protects the subject ("The Gaze in the Expanded Field," in Hal Foster, ed., *Vision and Visuality* [Seattle: Bay Press, 1988], 92).

34

On the atavism of this nexus of gaze, prey, and paranoia consider this remark of the novelist Philip K. Dick: "Paranoia, in some respects, I think, is a modern-day development of an ancient, archaic sense that animals still have—quarry-type animals—that they're being watched. . . . I say paranoia is an atavistic sense. It's a lingering sense, that we had long ago, when we were—our ancestors were—very vulnerable to predators, and this sense tells them they're being watched. And they're being watched probably by something that's going to get them. . . . And often my characters have this feeling. But what really I've done is, I have atavised their society. That although it's set in the future, in many ways they're living—there is a retrogressive quality in their lives, you know? They're living like our ancestors did. I mean, the hardware is in the future, the scenery's in the future, but the situations are really from the past" (extract from a 1974 interview used as an epigraph to *The Collected Stories of Philip K. Dick,* vol. 2 [New York: Carol Publishing, 1990]).

Bryson discusses the paranoia of the gaze in Sartre and Lacan in "The Gaze in the Expanded Field," where he suggests that, however threatened by the gaze, the subject is also confirmed by it, strengthened by its very alterity. Similarly, in a discussion of Thomas Pynchon, Leo Bersani intimates that paranoia is the last refuge of the subject: "In paranoia, the primary function of the enemy is to provide a definition of the real that makes paranoia necessary. We must then begin to suspect the paranoid structure itself as a device by which consciousness maintains the polarity of self and nonself, thus preserving the concept of identity. In paranoia, two Real Texts confront one another: subjective being and a world of monolithic otherness. This opposition can be broken down only if we renounce the comforting (if also dangerous) faith in locatable identities. Only then, perhaps, can the simulated doubles of paranoid vision destroy the very oppositions that they appear to support" ("Pynchon, Paranoia, and Literature," *Representations* 25 [Winter 1989]: 109. There is a paranoid aspect to other models of visuality—the male gaze, surveillance, spectacle, simulation. What produces this paranoia, and what might it serve—that is, besides this strange in/security of the subject?

35

Lacan relates this maleficent gaze to the evil eye, which he sees as an agent of disease and death, with the power to blind and to castrate: "It is a question of dispossessing the evil eye of the gaze, in order to ward it off. The evil eye is the *fascinum* [spell], it is that which has the effect of arresting movement and, literally, of killing life. . . . It is precisely one of the dimensions in which the power of the gaze is exercised directly" (118). Lacan asserts that the evil eye is universal, with no equivalent beneficent eye, not even in the Bible. Yet in biblical representation there is the gaze of the Madonna upon the Child and of the Child upon us. However, Lacan opts for the exemplum of envy in Saint Augustine, who tells of his murderous feelings of exclusion at the sight of his little brother at the maternal breast: "Such is true envy—the envy that make the subject pale before the image of a completeness closed upon itself, before the idea that the *petit a,* the separated *a* from which he is hanging, may be for another the possession that gives satisfaction" (116).

Here Lacan can be contrasted with Walter Benjamin, who imagines the gaze as auratic and replete, from within the dyad of mother and child, rather than as anxious and invidious, from the position of the excluded third. Indeed, Benjamin imagines the beneficent eye that Lacan refuses to see, a magical gaze that reverses fetishism and undoes castration, a redemptive aura based on the memory of the the maternal gaze and body: "Experience of the aura thus rests on the transposition of a response common in human relationships to the relationship between the inanimate or natural object and man. The person we look at, or who feels he is being looked at, looks at us in turn. To perceive the aura of an object we look at, means to invest it with the ability to look at us in return. This experience corresponds to the data of the *mémoire involontaire*" ("On Some Motifs in Baudelaire," in *Illuminations,* ed. Hannah Arendt, trans. Harry Zohn [New York: Schocken Books, 1977], 188). For more on this distinction see my *Compulsive Beauty* (Cambridge: MIT Press, 1993), 193–205.

36

For Lacan the gaze as *objet a,* as the real, is the stake not only of *trompe-l'oeil* painting but of all (Western) painting, of which he offers a short history. (Here again he might be contrasted with Benjamin, who presents a different history in "The Work of Art in the Age of Mechanical Reproduction.") Lacan relates three social regimes—religious, aristocratic, and commercial—to three pictorial gazes, which he terms "sacrificial" (the gaze of God; his example is Byzantine icons), "communal" (the gaze of aristocratic leaders; his example is the group portraiture of the Venetian doges), and "modern" ("the gaze of the painter, which claims to impose itself as being the only gaze" [113]; here he alludes to Cézanne and Matisse). For Lacan each pictorial gaze coaxes a laying down of the gaze as *objet a.* Some postmodernist art, I will claim below, wants to break this negotiation, this sublimation, of the gaze—which, for Lacan, is to break with art as such.

37

Fredric Jameson, *Marxism and Form* (Princeton: Princeton University Press, 1971), 105.

38

Ibid. (my emphasis).

39

Neither are productive modes, let alone social relations, representational forms, and so on, all of which Jameson knows.

40

See Georges Bataille, "The 'Old Mole' and the Prefix *Sur* in the Words *Surhomme* and *Surrealist,*" in *Visions of Excess,* ed. Allan Stoekl (Minneapolis: University of Minnesota Press, 1985).

41

This goal is rarely achieved in surrealism; indeed, its very possibility was questioned in the early days of the movement (see *Compulsive Beauty*, xv–xvi). In other words, surrealism may be on the side of the *automaton*, the repetition of the symptom as signifier, more than at the point of the *tuché*, the eruption of the real, as some contemporary art aspires to be.

42

This enveloping of the viewer (for example, in the entertainer images of Prince) is a property of the simulacrum defined by Deleuze: "The simulacrum implies great dimensions, depths, and distances which the observer cannot dominate. It is because he cannot master them that he has an impression of resemblance. The simulacrum includes within itself the differential point of view, and the spectator is made part of the simulacrum, which is transformed and deformed according to his point of view. In short, folded within the simulacrum there is a process of going mad, a process of limitlessness" ("Plato and the Simulacrum," *October* 27 [Winter 1983]: 49). This enveloping of the viewer also speaks to the confusions of self and image, inside and outside, in consumerist fantasy, as exploited in many advertising images and explored in some appropriation art. "His own desires had very little to do with what came from itself," Prince writes in *Why I Go to the Movies Alone* (1983), "because what he put out (at least in part) had already been out. His way to make it new was *make it again,* and making it again was enough for him and certainly, personally speaking, *almost* him" (New York: Tanam Press, 63). Sometimes this ambiguity makes his work provocative in a way that appropriation art overly confident of its criticality is not, for Prince is involved in the consumerist fantasy that he denatures. That is, sometimes his critique is effective precisely because it is compromised—because it lets us see a consciousness split before an image. But then, too, this splitting may be another version of cynical reason.

43

Consider this apposite remark of Slavoj Žižek: "Herein lies the fundamental ambiguity of the image in postmodernism: it is a kind of barrier enabling the subject to maintain distance from the real, protecting him or her against its irruption, yet its very obtrusive 'hyperrealism' evokes the nausea of the real" ("Grimaces of the Real," *October* 58 [Fall 1991]: 59).

Richard Misrach also evokes this obscene real, especially in his "Playboy" series (1989–91). Based on magazine images used as shooting targets in nuclear test ranges, these photographs reveal a powerful aggression against visuality in contemporary culture. (Some *décollages* of the 1950s and 1960s also attest to this aggression in the society of the spectacle.) Might this antivisuality be related to the paranoia of the gaze mentioned in note 34?

44

Rosalind Krauss conceives this desublimation as an attack on the sublimated verticality of the traditional art image in *Cindy Sherman* (New York: Rizzoli, 1993). She too discusses the work in relation to the Lacanian diagram of visuality. Also see the discussion of Sherman in Kaja Silverman, *The Threshold of the Visible World* (New York: Routledge, 1996), which appeared too late for me to consult.

45

See Julia Kristeva, *Powers of Horror,* trans. Leon S. Roudiez (New York: Columbia University Press, 1982).

46

Regarding these differences see "Conversation on the *Informe* and the Abject," *October* 67 (Winter 1993).

47

For an excellent analysis of such work see Mignon Nixon, "Bad Enough Mother," *October* 71 (Winter 1995). Nixon thinks this work in terms of a Kleinian concern with object relations. I see it as a turn in feminist art that is related to a turn within Lacanian theory from the symbolic to the real, a turn that Slavoj Žižek has advanced. Sometimes the "object" aspect of this art expresses little more than an essentialism of the body (let alone, as in Smith, an iconography of the maudlin), while the "real" aspect expresses little more than a nostalgia for an experiential grounding.

48

It is almost as if these artists cannot represent the body except as violated—as if it only registers as represented in this condition. In a similar way the staging of the body often drove performance art in the 1970s toward sadomasochistic scenarios—again, as if it only registered as represented if it was bound, gagged, and so on.

49

"Obscene" may not mean "against the scene," but it suggests this attack. Many contemporary images only stage the obscene, render it thematic or scenic, and so control it. In this way they place the obscene in the service of the screen, not against it, which is what most abject art does, contrary to its own wishes. But, then, it might be argued that the obscene is the greatest apotropaic defense against the real, the ultimate reinforcement of the image-screen, not its ultimate dissolvent.

50

Kristeva, *Powers of Horror,* 2.

51

See in particular Judith Butler, *Gender Trouble* (New York: Routledge, 1990) and *Bodies That Matter* (New York: Routledge, 1993), both of which contain critical elaborations of the Kristevan abject. Kristeva tends to primordialize disgust; in her mapping of abjection onto homophobia, Butler tends to primordialize homophobia. But then both might well be primordial.

52

To be abject is to be incapable of abjection, and to be completely incapable of abjection is to be dead, which makes the corpse the ultimate (non)subject of abjection.

53

Bataille, *Erotism: Death and Sensuality* (1957), trans. Mary Dalwood (San Francisco: City Lights Books, 1986), 63. A third option is that the abject is double and that its transgressivity resides in this ambiguity.

54

Kristeva, *Powers of Horror,* 18.

55

But then when is it not? The notion of hegemony suggests that it is always threatened. In this regard the concept of a symbolic order may project a stability that the social does not possess.

56

Radical art and theory often celebrate failed figures (especially of masculinity) as transgressive of the symbolic order, but this avant-gardist logic assumes (affirms?) a stable order against which these figures are posed. In *My Own Private Germany: Daniel Paul Schreber's Secret History of Modernity* (Princeton: Princeton University Press, 1996) Eric Santner offers a brilliant rethinking of this logic: he relocates transgression *within* the symbolic order, at a point of internal crisis, which he defines as "symbolic authority in a state of emergency."

57

"Everything tends to make us believe," Breton wrote in the *Second Manifesto of Surrealism* (1930), "that there exists a certain point of the mind at which life and death, the real and the imagined, past and future, the communicable and the incommunicable, high and low, cease to be perceived as contradictions. Now, search as one may one will never find any other motivating force in the activities of the surrealists than the hope of finding and fixing this point" (in *Manifestoes of Surrealism,* trans. Richard Seaver and Helen R. Lane [Ann Arbor: University of Michigan Press, 1972], 123–24). Many signal works of modernism fix this point between sublimation and desublimation (there are examples in Picasso, Jackson Pollock, Cy

Twombly, Eva Hesse, many others). They are privileged because we *need* this tension—need it to be treated somehow, both incited and soothed, *managed.*

58

See Breton, *Manifestoes of Surrealism,* 180–87. At one point Breton charges Bataille with "psychasthenia" (more on which below).

59

See Bataille, *Visions of Excess,* 39–40. For more on this opposition see my *Compulsive Beauty,* 110–14.

60

Georges Bataille, "L'Esprit moderne et le jeu des transpositions," *Documents,* no 8. (1930). The best discussion of Bataille on this score is Denis Hollier, *Against Architecture* (Cambridge: MIT Press, 1989), especially 98–115. Elsewhere Hollier specifies the fixed aspect of the abject according to Bataille: "It is the *subject* that is abject. That is where his attack on metaphoricity comes in. If you die, you die; you can't have a substitute. What can't be substituted is what binds subject and abject together. It can't simply be a substance. It has to be a substance that addresses a subject, that puts it at risk, in a position from which it cannot move away" ("Conversation on the *Informe* and the Abject").

61

This division is hardly absolute. Some female artists also mock the paternal law from an infantilist position, but this mocking tends to draw on an oral-sadistic vocabulary (e.g., Pondick, Hayt), not an anal-sadistic one, as with most male artists. So, too, some male artists also evoke the maternal body (e.g., the cuddly toys and blankets in Kelley, which, however, are soiled, even defiled, as if to register an aggression born of abandonment). In another register it is not only men who want to be bad boys; some women do too—an ambition registered in the 1994 "Bad Girls" shows in New York (New Museum) and Los Angeles (UCLA Wight Art Gallery). Regarding this bad-boy envy Mary Kelly has remarked: "Historically the avant-garde has been synonymous with transgression, so the male artist has assumed the feminine already, as a mode of 'being other,' but he does it, ultimately, as a form of virile display. So what the bad girl does that's so different from the previous generation is to adopt the masquerade of the male artist as transgressive feminine in order to display her virility. In zine speak you'd say: a girl thing being a boy thing being a girl thing to be a bad thing" ("A Conversation: Recent Feminist Practices," *October* 71 [Winter 1995]: 58).

62

"I am for an art of kid's smells. I am for an art of mama-babble" (Claes Oldenburg, *Store Days* [New York: The Something Else Press, 1967]).

63

See Benjamin H.D. Buchloh, "Figures of Authority, Ciphers of Regression," *October* 16 (Spring 1981): "This new icon of the clown is only matched in frequency in the paintings of that period [the 1920s] by the representation of the *manichino,* the wooden puppet, the reified body, originating both from shop-window decoration and from the props of the classical artist's studio. If the first icon appears in the context of the carnival and the circus as the masquerades of alienation from present history, the second appears on the stage set of reification" (53).

64

Abjected and repressed, "outside" and "underneath," these terms become critical, able to disclose the heterosexist aspects of these operations. Yet this logic may also accept a reduction of male homosexuality to anal eroticism. Moreover, as with the infantilist mocking of the paternal law, it may accept the dominance of the very terms that it opposes.

65

For an incisive reading of this discontent modernism see Rosalind Krauss, *The Optical Unconscious* (Cambridge: MIT Press, 1992), and for a comprehensive history of this antiocular tradition see Martin Jay, *Downcast Eyes: The Denigration of Vision in Twentieth-Century French Thought* (Berkeley: University of California Press, 1993).

66

Sigmund Freud, "On Transformations of Instinct as Exemplified in Anal Erotism," in *On Sexuality,* ed. Angela Richards (London: Penguin, 1977), 301. On the primitivism of this avant-gardist defiance, see my "'Primitive' Scenes," *Critical Inquiry* (Winter 1993). Evocations of anal eroticism, as in the Rauschenburg "Black Paintings" or early Twombly graffiti, can be more subversive than declarations of anal defiance.

67

Kelley pushes infantilist defiance toward adolescent dysfunction (he delves deeply into youth subcultures): "An adolescent is a dysfunctional adult, and art is a dysfunctional reality, as far as I am concerned" (quoted in Elisabeth Sussman, ed., *Catholic Tastes* [New York: Whitney Museum of American Art, 1994], 51).

68

See Janine Chasseguet-Smirgel, *Creativity and Perversion* (New York: W. W. Norton, 1984). Chasseguet-Smirgel views anality, problematically, indeed homophobically, as a site where differences are abolished.

69

However, this testing comes at the risk of an old racist association of blackness and feces.

70

Mike Kelley, *Theory, Garbage, Stuffed Animals, Christ,* quoted in Sussman, ed., *Catholic Tastes,* 86.

71

Freud, "On Transformations of Instinct," 298. Kelley plays on anthropological as well as psychoanalytic connections among these terms—feces, money, gifts, babies, penises.

72

Karl Marx, *The Eighteenth Brumaire of Louis Bonaparte,* in *Surveys from Exile,* ed. David Fernbach (New York: Vintage Books, 1974), 197.

73

Bataille, *Visions of Excess,* 15. Otherwise, Bataille warns, "Materialism will be seen as a senile idealism."

74

What was the music of Nirvana about if not the Nirvana principle, a lullably droned to the dreamy beat of the death drive? See my "The Cult of Despair," *New York Times,* December 30, 1994.

75

Roger Caillois, "Mimicry and Legendary Psychasthenia," *October* 31 (Winter 1984). Denis Hollier glosses "psychasthenia" as follows: "a drop in the level of psychic energy, a kind of subjective detumescence, a loss of ego substance, a depressive exhaustion close to what a monk called *acedia*" ("Mimesis and Castration in 1937," *October* 31: 11).

76

Ibid., 30.

77

This was first broached in "Postmodernism and Consumer Society," in Hal Foster, ed., *The Anti-Aesthetic: Essays on Postmodern Culture* (Seattle: Bay Press, 1983). For a critique of such psychoanalytic applications see Jacqueline Rose, "Sexuality and Vision: Some Questions," in Foster, ed., *Vision and Visuality.* This ecstatic version cannot be dissociated from the "boom" of the early 1980s, nor the melancholic version from the bust of the late 1980s and early 1990s.

78

See Sigmund Freud, *Beyond the Pleasure Principle* (1920), trans. James Strachey (New York: W. W. Norton, 1961) and Walter Benjamin, "On Some Motifs in Baudelaire" (1939), in *Illuminations.* This bipolarity of the ecstatic and the abject may be the affinity, sometimes remarked in cultural criticism, between the baroque and the postmodern. Both are drawn toward an ecstatic shattering that is also a traumatic breaking; both are obsessed with figures of the stigma and the stain.

79

To question this indifference is not to dismiss a noncommunitarian politics, a possibility explored in both cultural criticism (e.g., Leo Bersani) and political theory (e.g., Jean-Luc Nancy).

80

Kelley, quoted in Sussman, ed., *Catholic Tastes,* 86.

81

"Self-divestiture in these artists is also a renunciation of cultural authority," Leo Bersani and Ulysse Dutoit write of Samuel Beckett, Mark Rothko, and Alain Resnais in *Arts of Impoverishment* (Cambridge: Harvard University Press, 1993). Yet then they ask: "Might there, however, be a 'power' in such impotence?" If so, shouldn't it be questioned in turn?

82

A few supplemental comments: (1) If there is, as some have remarked, an autobiographical turn in art and criticism, it is often a paradoxical genre, for again, per trauma, there may be no "self" there. (2) Just as the depressive is doubled by the aggressive, so the traumatized can turn hostile, and the violated can violate in turn. (3) The reaction against poststructuralism, the return of the real, also expresses a nostalgia for universal categories of being and experience. The paradox is that this rebirth of humanism would occur in the register of the traumatic. (4) At moments in this chapter I have allowed trauma and abjection to touch, as they do in the culture, even though they are distinct theoretically, developed in different lines of psychoanalysis.

6

THE ARTIST AS ETHNOGRAPHER

1

Walter Benjamin, *Reflections,* ed. Peter Demetz, trans. Edmund Jephcott (New York: Harcourt Brace Jovanovich, 1978), 220–38. Unless otherwise indicated, all subsequent Benjamin references are to this text.

2

Benjamin explicitly charges only two movements, activism and *Neue Sachlichkeit* (new objectivity): the first, associated with writers like Heinrich Mann and Alexander Döblin, supplies the bourgeois apparatus with revolutionary themes, while the second, associated with the photographer Albert Renger-Patzsch, serves "to renew from within—that is, fashionably— the world as it is." Indeed, Benjamin continues in terms relevant today, this photography turns "even abject poverty . . . into an object of enjoyment."

3

See, for example, Benjamin Buchloh, "Since Realism there was . . . (on the current conditions of factographic art)," in Marcia Tucker, ed., *Art & Ideology* (New York: New Museum of Contemporary Art, 1984). Buchloh discusses the work of Allan Sekula and Fred Lonidier in particular.

4

"Author as Producer" arose out of the unique high-modernist conjuncture of artistic innova-tion, socialist revolution, and technological transformation, and even then Benjamin was late; Stalin had condemned avant-garde culture (productivism above all) by 1932, an event that must inflect any reading of this text. Today the high-modernist triangulation is long gone: there is no socialist revolution in the traditional sense, and technological transformation has only displaced artists and critics further from the dominant mode of production. In short, productivist strategies are hardly adequate alone.

Vestiges of productivism remain in postwar art and theory, first in the proletarian guise adopted by sculptors from David Smith to Richard Serra, and then in the production rhetoric of post-studio art and textual theory (e.g., *Tel Quel* in France). By the early 1970s, however, critiques of productivism emerged; Jean Baudrillard argued that the means of representation had become as important as the means of production (see chapter 4, note 50). This led to a situationist turn in cultural intervention (of media, site, address, and so on), now followed, I will suggest here, by an ethnographic turn. (I trace the productivist legacy in "Some Uses and Abuses of Russian Constructivism," in Richard Andrews, ed., *Art into Life* [New York: Rizzoli, 1990].)

5

To call it a myth is not to say that it is *never* true but to question whether it is *always* true— and to ask whether it might obscure other articulations of the political and the artistic. In a sense the substitution of politics for art now displaces the substitution of theory for politics.

6

This danger should be distinguished from "the indignity of speaking for others." In a 1983 "imaginary interview" with this title Craig Owens called on artists to go beyond the productivist problematic to "challenge the activity of representation itself" (in William

Olander, ed., *Art and Social Change* [Oberlin: Oberlin College, 1983]). Despite the poststructuralist language here, "the indignity of speaking for others" presents representation as literal displacement. This taboo pervaded the North American cultural left in the 1980s, where it effected a censorious silence as much as an alternative speech.

7

Roland Barthes, *Mythologies,* trans. Annette Lavers (New York: Hill and Wang, 1972), 146. Not only is revolutionary language mythical too (here it is also masculinist), but this very notion of language, which falls between the productivist and the performative, is almost magical: language here confers reality, conjures it up.

8

The primitivist fantasy may also operate in productivist modernisms, at least to the extent that the proletariat is often seen as primitive in this sense too, both negatively (the mass as primal horde) and positively (the proletariat as tribal collective).

9

For example, see Bataille, "The Notion of Expenditure" (1933), in *Visions of Excess,* ed. and trans. Allan Stoekl (Minneapolis: University of Minnesota Press, 1985), and Senghor, *Anthologie de la Nouvelle Poésie et Malagache d'Expression Française* (Paris: Presses Universitaires de France, 1948).

10

James Clifford describes the Leiris text as "self-ethnography" in *The Predicamant of Culture* (Cambridge: Harvard University Press, 1988), 170.

11

See Fanon, "The Fact of Blackness," in *Black Skin, White Masks* (1952), trans. Charles Lam Markmann (New York: Grove Press, 1967), and Soyinka, *Myth, Literature, and the African World* (Cambridge: Cambridge University Press, 1976).

12

Johannes Fabian, *Time and the Other: How Anthropology Makes Its Object* (New York: Columbia University Press, 1983), 11–12. For a discussion of related mappings in art history see my "The Writing on the Wall," in Michael Govan, ed., *Lothar Baumgarten, America: Invention* (New York: Guggenheim Museum, 1993).

13

Sigmund Freud, *Totem and Taboo,* trans. James Strachey (New York: W. W. Norton, 1950), 1. This strange association of the savage and the neurotic—indeed, of the primitive, the insane, and the child—was so fundamental to high modernism as to seem natural. Its disarticulation would expose several myths.

14

A new danger has arisen here, however: an aestheticizing, indeed a fetishizing, of signs of the hybrid and spaces of the in-between. Both not only privilege the mixed but, more problematically, presuppose a prior distinction or even purity.

15

See Franco Rella, *The Myth of the Other,* trans. Nelson Moe (Washington: Maisonneuve Press, 1994), especially 27–28. One can counter that this revaluing (e.g., of "black" or "queer") is part of any politics of representation. See Stuart Hall, "New Ethnicities," in Kobena Mercer, ed., *Black Film, Black Cinema* (London: Institute of Contemporary Art, 1988).

16

For example, the *négritude* movement associated colonized and proletariat as objects of oppression and reification (see Césaire, *Discourse of Colonialism* [Paris, 1955]), a political *affiliation* that prepared a political *appropriation*. In "Black Orpheus," his preface to the Senghor anthology (cited in note 9), Sartre wrote: "At once the subjective, existential, ethnic idea of *negritude* 'passes,' as Hegel puts it, into the objective, positive, exact idea of *proletariat*. . . . In fact, negritude appears as the minor term of a dialectical progression" (xl). To which Fanon responded: "I had been robbed of my last chance. . . . And so it is not I who make a meaning for myself, but it is the meaning that was already there, preexisting, waiting for me . . . waiting for that turn of history" (*Black Skin,* 133–34).

17

Michel Foucault, *The Order of Things* (New York: Vintage Books, 1970), 364. I return to this unveiling in chapter 7.

18

Paradoxically, this preservation of the self may also be effected through a *moral masochism* in the politics of alterity, which Nietzsche attacked in *The Genealogy of Morals* (1887) as the *ressentiment* at work in the master-slave dialectic. As Anson Rabinbach suggested to me, Sartre exhibits this masochism in his famous preface to *The Wretched of the Earth* where, as if in response to the charge of dialectical appropriation (see note 16), he now states that decolonialization is "the end of the dialectic" (1961; trans. Constance Farrington [New York: Grove Press, 1968], 31). Sartre then trumps the Fanonian argument that colonization has also dehumanized the colonizer with a masochistic call to redouble the redemptive vengeance of the colonized. Is this moral masochism a disguised version of "ideological patronage"? Is it resentment to a second degree, a position of power in the pretense of its surrender? Is it another way to maintain the centrality of the subject through the other?

19

On psychoanalysis in this regard see Mikkel Borch-Jabobsen, *The Freudian Subject,* trans. Catherine Porter (Palo Alto: Stanford University Press, 1988). I am also indebted here to Mark Seltzer, "Serial Killers, I and II," in *Differences* (1993) and *Critical Inquiry* (Autumn 1995).

20

Claude Lévi-Strauss, *The Savage Mind* (Chicago: University of Chicago Press, 1966), 247. This is his claim against the Sartrean dialectic.

21

See Foucault, *The Order of Things,* 340–43. "'Anthropologization' is the great internal threat to knowledge in our day" (348). But then this restoration may be what quasi-anthropological art intends; certainly it is effected in some cultural studies. *The Order of Things* concludes with the image of man washed away; *Crusoe's Footprints,* Patrick Bantlinger's overview of cultural studies, concludes with his prints in the sand (New York: Routledge, 1990). This multiplicity of *men* may not disturb the category of *man.*

22

Clifford develops the notion of "ethnographic self-fashioning" in *The Predicament of Culture,* in large part from Stephen Greenblatt in *Renaissance Self-Fashioning* (Chicago: University of Chicago Press, 1980). This suggests a commonality between new anthropology and new historicism, more on which below.

23

In "World Tour," a series of installations in different sites, Renée Green performs this nomadism of the artist reflexively. On the one hand, she works over traces of the African diaspora; on the other hand, she makes an art tour (her "World Tour" T-shirt plays on the model of the rock concert).

24

In *The Predicament of Culture* Clifford extends this notion to ethnography in general: "Is not every ethnographer something of a surrealist, a reinventor and reshuffler of realities?" (147). Some have questioned how reciprocal art and anthropology were in the surrealist milieu. See Jean Jamin, "L'ethnographie mode d'inemploi. De quelques rapports de l'ethnologie avec le malaise dans la civilisation," in J. Hainard and R. Kaehr, eds., *Le mal et la douleur* (Neuchâtel: Musée d'ethnographie, 1986); and Denis Hollier, "The Use-Value of the Impossible," *October* 60 (Spring 1992).

25

Not unique to the new anthropology, this artist envy is evident in the rhetorical analysis of historical discourse initiated in the 1960s. "There have been no significant attempts," Hayden

White writes in "The Burden of History" (1966), "at surrealistic, expressionistic, or existentialist historiography in this century (except by novelists and poets themselves), for all of the
vaunted 'artistry' of the historians of modern times" (*Tropics of Discourse* [Baltimore: Johns
Hopkins University Press, 1978], 43). Clifford Geertz put "textual" anthropology on the map
in *The Interpretation of Culture* (New York: Basic Books, 1973).

26

Clifford: "Interpretive anthropology, by viewing cultures as assemblages of texts . . . has contributed significantly to the defamiliarization of ethnographic authority" (*The Predicament of
Culture*, 41).

27

Pierre Bourdieu, *Outline of a Theory of Practice,* trans. Richard Nice (Cambridge: Cambridge
University Press, 1977), 1. Granted, the "discursive paradigms" of the new anthropology
are different—poststructuralist rather than structuralist, dialogical rather than decoding.
But a Bahktinian orchestration of informant voices does not void ethnographic authority. In
"Banality in Cultural Studies," Meaghan Morris comments: "Once 'the people' are both
a source of authority for a text and a figure of its own critical activity, the populist enterprise is not only circular but (like most empirical sociology) narcissistic in structure" (in Patricia Mellencamp, ed., *The Logics of Television* [Bloomington: Indiana University Press, 1990],
23).

28

See Fredric Jameson, *Ideologies of Theory* (Minneapolis: University of Minnesota Press, 1989).
As Jameson notes, the first textualist move was needed to loosen anthropology from its positivist traditions. In "New Historicism: A Comment" Hayden White points to a "referential
fallacy" (related to my "realist assumption") and a "textualist fallacy" (related to my "textualist
projection"): "Whence the charge that New Historicism is reductionist in a double sense: it
reduces the social to the status of a function of the cultural, and then further reduces the
cultural to the status of a text" (in H. Aram Veeser, ed., *The New Historicism* [New York:
Routledge, 1989], 294).

29

See Clifford, *The Predicament of Culture,* 30–32. "The ethnographic present" is passé in
anthropology.

30

For this aspect of conceptual art see Joseph Kosuth, "The Artist as Anthropologist," *The Fox*
1 (1975).

31

Marshall Sahlins, *Culture and Practical Reason* (Chicago: University of Chicago Press, 1976). This critique was written in the heyday of poststructuralism, and Sahlins, then close to Jean Baudrillard, favored (linguistic) symbolic logic over (Marxian) practical reason. "There is no material logic apart from the practical interest," Sahlins writes, "and the practical interest of man in production is symbolically constituted" (207). "In Western culture," he continues, "the economic is the main site of symbolic production. For us the production of goods is at the same time the privileged mode of symbolic production and transmission. The uniqueness of bourgeois society consists not in the fact that the economic system escapes symbolic determination, but that the economic symbolism is structurally determining" (211).

32

The role of ethnographer also allows the critic to recoup an ambivalent position between academic and other subcultures as critical, especially when the alternatives seem limited to academic irrelevance or subcultural affirmation.

33

These exchanges are not trivial at a time when enrollments are counted closely—and when some administrators advocate a return to old disciplines, while others seek to recoup interdisciplinary ventures as cost-effective programs. Incidentally, these exchanges seem governed by a used-car principle of discourse: when one discipline wears out a paradigm ("text" in literary criticism, "culture" in anthropology), it trades it in, passes it on.

34

Louis Althusser, *Philosophy and the Spontaneous Ideology of the Scientists & Other Essays* (London: Verso, 1990), 97. The ethnographic turn in cultural studies and new historicism is rarely questioned. In *Renaissance Self-Fashioning* (1980), a foundational text of new historicism, Stephen Greenblatt is explicit: "I have attempted instead [of literary criticism] to practice a more cultural or anthropological criticism—if by 'anthropological' here we think of interpretive studies of culture by Geertz, James Boon, Mary Douglas, Jean Duvignaud, Paul Rabinow, Victor Turner, and others." Such criticism sees "literature as a part of the system of signs that constitute a given culture" (4). Yet this seems a methodological circle: textual criticism approaches anthropological interpretation, but only because its new object, culture, is reformulated as text.

For Stuart Hall British cultural studies at the Birmingham Centre developed from literary to cultural to ideological criticism, with a "much broader, 'anthropological' definition" of culture as the result (quoted in Brantlinger, *Crusoe's Footprints,* 64). This turn was also basic to North American cultural studies. For Janice Radway the Birmingham Centre along with American studies programs prompted the move from a "literary-moral definition of culture to an anthropological one." Also important was reader-response criticism, which prepared the "ethnographies of reading" of cultural studies proper (*Reading the Romance* [Chapel Hill: University of North Carolina Press, 1991], 3–4). Here again an ethnographic basis is acknowledged but not questioned. The new anthropology does question ethnographic assumptions, of course, but *its* assumptions are rarely questioned, at least when taken up in cultural studies and new historicism.

35

Thus, for example, John Lindell, a member of the Gran Fury artist collective, has stated: "In terms of my own work, homosexual desire is a site and the gay world at large is a site. Again I'm trying to loosen up the notion of a physical site: a site may be a group of people, a community" ("Roundtable On Site-Specificity," *Documents* 4/5 [Spring 1994]: 18).

36

For Martha Rosler, see especially *3 Works* (Halifax: The Press of the Nova Scotia School of Art and Design, 1981); and for Allan Sekula see *Photography Against the Grain: Essays and Photo Works 1973–1983* (Halifax: The Press of the Nova Scotia School of Art and Design, 1984) and *Fish Story* (Düsseldorf: Richter Verlag, 1995). For Fredric Jameson on cognitive mapping see *Postmodernism* (Durham: Duke University Press, 1990), passim.

37

For Mary Kelly see *Interim* (New York: New Museum of Contemporary Art, 1990); and for Silvia Kolbowski see *XI Projects* (New York: Border Editions, 1993). Many other artists either question documentary representations and/or draw on ethnographic mappings (Susan Hiller, Leandro Katz, Elaine Reichek . . .). For one overview see Arnd Schneider, "The Art Diviners," *Anthropology Today* 9, no. 2 (April 1993).

38

See Bourdieu, *Outline for a Theory of Practice,* 2.

39

On these oppositions see Fabian, *Time and the Other,* and on Baumgarten see my "The Writing on the Wall" in Govan, ed., *Lothar Baumgarten, America: Invention.*

40

See the remarks of Miwon Kwon in "Roundtable on Site-Specificity." Again, a redemptive logic governs much site-specific work, from the reclamation projects of Smithson onward.

41

A recent instance was "The 42nd Street Art Project," a joint venture of an arts organization, a design firm, and the 42nd Street Development Project. Here again there were individual works of aesthetic and/or critical invention. Nonetheless, art, graphics, and fashion were deployed to improve the image of a notorious piece of real estate slated for redevelopment.

42

"Culture in Action" pamphlet (Chicago: Sculpture Chicago, 1993); also see Mary Jane Jacob et al., *Culture in Action* (Seattle: Bay Press, 1995).

43

Guy Debord, "Detournement as Negation and Prelude," *Internationale Situationniste,* no. 3 [December 1959], reprinted in *Situationist International Anthology,* ed. and trans. Ken Knabb (Berkeley: Bureau of Public Secrets, 1981), 55.

44

Put glibly, if the 1970s was the decade of the theorist and the 1980s the decade of the dealer, the 1990s may be the decade of the itinerant curator who gathers nomadic artists at different sites. With the art market crash in 1987 and the political controversies thereafter (Robert Mapplethorpe, "obscene" performance art, Andres Serrano . . .), support for contemporary art declined in the United States. Funding was also redirected to regional institutions, which often imported metropolitan artists nonetheless, as did European institutions where funding remained relatively high. Thus the rise of the migrant ethnographic artist.

45

See the remarks of Miwon Kwon and Renée Green in "Roundtable on Site-Specificity."

46

On trickstering see Jean Fisher, *Jimmie Durham* (New York: Exit Art, 1989); on playing dead see Miwon Kwon, "Postmortem Strategies," *Documents* 3 (Summer 1993). Again, postcolonial discourse now tends to fetishize personae like the trickster and places like the in-between.

I have focused on Native American artists, but others use these strategies as well. In a 1993 performance at Art in General (New York) Rikrit Tiravanija invited viewers to dance to the sound track of *The King and I* in a parody of popular stereotypes (in this case of Southeast Asian culture) as well as a reversal of ethnographic roles. In *Import/Export Funk Office* (1992) Renée Green also reversed ethnographic roles when she questioned the German critic Dietrich Dietrichsen about hip-hop culture.

47

See Leo Steinberg, *Other Criteria* (New York: Oxford University Press, 1972), 82–91.

48

Lawrence Alloway, "The Long Front of Culture" (1959), in Brian Wallis, ed., *This is Tomorrow Today: The Independent Group and British Pop* (New York: P.S. 1, 1987), 31.

49

This claim is made by critics like Fredric Jameson and developed by urban geographers like David Harvey and Edward Soja. I return to it in chapter 7.

50

A similar reaction against art burdened by politics occurred in the late 1930s with the rise of American formalism. Only today this reaction does not require the time of a generation; it can occur within the span of a Whitney Biennial, as suggested by its swing from political engagement in 1993 to stylish irrelevance in 1995. So, too, the old formalism sought to sublimate political renovation in artistic innovation; the contemporary version does not even attempt this.

51

For example, "race" is a historical construct, but this knowledge does not remove its material effects. As a fetishistic object, knowledge of "race" does not vanquish belief (indeed enjoyment) in it; they exist side by side, even or especially among the enlightened.

52

It is this impasse that prompted the cult of abjection mentioned in chapter 5. On the one hand, this cult is fatigued with the left politics of difference and dubious about its communitarian sentiments. On the other hand, it refuses the right politics of disidentification and sides with the wretched against the reactionary.

7

WHATEVER HAPPENED TO POSTMODERNISM?

1

See Jean-François Lyotard, *The Postmodern Condition* (1979), trans. Geoff Bennington and Brian Massumi (Minneapolis: University of Minnesota Press, 1984), and Fredric Jameson, *Postmodernism, or the Cultural Logic of Late Capitalism* (Durham: Duke University Press, 1991). The slippage between "modernity," "modern culture," and "modernist art" is notorious in discussions of postmodernism.

2

The range here is from Daniel Bell, *The Cultural Contradictions of Capitalism* (New York: Basic Books, 1978), a foundational text of neoconservatism, to Hilton Kramer, *The Revenge of the Philistines* (New York: Free Press, 1985).

3

See Ernest Mandel, *Late Capitalism* (1972), trans. Joris De Bres (London: Verso, 1978).

4

In spring 1992 I attended a centennial conference on Walter Benjamin in Detroit, a city occupied three times by the army, wounded by white flight, damaged by Reagan-Bush ne-glect. There the white tourist tends to travel from one cosmetic fortress to another. On one such trek my party of Benjamin scholars stopped at Highland Park, the birthplace of the Ford Model T, the first factory with an assembly line, the temple of Taylorist labor. On cue our taxi, a Ford, broke down and stranded us at this rusted plant, perhaps the most important site in twentieth-century industry, now lost between a deindustrial city core and a posturban residential ring, witness to the uneven development of our advanced-capitalist space-times, in a purgatory between modern and postmodern worlds. (Detroit, not New York or Los Angeles, is the Capital of the Twentieth Century.) There I saw that the notion of postmodern-ism was still needed to think this strange chronotropic terrain of fortressed cities armored against urban inhabitants and industrial remains suspended in twilight zones.

5

For some problems of this analogy see chapter 1, note 42. Even as I complicate development with deferred action, my extension of the (re)construction of the individual subject to the (re)construction of an historical subject is problematic. Can I address the logic of the subject historically if my model of history presupposes this logic? Is this a productive double bind or a paralytic one?

6

For the Benjamin remark see *Baudelaire: A Lyric Poet in the Era of High Capitalism* (London: New Left Books, 1973), 176. For the nonsynchronous see Ernst Bloch, *Heritage of Our Times* (1935), trans. Neville and Stephen Plaice (Berkeley: University of California Press, 1990), especially "Non-Contemporaneity and Obligation to its Dialectic." In "Answering the Ques-tion: What is Postmodernism?" (1982) Lyotard intimates the temporality of too early/too late: "*Post modern* would have to be understood according to the paradox of future (*post*) anterior (*modo*)" (*The Postmodern Condition*, 81).

7

This conflation occurs often in Freud (who referred to fantasy as a natural preserve). For the postmodernist version see Fredric Jameson, "Periodizing the 60s," in Sohnya Sayres et al., ed., *The 60s without Apology* (Minneapolis: University of Minnesota Press, 1984). The residual opposition of nature and culture may the problem here, for it sets up a romantic lapsarianism whereby the unconscious and the other, placed outside history, can only be contaminated by it.

8

Thus, for example, the discourse of the death of the subject is broached in the 1930s—not only by Benjamin (who, in "The Work of Art in the Age of Mechanical Reproduction" as well as "The Author as Producer," historicizes the function of the artist-author) but also by various figures in dada, surrealism, constructivism, and so on. In a sense this discourse is only recapitulated in the 1960s; yet this recapitulation *is* its articulation, at least as a characteristic ideologeme—that is my point.

"The subject" slips in this chapter: from the ego as body image (not yet properly a subject), to the artist-author function, to multicultural identities. Sometimes this slippage is due to my theoretical juxtapositions; sometimes it speaks to historical shifts. My scheme does not stress feminism because Julia Kristeva has already provided it with a tripartite narrative in "Woman's Time," in *The Kristeva Reader,* ed. Toril Moi (New York: Columbia University Press, 1986).

9

In "The Mirror Stage" (1936/1949) Lacan writes of "the armor of an alienating identity," a trope repeated in "Aggressivity in Psychoanalysis" (1948), its companion piece in *Ecrits* (trans. Alan Sheridan [New York: Norton, 1977]). In "Some Reflections on the Ego," a related paper read to the British Psychoanalytical Society on May 2, 1951, the trope reappears as the "narcissistic shield, with its nacreous covering on which is painted the world from which [the ego] is forever cut off." Could this aggressivity of the ego, "a correlative tendency" of its narcissistic basis and its paranoic structure, be part of its struggle to stabilize?

10

Lacan presented the first version of "The Mirror Stage" at the Fourteenth Congress of the International Psychoanalytical Association in Marienbad on August 3, 1936, at the time of the Nazi Olympics, which he may have attended. "The day after my address on the mirror stage," he tells us in *Ecrits,* "I took a day off, anxious to get a feeling of the times, heavy with promises, at the Berlin Olympiad. [Ernst Kris] gently objected '*Ça ne se fait pas!*'" (239). I suggested a fascistic association in the Lacanian account of the ego in "Armor Fou," *October* 56 (Spring 1991), where I discuss the dadaist and surrealist elaborations of this ego; for its futurist and vorticist elaborations, see my "Prosthetic Gods," *Modernism/Modernity* (Fall 1996). In both texts I am indebted to Klaus Theweleit, *Male Fantasies* (1977), trans. Stephen Conway (Minneapolis: University of Minnesota Press, 1987). Again, I mean to suggest not a historical

285

referent but a historical context for the theory. Jacques-Alain Miller has done a similar thing: "There is, therefore, a single ideology of which Lacan provides the theory: that of the 'modern ego,' that is to say, the paranoic subject of scientific civilization, of which a warped psychology theorizes the imaginary, at the service of free enterprise" (*Ecrits, 322*).

11

Foucault, *The Order of Things,* 387. "Since man was constituted at a time when language was doomed to dispersion, will he not be dispersed when language regains its unity?"

12

In Barthes, especially in *The Pleasure of the Text* (1973), *jouissance* is opposed to *plaisir;* its class enemy is not specifically fascist but generally (petit) bourgeois.

13

In the preface Foucault writes: "The major enemy, the strategic adversary is fascism. . . . And not only historical fascism, the fascism of Hitler and Mussolini—which was able to mobilize and use the desire of the masses so effectively—but also the fascism in us all, in our heads and in our everyday behavior, the fascism that causes us to love power, to desire the very thing that dominates and exploits us" (*Anti-Oedipus,* trans. Robert Hurley, Mark Seem, and Helen Lane [New York: Viking, 1977], xiii).

14

The status of the subject in multiculturalism is also ambiguous. On the one hand, even as multicultural critiques multiply the subject, they often reinstate its logic. On the other hand, they cannot be opposed to the death of the subject, for they are prepared by this discourse as well. On this last point see Ernesto Laclau, "Universalism, Particularism, and the Question of Identity," *October* 61 (Summer 1992).

15

In "Armor Fou" and *Compulsive Beauty* (Cambridge: MIT Press, 1993) I argue that some surrealists (like Hans Bellmer) countered the fascistic subject with images of the fragmented body, while others (like Bataille) did so with tropes of the *informe* and the acephalic.

16

On the modernist (ab)use of this analogy see my "'Primitive' Scenes," *Critical Inquiry* (Autumn 1993).

17

Catherine Clément, *The Lives and Legends of Jacques Lacan,* trans. Arthur Goldhammer (New York: Columbia University Press, 1983), 76.

18

In *Tristes Tropiques* (1955) Lévi-Strauss comments in retrospect: "There is no way out of the dilemma: either the anthropologist adheres to the norms of his own group and other groups inspire in him no more than a fleeting curiosity which is never quite devoid of disapproval, or he is capable of giving himself wholeheartedly to these other groups and his objectivity is vitiated by the fact that, intentionally or not, he has had to withhold himself from at least one society, in order to devote himself to all. He therefore commits the very sin that he lays at the door of those who contest the exceptional significance of his vocation" (trans. John and Doreen Weightman [New York: Atheneum, 1978], 384).

19

This is my conjecture only. His written references are scant and reminiscent: a few remarks on primitivist interests shared with André Breton, Max Ernst, and Georges Duthuit in New York in *The Way of the Masks* (1975) and *The View from Afar* (1983), and a 1947 note on the Collège de Sociologie (reprinted in Denis Hollier, ed., *The College of Sociology,* trans. Betsy Wing [Minneapolis: University of Minnesota Press, 1988], 385–86).

20

Lévi-Strauss, *Tristes Tropiques,* 37–44.

21

In other words, "correct distance" is potentially a primitivist ideologeme as well. It might not be entirely free of the evolutionist mapping of time onto space, whereby "back then" was conflated with "over there," with the most remote marked as the most primitive—a mapping that is rendered all the more absurd by the multinational implosion of metropolitan core and imperial periphery. (For the rhetoric of rescue in Lévi-Strauss, see James Clifford, "On the Salvage Paradigm," in Hal Foster, ed., *Discussions in Contemporary Culture* [Seattle: Bay Press, 1987].)

22

See Frantz Fanon, *The Wretched of the Earth* (1961), trans. Constance Farigan (New York: Grove Press, 1968), 206–48.

23

Ibid., 313, 311. As noted in chapter 6, Fanon felt that the *nègritude* movement succumbed to this last tendency. For a contemporaneous European response to the problematic of distance, see Paul Ricoeur, "Universal Civilization and National Cultures" (1961), in *History and Truth,* trans. Charles Kelbley (Evanston: Northwestern University Press, 1965).

24

This imbrication is explored in the work of Trinh T. Minh-ha.

25

Jacques Derrida, *Writing and Difference,* trans. Alan Bass (Chicago, University of Chicago Press, 1978), 280.

26

Roland Barthes, *The Empire of Signs* (1970), trans. Richard Howard (New York: Hill & Wang, 1982), 3–4. The other texts to which I allude here are, respectively, *Of Grammatology, The Order of Things, Chinese Women, Anti-Oedipus,* and *L'Echange symbolique et la mort.*

27

See Homi K. Bhabha, *The Location of Culture* (London: Routledge, 1994).

28

See Mandel, *Late Capitalism,* 191, and Jameson, "Periodizing the 60s," 204–9. Also see chapter 2.

29

Perhaps for these reasons Debord dates the emergence of the spectacle to the late 1920s in *Comments on the Society of the Spectacle* (1988), trans. Malcolm Imrie (London: Verso, 1990). Jonathan Crary discusses some of these transformations in "Spectacle, Attention, Counter-Memory," *October* 50 (Fall 1989).

30

Benjamin, *Illuminations,* 223–24. Might this withering be enacted, in deferred action, only in the poststructuralist death of the author and the postmodernist culture of the simulacrum? As I suggested in chapter 2, note 35, Benjamin was more ambivalent about aura than most of his postmodernist followers in the 1980s.

31

Ibid., 233. For important elaborations of these analogies see Miriam Hansen, "Benjamin, Cinema and Experience: 'The Blue Flower in the Land of Technology,'" *New German Critique* 40 (Winter 1987), and Susan Buck-Morss, "Aesthetics and Anaesthetics: Walter Benjamin's Artwork Essay Reconsidered," *October* 62 (Fall 1992).

32

Ernst Jünger, "Photography and the 'Second Consciousness,'" in Christopher Phillips, ed., *Photography in the Modern Era* (New York: Metropolitan Museum of Art, 1989), 207.

33

Martin Heidegger, "The Thing," *Poetry, Language, Thought* (New York: Harper & Row, 1968), 165–66.

———

34

In fact Debord invokes not the Benjaminian notion of distraction but the Lukácsian concept of contemplation used in *History and Class Consciousness* (1923) to think the subjective effects of capitalist mass production. For Barthes on myth, see *Mythologies* (1957), trans. Annette Lavers (New York: Hill & Wang, 1972).

35

"The spectacle thus unites what is separate," Debord writes, "but it unites it only *in its separateness*" (*The Society of the Spectacle*, trans. Donald Nicholson-Smith [New York: Zone, 1994], 22).

36

A primitivism returns in McLuhan when tropes of commonality, indeed commingling, are required—and this at a time of revolution in the third world.

37

Marshall McLuhan, *Understanding Media* (New York: McGraw-Hill, 1964), 60.

38

Ibid., 53. In McLuhan the psychic dimension of this screening of shock is elided more radically than in Benjamin. Consider too the different valuations given the media. Benjamin considers the problem of reproduction for values of art. For McLuhan (let alone Debord) art is no longer at issue, and the reproduced image is replaced by the metastatic media. Today the eccentric McLuhanian thesis, "the content of the medium is another medium," has become the everyday cyber slogan, "computers melt other machines."

39

Freud points to this logic in *Civilization and Its Discontents* (1930): "Man has, as it were, become a kind of prosthetic God. When he puts on all his auxiliary organs he is truly magnificent; but those organs have not grown on to him and they still give him much trouble at times" (trans. James Strachey [New York: W. W. Norton, 1950], 43). In "Prosthetic Gods" I examine this logic in its extreme (fascistic) versions, the futurism of Marinetti and the vorticism of Wyndham Lewis (who influenced McLuhan). On technology as prosthesis also see Mark Seltzer, *Bodies and Machines* (New York: Routledge, 1992).

40

Donna Haraway, "A Manifesto for Cyborgs," *Socialist Review* 80 (March–April 1985): 66. Also see her *Primate Visions* (New York: Routledge, 1989) and *Simians, Cyborgs, and Women* (New York: Routledge, 1991).

41

Haraway is suspicious of psychoanalysis, which she calls "much too conservative, much too heterosexual, much too familial, much too exclusive." She is right, but so is Constance Penley when she asks "if the way you have constructed your cyborg leaves any room for anything that could be called 'subjectivity,' and what the consequences of that possible omission may be," among which she numbers the forfeiting of "psychical mechanisms like displacement, projection, fetishism" ("Interview with Donna Haraway," in Constance Penley and Andrew Ross, eds., *Technoculture* [Minneapolis: University of Minnesota Press, 1991], 8–11). There is a voluntarism in cyborg discourse, as there is in most antipsychoanalytic constructs.

42

On our status as "dividuals" see Gilles Deleuze, "Postscript on the Societies of Control," *October* 59 (Winter 1992).

43

Here we see another reason why abject art insists on an untranscendable body. In the early 1990s cyber discourse attempted to resolve this contradiction of (dis)embodiment through an appropriation of psychedelic discourse—in movies, Microsoft-speak, *Mondo 2000* magazine (with Timothy Leary in particular), and so on.

44

On machine vision see Paul Virilio, *War and Cinema,* trans. Patrick Camiller (London: Verso, 1989). I presented this notion of splitting in a November 1991 lecture, published in Brian Boigon, ed., *Culture Lab* (New York: Princeton Architectural Press, 1993). In "Contingent Foundations: Feminism and the Question of Postmodernism," Judith Butler describes the subject-effects of the Gulf War in similar terms of dis/connection. In particular she notes the "fantasy of transcendence" staged by the smart bombs, which she describes as "optical phalluses" (in Judith Butler and Joan Scott, eds., *Feminists Theorize the Political* [New York: Routledge, 1992]). For another association of the media with oxymoronic pain-and-pleasure, see Patricia Mellencamp, *High Anxiety: Catastrophe, Scandal, Age and Comedy* (Bloomington: Indiana University Press, 1992).

45

As the example of the Gulf War made clear, the nation is hardly the limit of mediated collectivity. Consider in this regard the different valuations of the body in the discourse on technology. In Benjamin the body remains central as the object of technological prosthesis and as the figure of the polis. In McLuhan it is displaced by the trope of the nervous system: the social is seen as an electric network more than as an organic body. In contemporary culture the social has lost even this figural integrity; instead we have a psychic collective, a mass-mediated polis not only convoked around calamitous events (e.g., the Oklahoma City bombing) but also addressed as a traumatic subject (e.g., the generations that share the Vietnam War). I discuss these notions of mass subject and psychic nation in "Death in America," *October* 75 (Winter 1995).

46

Here too I can only point to a few landmarks. Paranoia was the subject of the 1932 thesis by Lacan, *De la psychose paranoïaque dans ses rapports avec la personnalité,* and it informed his account of the ego in "The Mirror Stage." It was also a primary subject of the surrealists, especially Salvador Dalí (then in contact with Lacan) and Max Ernst; and it drove the fascistic fear of the over-proximate other. In this extended moment its relation to discourses of subject and other is clear enough, but it is also bound up with discourses on technology (see especially "On the Origin of the 'Influencing Machine' in Schizophrenia" by Victor Tausk, where paranoia is thought in terms relevant here—as a confusion of distance and proximity, inside and outside). Paranoia also figures in these three discourses in the 1960s (when paranoia is captured by the left) and the 1990s (when it is captured by the right). Perhaps its centrality is due to its paradoxical status as the last refuge of the subject threatened by alterity and technology (see chapter 5, note 34).

47

Walter Benjamin, *Reflections,* ed. Peter Demetz, trans. Edmund Jephcott (New York: Harcourt Brace Jovanovich, 1978), 85. In *Postmodernism* Jameson offers the postmodernist version of this story of distance lost; it is essential to his notion of a schizophrenic postmodernism.

48

Ibid.

49

Benjamin admired Riegl, as is manifest in "Rigorous Study of Art" (1933), *October* 47 (Winter 1988). Also see Thomas Y. Levin, "Walter Benjamin and the Theory of Art History," in the same issue; Margaret Iversen, *Alois Riegl: Art History and Theory* (Cambridge: MIT Press, 1993), 15–16; and Antonia Lant, "Haptical Cinema," *October* 74 (Fall 1995).

50

Benjamin, *Illuminations,* 238.

51

Erwin Panofsky, *Studies in Iconology: Humanistic Themes in the Art of the Renaissance* (New York: Oxford University Press, 1939), 27–28. The question of distance is fundamental to art history, especially in its Hegelian dimension. Indeed, it is essential to Hegel in two primary ways: one function of art is "to strip the outer world of its stubborn foreignness" and one function of art history is to reflect on art as "a thing of the past"—which is also "to show how the art of alien or past cultures could become part of the mental life of the present" (Hegel, *Introductory Lectures on Aesthetics,* trans. Bernard Bosanquet [London: Penguin, 1993], 36, 13; Michael Podro, *The Critical Historians of Art* [New Haven: Yale University Press, 1982], xxii). For a meditation on distance closer to Benjamin, see the conclusion of Aby Warburg, *Images from the Region of the Pueblo Indians of North America,* trans. Michael Steinberg (Ithaca: Cornell University Press, 1995), first delivered as a lecture in 1923.

52

"Historicism contents itself with establishing a causal connection between various moments in history. But no fact that is a cause is for that very reason historical. It became historical posthumously, as it were, through events that may be separated from it by thousands of years" (*Illuminations,* 263).

53

Benjamin, *Illuminations,* 263. In the "Theses" Benjamin intimates a *Nachträglichkeit* at work in history (see note 52), which disturbs the Panofskyan picture of "comprehensive and consistent concepts of bygone periods."

54

This position, which ranges from the Heideggerian (see his "The Age of the World Picture" [1938]) to the feminist (as in Luce Irigaray), may play into the resentment against visuality remarked in chapter 5.

55

I mean distinction in the class-differential sense of Pierre Bourdieu; see *Distinction: A Social Critique of the Judgement of Taste* (1979), trans. Richard Nice (Cambridge: Harvard University Press, 1984).

56

Friedrich Nietzsche, *The Birth of Tragedy and the Genealogy of Morals,* trans. Frances Golfing (New York: Doubleday, 1956), 160. The "base" here is the bourgeoisie that advances "utility" as a value.

57

In a sense the critic caught between these imperatives remains in the place of the Baudelairean dandy caught between artistocratic "distinction" and democratic "leveling" (see chapter 4). As T. J. Clark remarks in "Clement Greenberg's Theory of Art" (*Critical Inquiry* [September 1982]), many critical terms retain aristocratic associations ("purity," "quality," and so on), and many critics remain in the compromise position of the early Greenberg—that is, in an "Eliotic Trotskyism" (143).

INDEX